D0039466

INSIDERS' GUIDE® TO
BELLINGHAM
AND MOUNT BAKER

MIKE McQUAIDE

INSIDERS' GUIDE®

GUILFORD, CONNECTICUT
AN IMPRINT OF THE GLOBE PEQUOT PRESS

The prices and rates in this guidebook were confirmed at press time. We recommend, however, that you call establishments before traveling to obtain current information.

INSIDERS' GUIDE®

Text design by LeAnna Weller-Smith
Maps by Bob's Map Service © Morris Book Publishing, LLC

ISSN: 1931-3977
ISBN-13: 978-0-7627-3845-8
ISBN-10: 0-7627-3845-6

Manufactured in the United States of America
First Edition/First Printing

CONTENTS

CONTENTS

Directory of Maps

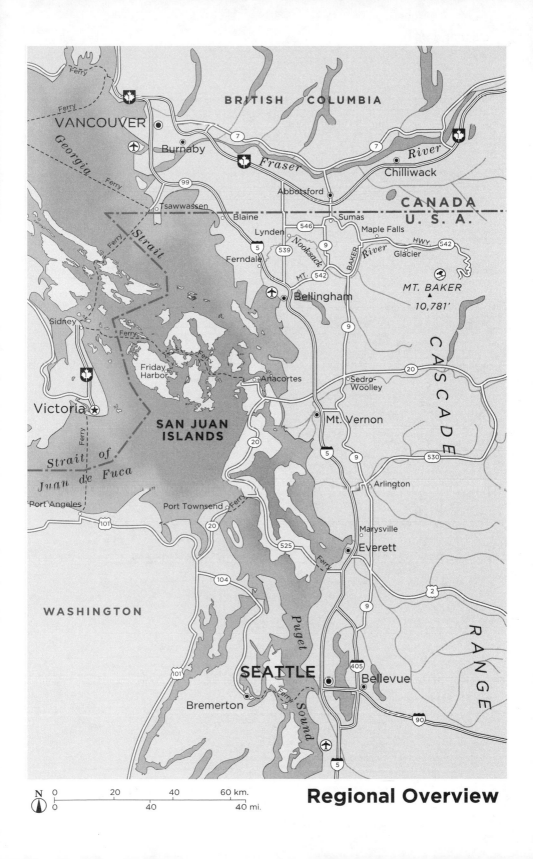

Regional Overview

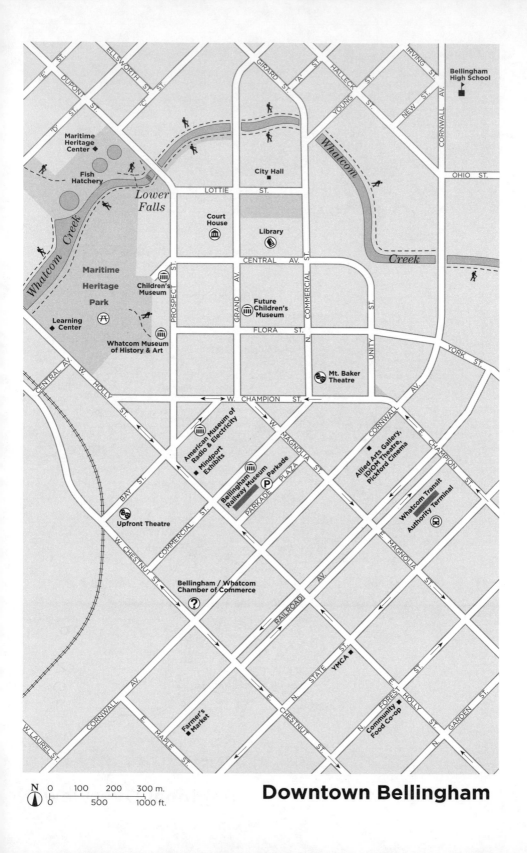

Bellingham
High School

Maritime
Heritage
Center

Fish
Hatchery

Lower
Falls

OHIO ST.

City Hall

LOTTIE   ST.

Court
House

Library

Maritime

Heritage

Park

Children's
Museum

CENTRAL   AV.

Learning
Center

Future
Children's
Museum

FLORA   ST.

Whatcom Museum
of History & Art

Mt. Baker
Theatre

YORK ST.

W. CHAMPION ST.

American Museum of
Radio & Electricity

Mindport
Exhibits

Allied Arts Gallery,
iDIOM Theatre,
Pickford Cinema

Bellingham
Railway Museum

Parkade
Plaza

Whatcom Transit
Authority Terminal

Upfront Theatre

Bellingham / Whatcom
Chamber of Commerce

YMCA

Farmer's
Market

Community
Food Co-op

W. LAUREL ST.

N   0   100   200   300 m.
     0   500   1000 ft.

Downtown Bellingham

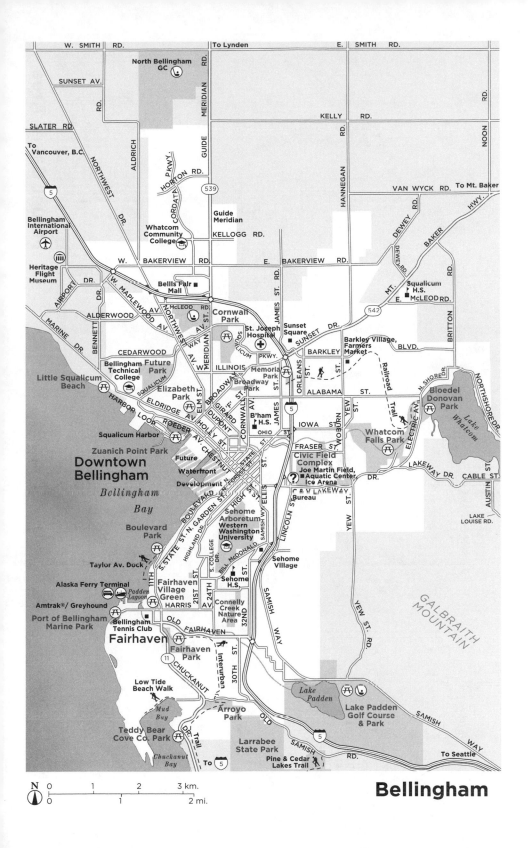

Bellingham

N

0   1   2   3 km.

0   1   2 mi.

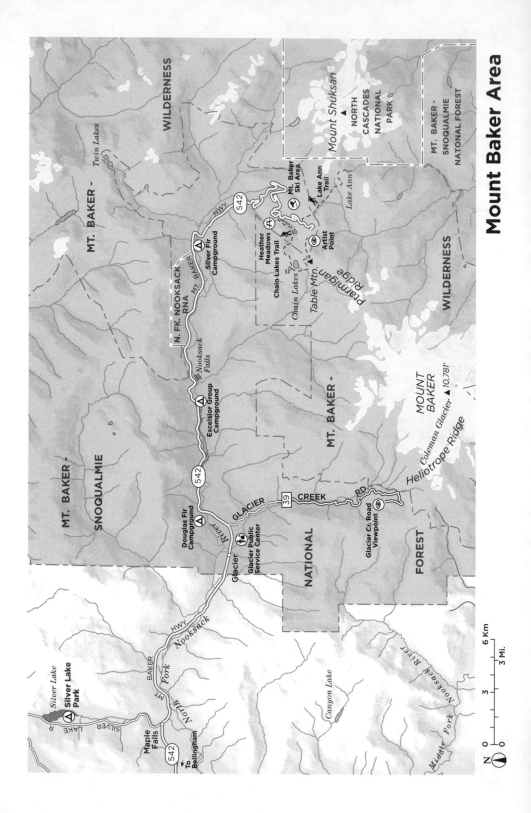

Mount Baker Area

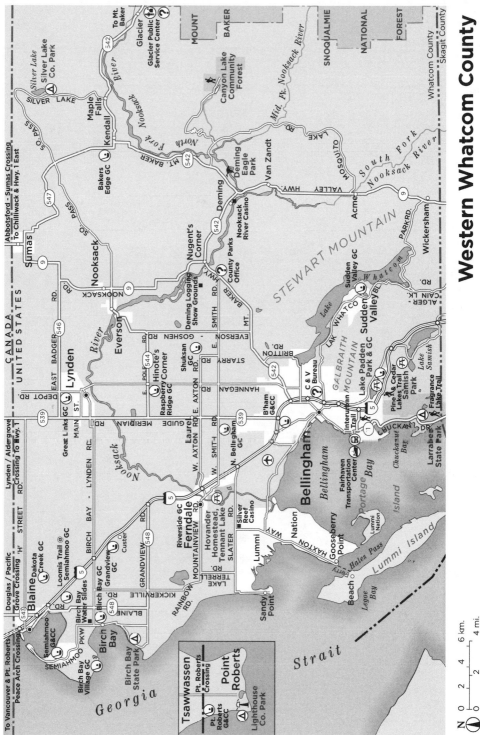

Western Whatcom County

N 0 2 4 6 km.
   0   2   4 mi.

PREFACE

When I first moved to Bellingham about 20 years ago to go to college, I experienced the strangest sensation. It was almost like déjà vu, or as if some mega-force had access to my daydreams and transformed them into reality. If I had ever imagined my perfect city and surrounding area, it would have been a place remarkably like Bellingham.

A place on the water so I could kayak and watch stunning sunsets, but also someplace with nearby mountains so I could scale the heights and snowboard into May. And since I like to run and bike and hike, a place laced with miles and miles of forested trails where I could lose myself in my thoughts without having to worry about getting hit by cars. A college town that wasn't too big—no big-city traffic jams, crime, or housing costs—but then again not too small, either. A place with great restaurants, movie theaters, and also a happening music and art scene that I wouldn't have to drive hours to get to. And if I *did* want the bright lights, big-city experience—to see the Rolling Stones, say, or visit a world-class museum—a place where I could do so without too much trouble. And not to be picky or anything, but I've always had a wildlife jones for critters like orcas and bald eagles, and owls so it'd be a place that had some of those thrown in as well.

I found all of it—and lots more—in Bellingham, and its big white watcher up in the hills, Mount Baker.

In the years I've lived here, I've watched Bellingham grow and only get better. More trails, parks, and greenbelts seem to be opening all the time. Entire neighborhoods are sprucing up and rejuvenating themselves, not in some generic sprawling fashion but by keying in on and accentuating their unique characteristics, such as Fairhaven, with its late 19th-century brick and Chuckanut sandstone, period streetlights, and hanging flower baskets. As Western Washington University's reputation continues to grow, its 215-acre campus continues to evolve, with more than $270 million worth of new buildings or renovation completed in the last 10 years. And downtown Bellingham is poised to transform its largely industrial waterfront into a bayside neighborhood with residences, shops, offices, parks, promenades, and a spectacular marina.

Bellingham is what I imagine some of the other great West Coast cities—Seattle, Portland, San Francisco—were like decades ago when they were undiscovered gems. When the only people who knew what great places they were, were the folks who lived there. Bellingham is where people from the rest of the Northwest go to escape, to decompress on its beaches and nearby mountainsides, or just to enjoy a few hours on a Saturday morning at a farmers' market.

When I tell Washingtonians from other parts of the state where I live, almost without fail, their response is, "Oooh, I looove Bellingham." And they smile and shake their heads as if wistfully recalling a great time they spent in the City of Subdued Excitement and how they wished they'd figured out a way to stay. Lucky for me, I did.

Upon graduation, I landed a features writing job with the *Bellingham Herald,* where I covered the arts and entertainment and outdoor recreation scenes. Talk about a dream job. I experienced firsthand and wrote about this area's vast outdoor and cultural riches, as well as its many fascinating people, the true essence of the area and what makes it so special. In recent years I've worked as a freelancer, gaining a larger perspective as I've written stories about people and places throughout the Northwest. But you know what? Bellingham and Mount Baker are still tops in my book. Far and away. How tops? Well, seven years ago my wife and I named our son Baker, after the mountain.

I welcome you to Bellingham and Mount Baker, and I think you'll agree: It's a special place.

ACKNOWLEDGMENTS

Numerous individuals and organizations in Bellingham and Whatcom County deserve thanks for helping put this book together. Far too many, in fact, to mention in a complete list here. Therefore, a partial one will have to do.

Sincerest thanks to Bellingham/Whatcom Chamber of Commerce & Industry, Bellingham Whatcom Tourism, Western Washington University (particularly geologist George Mustoe), Rich and Lylene Johnson at Johnson Team Real Estate, Bellingham School District, Mt. Baker Foothills Chamber of Commerce, the Steeles, the Hoyoses, Joshua Smith, Margaret Gerard, Columbia Elementary School, *Bellingham Business Journal,* the *Bellingham Herald,* Whatcom Museum of History and Art, Mount Baker-Snoqualmie National Forest, Bellingham Parks and Recreation Department, and Whatcom County Parks and Recreation Department.

Lastly, this book is dedicated to my two favorite Bellinghamsters—native son Baker and Jersey girl Jennifer.

HOW TO USE THIS BOOK ?

As the title suggests, the focus of this book is Bellingham and Mount Baker. A quick look at the map, however, reveals that the two are about 35 air miles, and some 50-plus miles of Mount Baker Highway, apart. Both are located in Whatcom County, but most of the county's population—and therefore attractions, accommodations, restaurants, cultural events, and recreation opportunities—are located in and around Bellingham.

That's not to say that Mount Baker, with its world-class skiing, snowboarding, hiking, and mountain climbing, isn't one of the region's top destinations. It definitely is. An estimated quarter of a million people visit the area annually. But for most it's just a day trip. Mount Baker is located in the Mount Baker–Snoqualmie National Forest, and the closest creature comforts—eateries and lodgings—are 17 miles away in the tiny town of Glacier.

As you've probably gathered, it's a spread-out landscape, so begin by reading the Area Overview chapter to get a feel of how it all fits together. (Check out the Close-up to find out how much it *really* rains out here.) And since this is the West, it was settled only a little more than 150 years ago, so check out the History chapter to get a sense of how it all came to be. You'll also find information there as to why the land itself looks the way it does—mountains, forest, and water, broken only by more water, more forests, and more mountains.

Once you know how Bellingham and Mount Baker are laid out, and how it got to be the way it is, take a look at the Getting Here, Getting Around chapter so you can figure out, well, how to get here and how to get around. Some nice tips on scenic driving approaches are included, as well as a heads-up about Bellingham's somewhat confusing street layout.

For the most part, chapters in this book dealing with things to do, places to go, and places to stay will be listed in alphabetical order. In general, if a street address is given but not a town or city name, assume that it means Bellingham. In certain instances, Fairhaven (though officially Bellingham but a distinct district) is listed, and, of course, if a location is in Ferndale or Lynden, that is pointed out. Annual Events like Ski to Sea and the Northwest Washington Fair are arranged chronologically and will include some of the bigger events in nearby towns (such as the Northwest Washington Fair, which takes place in Lynden).

If you're staying in Bellingham for a while and are looking for nearby worthwhile destinations—either for day or an overnighter—read the Day Trips and Weekend Getaways chapter. You'll find information on nearby places such as Vancouver and the San Juan Islands.

If you or a loved one is planning to attend Western Washington University, or you're looking for information about the local school systems, read the Education and Child Care chapter. In a related vein, the Retirement, Relocation, and Health Care chapters are useful to those who are thinking of making Bellingham their new home. And for those who do move here, the chapters Worship and Media provide helpful information, and Insiders' tips (indicated by ℹ️) provide quick insights for all readers.

AREA OVERVIEW

Just 20 miles down the road from the U.S.–Canada border, in the far northwest corner of the Pacific Northwest, sits Bellingham, a small bayside city poking its way out of the Great Northwest forest. A progressive college town of roughly 70,000, Bellingham isn't the kind of place that grabs folks with flash and neon, hustle and bustle, or high-powered moving and shaking. (In fact, the town's nickname is "the city of subdued excitement.")

What grabs folks, and as often as not, never lets go, is Bellingham's truly spectacular setting. The jewel-like San Juan Islands are a stone's throw away in one direction. Mount Baker, a massive 2-mile-high stratovolcano piled with more snow and ice than just about any other mountain in the Lower 48, is an hour's drive in another. And Bellingham itself is perched at water's edge and strung together by so many trails and parks and greenbelts that it's earned "Dream Town" status (and like accolades) from such national magazines and organizations as *Outside, National Geographic Adventure, Golf Digest, AARP* and others.

Yes, locals might be subdued and laid-back, but Bellinghamsters—as folks in B'ham are often called—are serious about immersing themselves in those spectacular surroundings. The region's notorious rainfall, which, truth be told, isn't nearly as bad as its reputation, slows them down not a drop. It's why people here dress so casually (Tevas sandals, hiking shorts, and a fleece pullover is de rigueur), so they can bolt out the door and run, walk, or cycle some of the city's 50 miles of trails. Or paddle the waters of Bellingham Bay. Or canoe or cast a line or swim in one of Bellingham's three large freshwater lakes.

Or, while we're at it, head out the Mount Baker Highway to the alpine splendor of Heather Meadows and its front-row

views of 10,781-foot Mount Baker—known to local Native Americans as the "Great White Watcher"—where, on even less than clear days, you swear you can see forever. Or maybe they're just heading to the backyard to tend to the roses and hostas and succulents and ceanothus and rhododendrons, all of which, like the cedars and firs along the Mount Baker Highway, seem to grow here to proportions seen only in Dr. Seuss books.

And every Memorial Day weekend, almost all of low-key, subdued Bellingham—and much of Whatcom County, really—shuts down so it can cut loose and party at the big Ski to Sea party, parade, and relay race.

Bellingham, like many desirable towns in the West, is dealing with what seems like exponential growth. Long considered an undiscovered gem, the town and Whatcom County (of which Bellingham is the county seat) are not so undiscovered anymore. Vancouver, B.C.'s Expo '86 did much to shine a light on the area as many festival-goers stopped in Bellingham on their way north from Seattle. They liked what they saw: a laid-back college town where waterfront property could be had for less than $80,000. Between 1990 and 2000, Bellingham's population increased almost 30 percent from 52,000 to 67,000.

The most recent boom, spurred largely by Californians heading north for a less expensive place to retire or just a better place to raise families, put 2006 population estimates at about 73,000. It's estimated that by 2020, Bellingham's population will hit 105,000, with Whatcom County projections at twice that.

To meet the demand—it's also anticipated that many more folks will be introduced to the area when they pass through on the way to the 2010 Winter Olympics in Vancouver, B.C, just 50 miles north—Bellingham is in the midst of a building

Mount Baker in early evening from Artist Point. DEBORAH CASSO

boom. (Regarding the Olympics, Washington State tourism expects to benefit to the tune of $150 million, with much of that money flowing into Bellingham and Whatcom County.)

Throughout a number of the town's neighborhoods and business districts, giant construction cranes, concrete pourers, and scaffolding are ubiquitous, as is the accompanying whirring, whizzing, and pounding of saws, hammers, and drills. Perhaps the biggest project is the major revitalization of the downtown waterfront. During the next 15 to 20 years, 137 acres of the downtown's industrial seafront will be transformed into a bayside neighborhood with homes, shops, parks, offices, an education center, and a marina with a pedestrian promenade.

But it's not just about hammers and nails and new construction. New parks and trails are always being added to the parks department's inventory, and the growing arts community has spawned a number of new local theater groups. Also in recent years, a burgeoning crop of local filmmakers has begun producing the NW Projections Film Festival, which draws entries from throughout the region.

What's fueling all this burgeoning, emerging, building, and booming? The area's QOL. That's quality of life. Time and again when residents are asked what's most important to them and what keeps them here as opposed to living somewhere else, and when visitors are asked what strikes them most about the area, they answer Bellingham and Whatcom

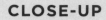

CLOSE-UP

Weather

Sure, tell someone you're visiting the Pacific Northwest and chances are the first thing they'll say is, "But doesn't it rain there all the time?" Truth be told, it don't. Bellingham's annual rainfall is 36 inches, about the same as New York or Boston. It just seems rainier than it really is because from October to April, it tends to be cloudy and overcast a lot. And to shower and spritz and precip a bit. But thunderstorms are rare, and lightning is maybe a once-a-year occurrence, if that. Precipitation rarely takes the form of an unrelenting downpour that keeps kids and families indoors and cancels outdoor plans. As long as you have a hat with a brim and shoes you don't mind getting wet, you can proceed mostly undaunted with your Bellingham plans. And, of course, the upside of all this is the incredible greenery that infuses the city and outlying areas year-round.

Summers are downright glorious. From mid-July (some years sooner) through September, it almost never rains, it's almost always sunny, and daytime highs are rarely above (or below) 75 degrees. With islands on one side, mountains on the other, and glistening water all around, it's hard to think of a better place to be in the summer than Bellingham. And because of Bellingham's northern latitude—it's higher on the map than any place in Maine—summer days are long, with the sun setting in late June at almost 9:30 P.M. and the sky staying light for another hour. Those who have friends they wish would relocate here know this is the time to invite them for a visit. Those who'd like to discourage their in-laws from retiring here, know that it isn't.

Summer temperatures range from 70 to 75 degrees during the day and from 50 to 55 degrees at night. While daytime temperatures can still be mild in late summer and early fall, the early sunset almost guarantees an evening chill. A common fashion accessory for both men and

County's quality of life. And certainly, the area's natural splendor contributes to that much-vaunted quality of life and fairly defines Bellingham's character.

To detail more of that natural splendor and in the process give the lay of the land so to speak, let's return to that annual Ski to Sea race, mentioned earlier. Quick facts: Ski to Sea is a relay race that's been held every year since 1970 in which eight-person teams cross-country ski, downhill ski, run, road bike, canoe, mountain bike, and kayak about 85 miles from the Mount Baker Ski Area to Fairhaven, Bellingham's historic South Side neighborhood. More than 400 teams compete (that's more than 3,000 people from all walks of Bellingham and Whatcom County life), and it's estimated that 80,000 spectators, volunteers, and revelers line the course as it snakes throughout much of the county. Way impressive considering that the county's total population is just a tad above 160,000.

In much the same way that the race's individual events reflect the various out-women is a flannel or other long-sleeve shirt tied around the waist to pull on when that chill hits.

As for winter, despite that high latitude and its propensity for precip, Bellingham itself receives very little snow. Puget Sound water temperatures are about 50 degrees year-round, which keeps Bellingham air temperatures fairly mild and from running to the extreme of either too hot or too cold. Average temperatures in January and February range from 40 to 45 degrees during the day, and from the low- to mid-30s at night. Annual snowfall is minimal, about 8 to 10 inches, and it's not uncommon for some years to have no snowfall in the city at all. As a result, the city doesn't have a lot of snow-clearing equipment. On those rare occasions when there is significant snowfall, Bellingham tends to come to a standstill. School is often postponed or delayed at even the threat of snow or freezing rain, and most organizations and institutions cancel operations until the snow has melted sufficiently.

Up at Mount Baker, the weather is just more of everything. It's rainier, colder, windier, the sun feels hotter and more blinding, and, of course, it's much, much snowier. Here are some nuggets of wisdom I've gleaned over the years from locals that give an idea of the difference in weather between coastal lowland Bellingham and the North Cascades Mountains, just 35 air miles away.

• When heading to the mountain, for every 1,000 feet of elevation you gain, it's three to five degrees cooler.

• If it's 50 degrees and raining in Bellingham, it's snowing at the Mount Baker Ski Area.

• Above 5,000 feet, it can snow any day of the year.

From November to April, snow is a given, a definite, and something that's made the Mount Baker Ski Area a destination spot for skiers and snowboarders the world over. The ski area receives about 650 inches of snow each year. During the 1998–99 ski season, it was dumped on by a world-record 1,140 inches—95 feet! But because the Department of Transportation stores its plows and sand trucks at the base of the mountain, the Mount Baker Highway is plowed clear of snow throughout the winter. (Under snowy conditions, chains are often required.)

door passions of the area's residents and visitors (the majority of participants are locals, but there are teams and individuals who come from all over the country and even the world for this race), the course itself reflects the various landscapes and communities that make up Whatcom County from Mount Baker to Bellingham.

The race begins with three events—cross-country skiing, downhill skiing and running—that take place at the Mount Baker Ski Area, almost a mile above sea level. This is the snowy flanks of regal Mount Baker, the most heavily glaciated mountain in the contiguous United States save for Mount Rainier, and a place where just a few winters ago, 95 feet of snow fell in a single season, setting a world record. That's winter. In summer, it's a place known as Heather Meadows, a hiker, sightseer, and photographer's dream, crisscrossed by alpine trails through rainbows of wildflower meadows with jaw-dropping views to some of the most jagged, rocky, and icy peaks in the country.

From the ski area, Ski to Sea runners

descend the alpine in a hurry, dropping past exposed outcrops of columnar basalt, snaking their way down the Mount Baker Highway, and finally handing off to a road cyclist near the banks of the Nooksack River. Glacier-fed, the chilly Nooksack has spent the last few million years gouging out steep-walled canyons on its way down the mountains and west to Bellingham Bay and Puget Sound. Along the way, it squeezes through boulder- and timber-choked gorges and plunges in a series of cascades, the most impressive being Nooksack Falls, one of the area's popular roadside, drive-up attractions. Here two mighty threads of the Nooksack plunge about 90 feet to a jumble of boulders below.

On their way to Everson, Ski to Sea cyclists follow the highway through dense, dark forests where the rain falls by the bucket, and through stands of massive firs and cedars so old they were already into their third century when Shakespeare was writing about melancholy Danes and the like. They pass through the small communities of Glacier (population 90, perhaps 87 of whom are snowboarders) and Maple Falls (population 277), tiny towns set against the edge of the national forest and that boast a surprising number of places to stay and eat at, mostly catering to folks heading up to Mount Baker.

At Kendall (population 156), another tiny forest community, riders head north near the border town of Sumas (population 960), one of Whatcom County's four U.S.–Canada border crossings. In yet

In August you're likely to see cars pulled over on the side of the road and driver and passengers poking around in the bushes and filling their mouths (and likely a pail) with the bounteous blackberries that grow seemingly everywhere. Popular pickin' spots are State Street south of downtown, along the Boulevard, Samish Way along Lake Padden, and the Squalicum Parkway.

another small town, Everson (population 2,035), riders regain the Nooksack, where they hand off to a couple canoeists, who paddle the river for 18 miles as it winds a gentle arc through the heart of the county's wide-open farmland. Apple orchards. Dairy farms. Produce farms. Organic farms. Wineries. Berry farms. Lots of berry farms. (Whatcom County is the top raspberry producer in the nation with 116 growers producing 46 million pounds of berries. That's 65 percent of North America's total!)

The river passes Lynden (population 9,020), the county's second biggest town and one of the state's largest Dutch settlements. Windmills, wooden shoes and, come the annual Holland Days Festival each May, klompen dancing are the town's calling cards. Surely one of the cleanest towns you'll find anywhere, Lynden boasts more churches per capita than just about any town in the United States.

Here in the flatlands, away from the mountains, the river, while still swift in places, is wider and easier to navigate. It's how the area's earliest settlers made their way east in search of gold near the mountains and how they gained access to the Fraser River just north of the border in British Columbia. Others, seeking big timber from which to make their livings, floated big logs down the river to Whatcom—later to become the town of Bellingham—where they were shipped to San Francisco and other ports down the West Coast. And for many years before that, the Nooksack was the lifeblood of local Indian tribes who had some 30 villages along the river. They harvested berries along its banks and caught, cleaned, and dried thousands of salmon each day in multifamily smokehouses.

Back to the race. Soon enough, Ski to Sea canoeists reach Ferndale (pop. 8,758), Whatcom County's third largest town, located just 6 miles northwest of Bellingham. In the late 1800s, with the towns that became Bellingham often experiencing more bust than boom, many residents decided to try farming and settled here, a few miles upriver. Back then Ferndale was known as Jam, because of a massive log-jam here that was more than a mile long. It so clogged the river and had become so entrenched that the forest was growing right on top of it. A man could truly walk right across it and not be aware he was on top of the river. These days Ferndale is still largely agricultural, as well as being the home of a large aluminum producer and a couple of oil refineries.

Just south of Ferndale at Hovander Homestead Park, a place where visitors can experience a preserved turn-of-the-twentieth-century farm and homestead, Ski to Sea canoeists hand off to their team's mountain biker, who makes a mad 9-mile dash south over trail, road, and beach, finally arriving at Bellingham's Squalicum Harbor. The second largest harbor on Puget Sound—only Seattle's are bigger—it's also one of the busiest with more than 1,800 commercial and pleasure boats. Adjacent to downtown waterfront that's being revitalized, Squalicum Harbor is itself undergoing a renaissance with new shops, galleries, and restaurants anchored by the circa-2001 way-posh Hotel Bell-wether, one of only three four-star hotels in the Northwest.

Here at the harbor, Ski to Sea mountain bikers hand off to kayakers, who paddle the 5-mile homestretch across Bellingham Bay to Fairhaven and the Ski to Sea finish line. From the water, all of Bellingham is laid out before them. It's a town built atop forested bluffs, a slopeside city that seemingly spills right into Puget Sound, with buildings of brick and Chuck-anut sandstone, neighborhoods stuffed with meticulously maintained craftsman homes, hilltop Queen Annes ringed with wraparound porches, waterfront condos with decks pointing toward the sunset, and wild English gardens making backyard rainbows.

There're the distinctive red Victorian cupolas of the Whatcom Museum of History and Art, a Bellingham icon, and formerly the town's City Hall building, circa 1892. There's Western Washington Univer-

It's not uncommon in spring to see a lone gray whale that's broken away from the mass whale migration out in the Pacific Ocean swimming about in Bellingham Bay. In 1999, however, half a dozen whales spent about six weeks frolicking and feeding in Bellingham Bay, providing quite a show for residents.

sity, perennially ranked one of the region's top public universities, set against densely wooded Sehome Hill, and looking like a college in the woods. And there's where Whatcom Creek spills into Bellingham Bay, where in 1852 the first white settlers rowed to shore having found what they were looking for—a seemingly endless supply of trees and enough moving water to start a lumber mill.

Nearing Fairhaven, paddlers pass waterfront Boulevard Park and Taylor Avenue Dock, a recently constructed 0.3-mile promenade over the bay. Approaching Marine Park, they pass the Alaska Cruise Terminal, from which ferries sail twice weekly for Alaska. And they pass the Padden Creek inlet, where a notoriously unkempt smuggler named Dirty Dan Harris first made land in 1853, and who, over the next 35 years, would plat the streets and essentially found the town of Fairhaven. At Marine Park, kayakers come ashore, sprint across the sandy beach, and ring a brass bell, marking the end of their race.

In one broad, bold, and beautiful Ski-to-Sea stroke, that's the width and breadth of Bellingham, Whatcom County, and Mount Baker. From an ancient, snow- and ice-clad volcano more than 2 miles high to a handful of foothill and farmland communities, to a burgeoning city of 70,000 on a tidewater bay at the northernmost reaches of Puget Sound.

QUALITY OF LIFE

Between 1990 and 2000, Bellingham's population went from 52,179 to 67,171, a 29

The Taylor Avenue Dock offers a ⅓-mile promenade over Bellingham Bay. MIKE MCQUAIDE

percent increase. (2005 estimates put the population at 72,320.) It's estimated that between 2000 and 2020, Bellingham's population will increase another 31,601. Bellingham is the 11th largest city in Washington State, and less than 40 percent as densely populated as Seattle, the state's largest city.

Overall, Whatcom County, which also includes the small towns of Lynden, Ferndale, and Blaine—each with populations of about 10,000 or below—is largely rural and has a 2004 estimated population of 180,800. (It's estimated the county's population will increase to 212,000 by 2010.) Washington State's population grew 21 percent between 1990 and 2000. (2004 estimates put the state's total at 6,203,788, making it the 15th most populous state in the United States.)

Like many desirable places to live in the West (or anywhere), Bellingham's cost of living has risen in recent years, but not to exorbitant levels. According to Sperling's BestPlaces, which takes into account such things as housing, food, transportation, utilities, and health care, Bellingham scores a 110, with 100 being average.

By comparison, Seattle scored 136; Portland, Oregon, 119; Austin, Texas, 103; Flagstaff, Arizona, 113; Phoenix, 101; Santa Fe, New Mexico, 155; Sedona, Arizona, 127; San Francisco, 217; San Clemente, California, 181; San Diego, 143; New York 193; Orlando, 97; Madison, Wisconsin, 107; Virginia Beach, Virginia, 101; Bend, Oregon, 112.

TOURISM

- *Outside* (2001) magazine names Bellingham one of its Top Ten Dream Towns.
- *National Geographic Adventure* (2004) magazine calls Bellingham one of the

U.S.'s Top Ten Adventure Towns.
- AARP (2003) lists Bellingham as one of the nation's Top Fifteen "Dream Towns" for baby boomers looking to relocate.
- *Forbes* Magazine (May 2001) ranks Bellingham as the best small city in Washington State and 14th best small city nationally for doing business and advancing one's career.
- *Golf Digest* (2002) rates Bellingham seventh on its list of "best little golf towns in America."
- The American Lung Association names (2004) Bellingham one of the top 20 cities for clean air for the fifth year in a row.
- John Villani (2005), author of *100 Best Art Towns in America*, names Bellingham 1 of the top 10 small-city art communities in the United States.

Accolades such as these have helped fuel a $360 million tourism industry in Bellingham and Whatcom County as of 2005, the most recent year for which figures are available. That's up from $266 million in 1998, an increase of 35 percent. This booming tourism industry employs some 6,280 individuals, or about 10 percent of the workforce.

Much of this spending takes place in May during the venerable Ski to Sea race, parade, and party that, according to the Bellingham and Whatcom Visitors Bureau, draws some 80,000 spectators and pumps $5 million into the local economy.

Bellingham itself has about 1,500 hotel rooms with about another 850 available throughout the county. During the next few years, planned projects in Fairhaven, Glacier, and the Silver Reef and Nooksack River casinos should increase those numbers significantly.

Rooms can be a little tougher to come by on weekends in July and August when the good weather hits and also in mid-June, around the time of Western Washington University's and area high schools' graduations. In January and February when all is rain and clouds down in Bellingham but the snow is piling up at Mount Baker where the snowfall is measured in

Until just a few years ago, when the wind was right—or perhaps more accurately, wrong—Bellingham stunk. Well, not really stunk but had a certain aroma to it. Some say it smelled like hot dogs being boiled in water. Some said it was not unlike that of a beached whale rotting in the sun. Others had more graphic descriptions not suitable for print. As the downtown Georgia Pacific plant curtailed operations, the stench left, and Bellingham's air quality improved dramatically. The American Lung Association now perennially ranks Bellingham as one of the nation's top 20 cities for clean air.

triple digits (as in 600-plus inches per year), rooms fill quickly, especially in the foothills communities. Overall, occupancy rate is 61 percent, about the state average.

Whatcom County doesn't have a convention center per se, but its setting makes it an attractive destination for smaller groups of 300 and fewer. Western Washington University hosts a number of education and sports conferences with various hotels, including the Semiahmoo Resort, the Hotel Bellwether, and the Chrysalis Inn, where business, trade, reunion, and fraternal group meetings are held. The Mount Baker Theatre and Northwest Washington Fairgrounds are also popular with groups.

THINGS TO DO

What to do—whew!—there's lots. Head to Fairhaven, Bellingham's artsy-historic century-old neighborhood, and peruse its many shops, galleries, and cafes, its cobblestone streets and alleys. Don't miss beloved Village Books, one of the Northwest's largest independent bookstores, newly settled in a three-story corner building, with views from its stacks that extend far across Bellingham Bay to Vancouver and Canada's Coast Mountains.

Bellingham's charming Fairhaven district. BELLINGHAM WHATCOM COUNTY TOURISM/TAIMI GORMAN

Add some exercise by starting your stroll 0.5 mile north of Fairhaven at Boulevard Park at the edge of Bellingham Bay. Follow the wide trail south to the newly built (2004) Taylor Avenue Dock, which extends above the Bellingham Bay for a third of a mile. Scan the seas for seals and whales, and marvel at island after island spread out before you. For the true Bellingham experience, time your walk so your return coincides with sunset. Watch from the dock or, if you're in the mood for a glass of Cinzano Bianco, step inside the Fino Wine Bar at the Chrysalis Inn, a classic Northwest waterfront hotel and spa.

Head up the hill and stroll the 215-acre Western Washington University campus, perusing its nationally recognized Outdoor Sculpture Collection. Hike or drive to the top of the Sehome Hill Arboretum, crowned by a 40-foot watchtower, from which the bird's-eye views of Bellingham,

Northern Puget Sound, and seemingly all of Whatcom County are the best around.

If it's summer, while on campus attend a Bellingham Festival of Music or Summer Stock performance. Head for the distinctive crimson cupolas of the old City Hall building and take in one of the many exhibits at the Whatcom Museum of History and Art. Or grab the little ones and head next door to Whatcom Children's Museum. If you're in the mood for a shock, mosey over to the nearby American Museum of Radio and Electricity, which details the several-century attempt to bottle lightning. Or if railroads are your thing, chug 1 block over to the Bellingham Railway Museum.

Pick up some fresh fruits, flowers, and veggies at the Bellingham Farmer's Market and have a picnic while enjoying one of the dozens of free concerts held throughout the summer at various city parks. Live

Point Roberts

Fifteen miles south of Vancouver, British Columbia, a nubbin of land hangs down across the U.S.–Canada border like a limb from a neighbor's tree. At only 4.9 square miles, Point Roberts, Washington, might lack size, but this curiosity of cartography is blessed with a couple small beaches that are more than worthy of a visit.

But first things first: How is it that this seemingly stranded peninsula is part of the United States and not Canada? In 1846, Great Britain and the United States established the 49th Parallel as the border in this area. Just west of here, they bent the border so that all of Vancouver Island became British territory, but across the Delta Peninsula they adhered to the 49th. All along the U.S.–Canada border, markers identify it as the longest undefended border in the world.

Marker No. 1, a 20-foot-high obelisk erected in 1861, is here at Point Roberts. These days, getting to Point Roberts from the rest of Washington State requires two border crossings and a 25-mile drive through Canada. (Captain George Vancouver named the point after his friend Capt. Henry Roberts.)

Who lives in Point Roberts? A mostly retired and mostly Canadian population of about 900 calls Point Roberts their year-round home. In summers, however, that number swells to about 5,000. What draws the crowds? The beaches, among other things. About 1.5 miles due east of that second border crossing, Maple Beach, at the point's northeast corner, offers a sandy spot that's perfect for spreading the blanket and basking in the sun. When the tide is in, Boundary Bay's shallow, protected waters are often warm enough for swimming, an oddity so far north. When the tide is out, it's out—as in a mile or more, and there's no better place on the peninsula for beachcombing. Maple Beach treats visitors to an otherworldly view too—from the glittering skyscrapers and bridges of Vancouver to the north, majestic Mount Baker and her Cascade siblings to the east, and the jewel-like San Juan Islands to the south.

Looking for whales? Head for Point Roberts' opposite corner and the top of Lighthouse Marine Park's 20-foot-high whale-watch observation tower. From June through September, members of orca pods J, K, and L cruise by, drawn by salmon making their annual run past the peninsula's southwest tip. Don't bother looking for the lighthouse; the park hasn't had one for decades. The Point Roberts Lighthouse Society, an enthusiastic group of locals that's seeking funds to build a new lighthouse, hopes to change that in the coming years.

Point Roberts' beaches aren't particularly big—there's only so much space on this peninsula below the 49th Parallel—but each offers its own charms. And they're close enough that it's a cinch to enjoy both in an afternoon.

To get there: From Interstate 5 in Washington State, cross into Canada at the Peace Arch border crossing. Drive north 17 miles on Highway 99 to Highway 17, then west for 5 miles to the Tsawwassen exit. Follow 56th Street for 3 miles to the Point Roberts border crossing and Tyee Drive.

Maple Beach: From Tyee Drive, turn left onto Johnson Road, then left onto Goodman Road to the end.

Lighthouse Marine Park: Take Tyee Drive south to where it turns into Marina Drive and follow to the southwest corner.

Contact Lighthouse Marine Park, 811 Marine Drive, Point Roberts; (360) 945-4911.

a little bit of Americana—fork over five bucks for a bleacher seat at a Bellingham Bells minor league baseball game. Head north to Lynden for the farm-themed Northwest Washington Fair and marvel at bulls big enough to carry four men, hogs the size of sofas, tractor pulls and demolition derbies, and farm-fresh ice-cream sandwiches so good that once you're finished you'll cry for Mommy.

Rent a mountain bike and check out the seemingly endless miles of trails on Galbraith Mountain and at Lake Padden, or the wide, gentle Interurban Trail. Rent a kayak and paddle along the sculptured sandstone cliffs of Chuckanut Bay. Go for a swim or cast a line in one of the city's three large freshwater lakes. Drop some crab pots, dig for clams along some of Bellingham and Whatcom County's 143 miles of shoreline. Ski or snowboard the slopes at the Mount Baker Ski Area, which receives more snow than any other ski area in North America and has just about the longest ski season, too. Watch salmon return to the creeks of their birth, swimming upstream to spawn (and die).

Stroll the paved promenade along Squalicum Harbor, and ogle some of the 1,800 commercial and pleasure boats. Score some fresh salmon right off the boat, or sign up for a summer whale-watch cruise to the San Juan Islands, where you're pretty much guaranteed to see some of the 90 orcas that summer there.

Tee off on one of the county's 16 golf courses, maybe even Semiahmoo Golf and Country Club, designed by Arnold Palmer and ranked by Golf Digest as one of the 75

top resort courses in the United States. Treat yourself to a hot stone or Hawaiian Lomi Lomi massage at the Chrysalis, or maybe a Hydrolicious foot treatment or Stress Buster hand and scalp massage at Bellwether's Zazon Spa is more your speed. Spend a rainy afternoon browsing the used bookstores of Grand Avenue—one store claims to have 100,000 books, and another across the street says it has 100,001. If antique hunting is your thing, Old Town, so named because it's where the area's first settlers settled, is the place to go.

Take a drive east to Mount Baker and the snowy Cascade Mountains, or south along Chuckanut Drive, with its Big Sur–like twists and turns high above Chuckanut and Samish Bays. Take a five-minute ferry ride to Lummi Island, where the slow pace will have you checking your watch to make sure time hasn't stood still. Check out a performance at one of the local theaters—the Bellingham Theatre Guild (the state's oldest), the cutting-edge Idiom Theater, or the Upfront Theatre, an improv venue opened in 2004 by TV's Ryan Stiles. Follow along as a period-costumed Dirty Dan Harris takes you on a Friday-morning guided tour of Fairhaven.

Or just check out one of Bellingham and Whatcom County's many festivals—Chalk Art Festival, Holiday Festival, Kids Fair, Bellingham Festival of Music, NW Projections (a local film festival), Ski to Sea, Pacific Northwest Rain Celebration, Dirty Dan Days, Outdoor Cinema at various outdoor locations throughout the summer, Holiday Tour d'Art Gallery Walk, Deming Log Show, Sumas Junior Rodeo, Barkley Pumpkin Patch and Autumn Festival, Pioneer Days, Bellingham Storytelling Festival, Holiday Port Festival, and more. As you can see, there's much to do here in Bellingham and up at Mount Baker, and you'll find details on these and many other things to do and places to go within the pages of this book.

Vital Statistics

Mayor: Mark Asmundson

Washington governor: Christine Gregoire

Population: Bellingham: 67, 171 (72,320 by 2005 estimates)
Whatcom County: 180,800
Washington State: 6,203,788

Area (square miles): 25.6

Nickname: City of Subdued Excitement, Belliwood (a reference to the number of local aspiring filmmakers)

Average temperatures: July: 66.3 degrees (72.5/54)
January: 40.4 degrees (46.1/34.7)

Average annual rain: 36 inches, with most falling between November and April

Average annual Bellingham snowfall: 10 inches

Average annual Mount Baker Ski Area snowfall: 647 inches

Average annual Bellingham sunny days: 71

Average annual Bellingham partly sunny days: 93

Average annual Bellingham cloudy days: 201

Bellingham founded: Whatcom (first of Bellingham's four preceding towns) 1852; Bellingham incorporated: 1903

Colleges and universities: Western Washington University, Whatcom Community College, Bellingham Technical College, Northwest Indian College

Major area employers.
Public sector: Western Washington University, Bellingham School District, Whatcom County, Ferndale School District, City of Bellingham, Whatcom Community College, Lummi Indian Business Council, Mount Baker School District, Bellingham Technical College, Blaine School District
Private sector: St. Joseph Hospital, Haggen Food & Pharmacy, Sodexho Services, Brown & Cole Stores, BP (Cherry Point), Intalco, T-Mobile, Fred Meyer, Everyday Staffing LLC, Diamond B Constructors, Haskell Corp, Wal-Mart, Anvil Corp., Madrona Medical Group, Silver Reef Casino, Olympic Health Management, Semiahmoo Resort, Bellingham Cold Storage, Premier Graphics, Homestead Northwest

Famous sons and daughters: Hilary Swank, Doug Pederson (NFL player), Loretta Lynn (lived and played music here in her early 20s), Luke Ridnour (Seattle Supersonics guard), Ryan Stiles (lives here now), author Steve Martini (lives here now), Deathcab For Cutie, The Posies

State/city holidays:

January 1	New Year's Day
Third Monday in January	Martin Luther King Jr.'s Birthday
Third Monday in February	Presidents' Day
Last Monday in May	Memorial Day

July 4	Independence Day
First Monday in September	Labor Day
November 11	Veteran's Day
Fourth Thursday in November	Thanksgiving
December 25	Christmas

Resources and visitor centers:
Bellingham/Whatcom Chamber of Commerce and Industry
1201 Cornwall Avenue, Suite 100 or
P.O. Box 958
Bellingham, WA 98227
(360) 734-1330
www.bellingham.com

Bellingham/Whatcom County Convention and Visitors Bureau
904 Potter Street
(360) 671-3990
www.bellingham.org

Mt. Baker Foothills Chamber of Commerce
P.O. Box 866
Maple Falls, WA 98266
(360) 599-1518
www.mtbakerchamber.org

Mount Baker Ranger District
Glacier Public Service Center
10091 Mount Baker Highway, Glacier
(360) 599-2714

Mount Baker–Snoqualmie National Forest 810 State Route 20, Sedro-Woolley
(360) 856-5700
www.fs.fed.us/r6/mbs

Public transportation: The Whatcom Transit Authority (WTA) serves Bellingham and most populated areas of Whatcom County. Call (360) 676-RIDE (7433) for route information. For specialized transportation, call WTA at (360) 733-1144. Web site: www.ridewta.com.

Driving laws: Seat belts must be worn by all persons seated in the front or back seats of cars and light trucks. Under state law, children six years old and younger and weighing 60 pounds or less are required to be in a child safety seat or booster seat. Children age five and younger are required to sit in the back seat. The fine for failing to use a seat belt or child safety restraint device is $101. The driver is only responsible for ensuring that those age 15 and younger wear a seat belt; those not wearing a belt who are age 16 and older can be ticketed individually.

Automobile insurance is required. The maximum speed limit on interstate highways in Washington is 70 mph. On Bellingham city streets, the speed limit is 25 mph, unless marked otherwise. On the way to Mount Baker, the speed limit varies along the Mount Baker Highway (State Route 542) from 35 mph in populated areas to 55 mph in undeveloped sections.

Motorcycle helmets are required.

Alcohol laws: You must be age 21 or older to drink in Washington. Beer and wine can be sold from 6:00 A.M. to 2:00 A.M. six days per week. Liquor is sold at state liquor stores, which are open from 10:00 A.M. to 9:00 P.M. every day but Sunday. Some test stores have recently opened on Sundays on a trial basis. Bars stay open until 2:00 A.M.

The legal limit for blood-alcohol content for drivers is .08. The state has a zero-tolerance policy for minors: Anyone younger than age 21 who obtains, possesses, or consumes alcohol will be charged with a gross misdemeanor and face a maximum penalty of a year in jail and a $5,000 fine. Anyone younger than age 21 who drinks and drives may get their driver's license revoked.

Newspapers: the *Bellingham Herald* (daily), the *Cascadia Weekly* (weekly), the *Whatcom Independent* (weekly).

Sales tax: Sales tax in Whatcom County (which includes Bellingham) is 8.3 percent and is levied on most purchases except for food and prescription drugs.

Income tax: Washington State has no income tax.

GETTING HERE, GETTING AROUND

On a map of the United States, Bellingham is located high in the far left corner, the city in the Lower 48. Less than 20 miles from the U.S.–Canada border, Bellingham is closer to Vancouver, B.C. (50 miles) than Seattle (90 miles). With Bellingham Bay to the west and the snowy Cascade Mountains to the east, Bellingham is approachable only from the north or south. No road crosses the mountains this far north in Washington State. Spokane is 360 miles east of Bellingham and Portland, Oregon, is 250 miles south. While daily flights to and from both cities to Seattle are frequent, there are no direct flights to Bellingham from either city.

Bellingham International Airport provides commercial service to Seattle-Tacoma International Airport (Sea-Tac) and smaller ports such as Las Vegas and Friday Harbor on San Juan Island. Charter flights can also be arranged at Bellingham's airport.

COMMERCIAL AIRLINES SERVING BELLINGHAM INTERNATIONAL AIRPORT

Horizon Air: (800) 547-9308; www.horizonair.com

Allegiant Air: (800) 432-3810; www.allegiantair.com

San Juan Airlines: (800) 874-4434; www.sanjuanairlines.com

Most visitors who fly to the area arrive in Seattle and connect to Bellingham via Horizon Air. Or they'll rent a car at Sea-Tac and drive north to Bellingham or take the Airporter Shuttle van service.

RENTING A CAR AT SEA-TAC

The companies below have rental counters in the baggage claim area. Alamo, Avis, Budget, Hertz, and National have pickup and drop-off just outside the airport in the first-floor garage. The remaining have off-site cars but provide courtesy van service to and from the airport.

Alamo: (800) 462-5266; www.alamo.com

Avis: (800) 331-1212; www.avis.com

Budget: (800) 435-1880; www.budget.com

Hertz: (800) 654-3131; www.hertz.com

National: (800) 328-4567; www.nationalcar.com

Advantage: (800) 777-5500; www.arac.com

Dollar: (800) 800-4000; www.dollarcar.com

Enterprise: (800) 736-8222; www.enterprise.com

Thrifty: (800) 847-4389; www.thrifty.com

SHUTTLE SERVICE

The Airporter Shuttle provides service to and from Sea-Tac International Airport with buses arriving in Bellingham every two hours between 2:00 A.M. and 7:00 P.M. Because the shuttle stops at several points along Interstate 5, the airport trip takes about 2½ hours.

Cost is $32 for adults and $17 for those age 2 through 16. For reservations call (866) 235-5247 or visit www.airporter.com.

RENTING A CAR IN BELLINGHAM

Bellingham International Airport is served by the following rental car companies: Avis, Hertz, Budget, Alamo, and Enterprise. See the above phone numbers and Web sites for contact information.

BUS TOURS

Bellair Charters and Hesselgrave International Tours offer charter buses and tours to Mount Baker; Seattle; Vancouver, B.C.; the San Juan Islands; and various other destinations. In addition, during the winter months, Bellair Charters provides service to the Mount Baker Ski Area. Contact Bellair Charters (800-221-4548; www.bellair charters.com) or Hesselgrave International Tours (800-457-5522, 360-734-3570; www.hesselgrave.com).

AMTRAK

Bellingham is served by Amtrak with two trains leaving daily for Seattle and two for Vancouver, B.C. The Amtrak station is located at Fairhaven Station, 401 Harris Avenue, next to the Bellingham Cruise Terminal.

Hours: 8:00 A.M. to 9:00 P.M., seven days a week.

Contact information: (800) 872-7245, (360) 734-8851, for Bellingham station information only; www.amtrak.com.

GREYHOUND

Greyhound also serves Bellingham with five buses leaving daily for Seattle and five for Vancouver, B.C. The bus depot is located in the Fairhaven Station in Fairhaven, next to the Bellingham Cruise Terminal.

Hours: 8:00 A.M. to 5:30 P.M. seven days a week.

Contact information: (800) 231-2222, (360) 733-5251 for station; www.grey hound.com.

TAXICABS

A number of cab companies serve Bellingham and offer reliable service from the airport and other transportation hubs.

Bellingham Yellow Cab: (360) 738-8294

City Cab: (360) 733-8294

Evergreen Taxi: (360) 714-0502

Scott's Taxi: (360) 733-8900

Superior Cabs: (360) 734-3478

Yellow Cab of Whatcom Skagit: (360) 734-8294

DRIVING TO BELLINGHAM

Most visitors driving to Bellingham from points east take Interstate 90 to Seattle, then head north on I-5 for about 90 miles to Bellingham. While this all-interstate route is theoretically the quickest, given the growing sprawl from Seattle north for about 35 miles to above Everett—and the ever-slowing down of traffic that follows, it doesn't always turn out that way.

A couple scenic alternatives for crossing the Cascade Mountains from Eastern Washington to Western Washington are Highway 2 (Stevens Pass Scenic Byway) or State Route 20 (North Cascades Scenic Byway). Both are spectacular drives that offer scenic vistas as well as interesting places to overnight or just pick up an Italian soda or espresso float. (The town of Leavenworth, along Highway 2, sports a Bavarian theme; Winthrop, along the North

Cascades Highway, is decked out like a town from the Old West. Like Bellingham, both are chock-full of year-round recreation opportunities and beloved by outdoor geeks.)

Highway 2 and Route 20 might be slightly slower routes than I-90, but if you're going to be slowed by traffic in the Seattle metro area anyway, you might as well hook up with I-5 north of that city, as both these highways do. Highway 2 connects to I-5 at Everett exit 194, about 60 miles south of Bellingham (and 30 miles north of Seattle); and Route 20 connects at Burlington exit 230, about 25 miles south of Bellingham.

There's a scenic noninterstate approach to Bellingham for the final 20 miles too. At I-5 exit 231 (the first exit following the intersection with Route 20), head north on Chuckanut Drive (State Route 11), which leads 20 miles to

Fairhaven, Bellingham's historic, turn-of-the-century South Side neighborhood. Along the way Chuckanut Drive traverses the lower flanks of Blanchard and Chuckanut Mountains, winding above the shoreline of Northern Puget Sound, and boasting jaw-dropping views east to the San Juan Islands. It's a mini–Big Sur and makes for a dramatic entrance to Bellingham. (See the Day Trips chapter for more detailed information.)

FERRIES

Victoria San Juan Cruises, a local company, offers seasonal passenger-only ferry service to the San Juan Islands and Victoria, British Columbia, at the southern tip of Vancouver Island. They also provide ferry service across Bellingham Bay from Fairhaven at the South Side to Squalicum

A ferry about to dock in Seattle. WWW.PHOTOS.COM

Harbor at the north. Service runs from May to September. The company also does whale-watching tours, which look for some of the 90 or so orcas who call the nearby waters home.

Information and reservations: (800) 443-4552; www.islandcommuter.com.

The Whatcom County ferry to Lummi Island runs every 20 minutes from Gooseberry Point, which is about 12 miles west of downtown Bellingham on the Lummi Indian Reservation Island. Round-trip fares are $1.00 for walk-ons and bicycles, $3.00 for cars, and $1.00 for each person in the car. Information: (360) 676-6759.

The Alaska Marine Highway offers ferry service—both car and passenger— from Bellingham to Southeast Alaska (with connections cross-gulf to Southcentral Alaska). Boats leave the Alaska Cruise Terminal in Fairhaven on Tuesday and Friday at 6:00 P.M. for Southeast Alaska, with stops at Ketchikan, Wrangell, Petersburg, Juneau, Haines, and finally Skagway, 900-plus miles from Bellingham. Passengers can either rent a room or camp out—even set up a tent—on the ferry deck. Along the way, views are almost beyond description, with countless glaciers, fiords, humpback whales, orcas, and eagles on the daily itinerary.

Sailing times range from about 40 hours to Ketchikan at the southern end to 85 hours to Skagway at the north end. (Juneau is 61 hours.) From Juneau, riders can catch ferries to Southcentral Alaskan ports such as Valdez and Homer, as well as other Southeast ports such as Sitka. So while there's no direct ferry service from Bellingham to points such as Valdez, it is possible to ride public transportation from Bellingham to Southcentral Alaska.

For reservations and information, contact the Alaska Marine Highway at (800) 642-0066 or www.ferryalaska.com.

WATER TAXI

Pacific Sea Taxi is the only company that offers chartered sea taxi service from Bellingham to the San Juan Islands. A couple nice features are that they serve a number of the smaller, less-visited islands (i.e., Sucia, Cypress, and Sinclair Islands) as well as the four main Washington State ferry-served islands and that service is year-round rather than just during summer months. Rates vary according to the size of the group. For example, a one-way trip for one to Sucia Island costs $85; for a group of six or more, the individual fare is $25. Bikes and kayaks are an additional $5.00. Boats leave from the Bellingham Cruise Terminal.

Information: (360) 393-7123; www.pstaxi.com.

WASHINGTON STATE FERRIES

Car and passenger ferry service to the San Juan Islands and Sidney, British Columbia, is available from Anacortes, about 45 minutes southwest of Bellingham. Depending on the tides, there are more than 400 San Juan Islands. Some "islands" are mere rocks, visible only at the lowest of tides, but only four are served by Washington State ferries. (There are 176 named San Juan Islands.) Lopez Island is a quiet one, favored by bicyclists because it's relatively flat; Shaw Island is smallest and is *really* quiet with nary a commercial business save for a small general store that until recently was run by some nuns from the Franciscan center up the hill. Orcas Island and San Juan are the most heavily visited, each with numerous lodgings, restaurants, and attractions, including Orcas' Moran State Park, the town of Friday Harbor on San Juan Island, and Lime Kiln Point State Park, also on San Juan.

To get to the Washington State Ferry terminal in Anacortes, head south on I-5 to exit 230. Head west on Highway 20 for about 16 miles to Anacortes and follow the ferry terminal signs. Once in town, turn left onto 12th Street, and the ferry terminal is about 4 miles ahead.

Slalom race at the Mount Baker Ski Area. MIKE MCQUAIDE

In recent years, because of rising fuel costs, ferry rates have risen dramatically. Round-trip peak-season (early May through mid-October) rates for two adults with one child age 18 or younger, and a vehicle range from $55 to Lopez Island, the closest of the ferry-served islands, to $69 for Friday Harbor on San Juan Island, the farthest island. Off peak-season rates are $13 to $18 less. Rates are also $3.00 to $8.00 cheaper if you leave Anacortes Sunday through Tuesday.

Contact Washington State Ferries at (888) 808-7977 (in-state) or (206) 464-6400 from outside Washington. Go to www.wsdot.wa.gov/ferries for a very comprehensive Web site with route maps and fare calculator.

DRIVING TO MOUNT BAKER

Get on the Mount Baker Highway (State Route 542) and head east for as far as you can. Most years, the road is plowed and free of snow from October to some-time in July to just beyond the Mount Baker Ski Area, about 54 road miles east of Bellingham. From July until the snow starts piling up again in late September or early October, the road is plowed for another 3 miles—and about 600 feet higher—to the road's end at Artist Point. (The ski area is at an elevation of 4,300 feet and receives about 650 inches of snow each year, the most of any ski area in North America; the last 3 miles of the

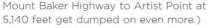

Mount Baker Highway to Artist Point at 5,140 feet get dumped on even more.)

The Mount Baker Highway (the last 24 undeveloped miles of the roadway have been aptly designated the Mount Baker Scenic Byway) is a two-lane roadway that becomes progressively more winding, more hilly, and potentially more intimidating the farther east one goes. That's especially true given that the word "guardrail" is apparently not in local Department of Transportation officials' vocabularies. There's little chance Paul McCartney was thinking of the Mount Baker Highway when he wrote "The Long and Winding Road," but it's certainly an apt description.

All that said, it's only on the last 10 miles that the road really starts to climb up the mountain in a hurry. And though guardrails might not be as present as one might want (the area's prodigious snowfall would make mincemeat out of them) for most of the way, adequate tree cover keeps one from feeling dangerously exposed.

Along with leading to the Mount Baker Ski Area, the highway provides access to Heather Meadows, a spectacular hiking, sightseeing, and picnicking spot that includes Picture Lake, the Austin Pass Picnic Area, and Artist Point, a simply sublime alpine setting at the road's end. On the way the highway passes through foothills communities such as Deming, Maple Falls, and Glacier, each with its own services, accommodations, and restaurants that are worthy of a stop.

For those not comfortable with the drive, or for those who'd just like some company, some Bellingham groups such as Whatcom County Parks and Recreation, The Whatcom Family YMCA, and Bellingham Parks and Recreation offer hiking, snowshoeing, and cross-country skiing outings that include transportation to the Mount Baker Ski Area–Artist Point area. In addition, Bellair Charters (see the Bus Tours section) offers bus trips to the ski area in winter and Artist Point in summer.

For more information on the Mount Baker Highway, including the current con-

ditions, go to www.wsdot.wa.gov/traffic/passes and click on "Mount Baker Highway," or call (800) 695–7623.

CROSSING THE U.S.–CANADA BORDER

Whatcom County has five U.S.–Canada border crossings. From west to east, they are Point Roberts, Peace Arch (I–5), Blaine Truck Crossing (Pacific Highway), Lynden, and Sumas. All are open 24 hours except for Lynden, which is open from 8:00 A.M. to midnight. (Because the Point Roberts crossing is on a mini-peninsula that extends south from the British Columbia mainland and Americans have to go through Canada for more than 20 miles to get to it, it's not a viable entrance point into Canada for Bellinghamsters or visitors thereof.)

Since the terrorist attacks of September 11, 2001, security has been tightened, particularly when crossing into the United States. Travelers, including children, who are U.S. citizens should have either a valid passport or a certified copy of their birth certificate or baptismal record as well as a current photo ID issued by a government agency, i.e. driver's license or ID card. Minors younger than age 14 are not required to show a photo ID.

An individual parent crossing the border (and eventually back into the United States) with children younger than 18 should have a note (preferably notarized) from the child's other parent stating that the child has permission to do so. Similarly,

---

Though the name might be misleading, the Blaine Truck Crossing (Pacific Highway) at the U.S.-Canada border permits cars and, in fact, usually has shorter wait times than the I-5 Peace Arch crossing. Before crossing, check http://apps.cbp.gov/bwt for current wait times.

relatives traveling with children should have a letter giving permission to do so.

In most cases, border agents check ID, ask where you're going, how long you'll be there, and then send you on your way. Occasionally car searches take place. For current border wait times, check http://apps.cbp.gov/bwt.

GETTING AROUND BELLINGHAM

In town the city's popular trail system and wide bike lanes on most of the major arterials make biking a good way to get around Bellingham. Consider renting a bike as a way to familiarize yourself with the city. Fairhaven Bike and Mountain Sports (360-733-4433 or www.fairhaven bike.com) and Jack's Bicycle Center (360-733-1955) rent bikes.

With main sections of town miles apart (i.e., downtown and Fairhaven) and connected by non-motorized-use rail trails, Bellingham is popular with walkers, too. Bellingham pedestrians as a rule adhere to WALK/DON'T WALK signs (on deserted streets, this prompts some serious head-scratching from visiting Easterners) and most drivers stop to let pedestrians pass at crosswalks.

LOCAL TRANSIT

The Whatcom Transit Authority (WTA) serves Bellingham and most populated areas of Western Whatcom County. For route information, call (360) 676-RIDE (7433). For specialized transportation,

Bellingham drivers stop for pedestrians, not just at crosswalks but pretty much anytime they see someone who looks like they have the slightest inclination to cross the street. Thus, if you happen to drive past pedestrians without letting them cross, don't be surprised if you garner some askance looks.

contact WTA at (360) 733-1144. or www.ridewta.com.

STREET LAYOUT

Bellingham city streets can be confusing to newcomers. The city is a merger of four former towns, Whatcom, Sehome, Bellingham, and Fairhaven, each of which platted its streets along the shoreline. The shoreline slants and curves, in fact, makes a 90-degree elbow bend to the northwest in present-day downtown, and the city's bending, slanting streets somewhat reflect this. Add to this the fact that many of those downtown streets are one-way and/or change their names (Prospect Street turns into Dupont Street which turns into Elm Street which turns into Northwest Avenue, all in less than a mile) and even longtime residents (I'm raising my hand here) can sometimes find themselves confused.

Interstate 5 (a north-south route) bisects the city with nine exits offering access to a wide range of neighborhoods, parks, attractions, and, in some places, fast food–big box sprawl and its accompanying congestion.

For **Lake Padden,** get off at exit 246 (if you're coming from the south) or 250 (if you're already in town). For **Fairhaven,** including the Fairhaven Transportation Center (Amtrak and Greyhound stations) and Bellingham Cruise Terminal (Alaska Ferry), exit 250 works best. For **Western Washington University** and Sehome Village shopping center (including REI), try exit 252. For **downtown** Bellingham, Squalicum Harbor, Whatcom Falls Park, and Lake Whatcom, exits 253 and 254 will work. Exit 255 leads to some of Bellingham and Whatcom County's least and most scenic areas—the urban sprawlville and mega traffic of Sunset Square shopping center at the less picturesque side and the **Mount Baker Highway** and its stunning mountain scenery at the other end. St. Joseph Hospital is also accessed at this exit.

For **Bellis Fair Mall** and the city's real big box–fast food strip, Bellingham Golf and Country Club, Cornwall Park, and outlying points in northern Whatcom County such as the town of Lynden, use exit 256. Exit 258 offers access to **Bellingham International Airport,** other points in north Bellingham, a new Fred Meyer's shopping center, and numerous recently constructed condominium and apartment complexes.

Newcomers and first-timers heading to **downtown Bellingham** most likely enter the town via Holly Street after leaving I-5 at exit 253 (Lakeway Drive). Holly leads (one-way) to Bellingham's central business district, a downtown core of shops, businesses, eateries, cafes, galleries, antique shops, and, in recent years, more and more residential units. Colorful awnings, hanging flowers, and sidewalk cafes add color and character to this part of town, some of which dates from the 1850s. Here's where you'll see Bellingham's workaday hustle and bustle, such as the city of subdued excitement can muster. Once in a while, you may even see someone wearing a suit and tie.

Fairhaven, Bellingham's artsy-historic neighborhood, with its brick architecture and with chunky Queen Anne–style homes that sit on the hillside, is about 2.5 miles south of downtown Bellingham and usually one of the first stops for newcomers to the area. Charming cafes, restaurants, hotels, and shops—including Village Books, one of the top independent bookstores in the Northwest—attract visitors and locals who tend to just linger and dawdle, enjoying that extra latte refill or browsing another floor of books. Streets are tree-lined, and the neighborhood's brick and sandstone buildings (Chuckanut sandstone, quarried from slopes just south of here) belie its rough-and-tumble beginnings as a turn-of-the-20th-century port town (with a brothel or two on every corner) founded by one Dirty Dan Harris, by most accounts a rapscallion of a man.

Get to Fairhaven by heading west from I-5 exit 250 for a little more than a mile on Old Fairhaven Parkway. From downtown

Bellingham residents are faithful to WALK/DON'T WALK *signs, especially in the downtown business core. So faithful it's not uncommon to see pedestrians waiting patiently for the* WALK *sign even in early morn when the streets are deserted.*

Bellingham, follow State Street south for about 2.5 miles right into Fairhaven. Harris Avenue, named for Dirty Dan, is the main east-west drag. (State Street follows the shoreline and along the way becomes Boulevard and then 11th Street but requires no turns.) As mentioned above, Chuckanut Drive leads north right into Fairhaven and is a scenic option for those approaching Bellingham from the south.

The 215-acre campus of **Western Washington University** is atop a forested hill (actually a couple hills—South and Sehome Hills) that rises some 400 feet above Bellingham Bay, pretty much equidistant between downtown and Fairhaven. Western, as it's known locally, is an extremely scenic campus with a renowned outdoor sculpture collection and spectacular views that extend across the San Juan Islands and Vancouver's North Shore Mountains.

Whatcom Transit Authority buses leave downtown for campus several times each hour. And Western Washington University campus tours, both student-led and self-guided, are available daily. For information call (360) 650-3861 or check www.wwu .edu and click "Visit."

To get to Western from the freeway, take I-5 exit 252 to Bill McDonald Parkway

Sperling's BestPlaces says that the average B'ham commute is 14 minutes versus the national average of 19. Also, the percentage of Bellingham residents who walk or bike to work is almost twice the national average.

If you head over to Lummi Island, don't be surprised if drivers heading in the opposite direction wave as they pass. It's an island thing. For whatever reason, residents on some of the smaller San Juan Islands—i.e., Lopez, Guemes—are inclined to wave when they pass by. So wave back.

and follow the signs about a mile to campus. From downtown Bellingham, head up the hill via Chestnut and High Streets. From Fairhaven, take Harris and 21st Street.

LOCAL TRAFFIC

Longtime residents may gripe from time to time about how traffic is gradually getting worse, but it's all relative. All it takes is a trip south to Seattle, where the congestion starts about 40 miles north of the Emerald City at Marysville, for residents to realize how good they've got it. Sure, maybe now with the recent construction boom it takes maybe 15 minutes to get from one end of town to the other instead of 10.

Along with I-5, which essentially bisects the city smack down the middle, Bellingham's major streets include:

• State Street, a north-south (northeast-southwest, really) boulevard that follows the shoreline and connects downtown to Fairhaven. Along the way, it melds into Boulevard and 11th Street closer to Fairhaven. In much of downtown, State Street is a one-way street heading south; North Forest Street is its parallel and offers one-way access north.

• East Holly Street, a one-way street heading west, is the most direct route downtown from I-5 (exit 253). It heads west (northwest, really) and after passing through downtown, the Central Business District (where it becomes West Holly Street), Old Town, and the Columbia neighborhood (where it becomes Eldridge Avenue), it leaves the city limits and becomes Marine Drive. This road continues along the shoreline eventually leading to the Lummi Nation. East Magnolia and East Chestnut are east-heading one-way streets that parallel much of Holly and lead to Lakeway Drive.

• Lakeway Drive, which leads east from downtown to Lake Whatcom and Sudden Valley.

• Meridian Street, which heads north from downtown to retail centers, the outlying county (where it becomes Guide Meridian) including the town of Lynden, and eventually, the U.S.–Canada border.

• Sunset Drive, which, after passing through retail and residential areas at the northeast end of town, becomes the Mount Baker Highway and heads east for 57 miles toward its namesake, Mount Baker.

• Harris Avenue, the main east-west drag in Fairhaven, leads down the hill toward Bellingham Bay and the Alaska Cruise terminal and Fairhaven Transportation Center.

• Squalicum Parkway, a trucker's route favored by folks who want to avoid midday or rush-hour downtown congestion but don't want to jump on I-5, offers west city access and leads to Squalicum Harbor. It continues southeast along the Bellingham waterfront as Roeder Avenue and eventually becomes East Chestnut Street.

• Chuckanut Drive, which leads south for 21 winding and scenic miles to the Skagit Flats Area, offers access to the Interurban Trail and Larrabee State Park.

HISTORY 🏛

MOUNTAINS

Bellingham, Mount Baker, and the surrounding area are a geologist's jungle gym. With Puget Sound, the San Juan Islands, and the North Cascade Mountains at the area's doorstep, its natural history is written large in many of its prominent features, much of it accessible to even the most casual armchair geologist.

While Bellingham might be known as the city of subdued excitement, geologically it's been anything but subdued. Deep underground, tectonic plates are slipping and sliding and faults are bumping and grinding all the time. In the process called subduction, the Juan de Fuca plate is slipping easterly under the westward-moving North American Plate. It's not moving fast, usually less than 1 inch per year, but sometimes it's moved as much as half a foot.

Over millions of years, this colliding and grinding has forced rock upward from underneath the surface; about 30 million years ago, it's how much of the Cascade Mountains Range, those snowy peaks to the east, were formed. Thirty million years sounds like a long time but compared to mountains on the East Coast, the Cascades are mere babes. The Appalachians, for instance, formed about half a billion years ago and have been gradually wearing out through erosion ever since.

Mount Baker, however, is a slight variation on the subduction story. As you might expect, subduction produces a lot of heat, much of which manifests itself in the ring of fire volcanoes on the West Coast—from Mount Garibaldi in British Columbia south to Lassen Peak in Northern California—and includes such notables as mounts Baker, Rainier, and St. Helens, which, as most everybody knows, blew its top in 1980.

These volcanoes are all—geologically speaking—very young mountains. Mount Baker dates from only about 30,000 years

ago, though it sits upon the remnants of a much larger and older volcano that was located a little less than 3 miles west of the present-day Mount Baker. That volcano was active about 300,000 to 500,000 years ago, and its remains are visible today in the aptly named Black Buttes, fractured rock outcrops seen (from the west) in Mount Baker's foreground.

Mount Baker has never had a Mount St. Helens-esque eruption. About 10,000 years ago, however, lava flowed from a small cinder cone—a kind of parasitic mini-volcano—on the mountain's south side near today's Schreibers Meadow, a popular hiking area. In the 1840s a major steam blast erupted from Sherman Crater, the 1,200-foot-wide "bite" about 1,000 feet below the summit on Mount Baker's south side. Ash spread throughout the landscape, which set the forest aflame and resulted in a major fish kill in nearby Baker River.

Mount Baker is still an active volcano. Steam plumes emanating from Sherman Crater can occasionally be seen from Bellingham, particularly in winter. In 1975, increased heat, gas, and steam activity in the crater caused a major steam plume, melted glacial snow near the summit, and caused such concern that nearby Baker Lake was closed to public access. Scientists felt that in the event of an eruption,

---

Edmund Coleman, an Englishman living in Victoria, B.C., is credited with being the first person to climb Mount Baker. (There are no records of early Native Americans summiting Koma Kulshan, their name for Mount Baker.) On August 17, 1868, Coleman and climbing partners John Tennant, David Ogilvy, and Thomas Stratton reached the summit after a couple of unsuccessful 1866 attempts.

The Cascades. WWW.PHOTOS.COM

the attendant avalanches, lahars (mud and debris flows), and flooded creeks and rivers would fill the lake to overflowing in no time, and the water level of the dam-impeded lake was lowered 10 feet. Volcanologists and other scientists flocked to the area to monitor the mountain's geothermal activity. Mount Baker never blew, but five years later, Mount St. Helens, a similar-size volcano less than 200 miles to the south, erupted cataclysmically, killing 57 people and shearing off the mountain's upper 1,300 feet. Today Mount Baker is still monitored closely.

Mount Baker is the most heavily glaciated of the Cascades volcanoes, except for Mount Rainier, and it boasts more permanent snow and ice than the others put together.

The Twin Sisters, the two 6,500-foot side-by-side pyramids that are also prominent in the skyline east of Bellingham, tell an interesting story themselves: The massif is one of the largest slabs of exposed mantle rock found anywhere. In the tectonic scrum that is the North Cascades, the rock thrust forth from deep in the earth—some say 10 miles—and emerged mostly unchanged. Composed of dunite, the Twin Sisters have a distinct reddish tint, and at sunset (and sunrise, from the east), they are quite spectacular.

Those are the mountains. Puget Sound and the lowlands of Bellingham and Whatcom County tell a different story.

LOWLANDS

While all this underground shifting and thrusting and faulting was taking place, the earth's surface was experiencing climate changes. The change with perhaps the most impact on what we can see here today occurred during the various Ice Ages and their attendant periods of glaciation. Between two million and 10,000 years ago, scientists believe that Puget Sound experienced at least six episodes of glaciation.

Wanna see what Bellingham was like a long time ago? I mean, a really long time ago? Head south on Chuckanut Drive for about 7 miles to an unmarked pullout just past a Heritage Marker pullout. At an obvious road cut on the east side of Chuckanut Drive are several well-preserved imprints of palm fronds from 50 million years ago, when this part of the coast was a warm, damp, tropical swampland.

The Cordilleran Ice Sheet, which was more than a mile thick, flowed south from what's now British Columbia, receding and advancing, receding and advancing—six times—like a giant window shade being raised and lowered by someone who can't make up their mind. The result was the gouging out of Puget Sound and the carving and deposition of landforms that would become the San Juan Islands and various Western Washington features.

Of course, with 4.6 billion years to cover, geologic history has many layers to it. On Chuckanut Mountain, just south of Bellingham, fossils of palm fronds can be found that date from 50 million years when this area was swampland in a subtropical rainforest. Chuckanut Mountain itself is largely made up of a layer of sedimentation 20,000 feet thick, which has been toppled and folded, accordion-style by subduction and other geologic forces. It's one of the thickest layers of non-ocean sedimentary rock in the world.

The flatlands north and west of Bellingham that today are so conducive to farming are the result of ancient meandering rivers that swept back and forth over many millennia, depositing sediment and leaving great floodplains and deltas in their path. As the Ice Age's massive glaciers melted, rivers such as the Nooksack, Fraser in lower British Columbia, and Skagit, down near Mount Vernon, were much larger and played huge roles in sculpting the region's landforms.

THE FIRST HUMANS

Humans first began inhabiting the Bellingham–Whatcom County area about 12,000 years ago. They migrated from Asia and were drawn to the area's relatively mild climate and rich supply of timber, salmon, and other natural resources. Coast Salish tribes, especially the Lummis, Semiahmoos and Nooksacks, were the predominant groups living here in the mid-1850s when white settlers first started putting down roots. The Lummis and Semiahmoo were located mostly along the coast, and the Nooksacks were settled farther up the river that now bears their name.

Legend has it that in late 1500s, Juan de Fuca, a Greek pilot of a Spanish ship, explored the area while searching for the elusive Northwest Passage. Subsequent explorers named the waterway that separates Washington's Olympic Peninsula from Canada's Vancouver Island—the Strait of Juan de Fuca—after him. It's not known whether de Fuca and his crew ever made land, but stories of a three-day battle between the Spanish and local Native Americans having taken place in present-day Fairhaven persist to this day. A Spanish chalice from those days is also said to have been found.

It was Britain's Capt. George Vancouver, who, in the late 18th century, really put Northwest Washington on the map, literally and figuratively. On his 1792 voyage aboard the *Discovery* to map the West's coastline—a trip on which he somehow missed the mouth of the massive Columbia River that separates Washington from Oregon—Vancouver and his crew sailed east into the strait named after Juan de Fuca. While anchored near Dungeness Spit on the Olympic Coast, Third Lt. Joseph Baker was taking his turn as the ship's watch when he spotted a certain ice- and snow-clad volcano about 100 miles to the east across Puget Sound. As a reward, Vancouver named Mount Baker for him. Local Native Americans called Mount Baker "Koma Kulshan," which, depending on the source, means "the white watcher" or "the shining one" or refers to a peak that has been damaged or exploded.

After crossing Puget Sound, the *Discovery* anchored in today's Birch Bay. Joseph Whidbey, the *Discovery*'s master, sailed south on a smaller boat and discovered Bellingham Bay, which he named after Sir William Bellingham, controller of the storekeeper's accounts of the British navy.

Throughout the first half of the 19th century, as the rest of America was coming into being as Louisiana was purchased, New York City became one of the world's major seaports, Lewis and Clark searched for the Great Northwest Passage, and thousands rushed West for California gold, this far corner of the Northwest remained largely unsettled.

During this time, local Indian tribes did have contact with Russian, Spanish, Japanese and British traders, and Catholic missionaries migrated north from Oregon and converted many to Christianity. But it wasn't until mid-century that white people began settling in the area, dramatically altering it forever. About 1,000 Native Americans populated the area at the time. About 75 years earlier that number was closer to 3,000, but many Native Americans died from various epidemics.

In 1852, a couple of less-than-supersuccessful California gold miners headed north in search of lumber to help rebuild San Francisco, which tended to burn down from time to time. With the help of Lummi Chief Chawitzit, Henry Roeder and Russell Peabody found what they were looking for—falling water in a protected bay—at the mouth of Whatcom Creek, located in

ℹ️ *In the late 19th century, Bellingham was four separate bayside towns. Whatcom was basically where Old Town is located today. Sehome was where downtown is. Bellingham was about where Boulevard Park is, and Fairhaven has remained in the same South Side spot.*

today's Maritime Heritage Park, just below the Whatcom Museum of History and Art.

With the help of local Native Americans, Roeder and Peabody built a mill, and Whatcom, the first of what would eventually be four waterfront towns, sprang up. Whatcom is a Lummi word for "noisy all the time" (or "noisy, rumbling water," depending on the source), a reference to the creek on which the town was founded. Not long after, coal was found just east of Whatcom under a tree stump.

A San Francisco syndicate purchased rights to the coal property and formed the Bellingham Bay Coal Company. Soon the mine employed 125 people, far more than Roeder and Peabody's mill. Sehome, the second town on the bay, which is named after Chief Sehome of the Clallam tribe, sprung up at about the location of today's downtown.

It was the only coal producer in the region, and since Indian tribes from Southeast Alaska and coastal British Columbia tended to make annual raids to terrorize area Lummis, the government realized that their commercial interests were at stake. In 1856 the U.S. Army built Fort Bellingham on the bay a couple miles west of Whatcom. Its commanding officer was George Pickett, who would later gain fame as a Confederate general, particularly for his role in the battle at Gettysburg.

In 1858 gold was discovered in the Fraser Valley in southern British Columbia, about 80 miles northeast of Whatcom. Work was begun on the trail through the nearly impenetrable forest, and the towns boomed as thousands made their way to the area in search of riches. Estimates from the time say as many as 10,000 potential prospectors and the like were camped out on the shores of Bellingham Bay waiting to make their way up the trail.

The boom was short-lived, however, as B.C.'s Gov. James Douglas realized that Victoria was missing out on a gold rush in its own country. He passed a law requiring that prospective miners obtain mining permits in Victoria at the southern tip of Vancouver Island on their way to the Fraser.

The oldest brick building in Washington State still stands at 1308 E Street in Old Town. Built in 1858, the one-story Richards Building (formerly a two-story until E Street was raised) has served as a general store, bank, warehouse, and courthouse.

Around the same time that these towns on the north end of the bay were bouncing from boom to bust and bust to boom and back again, a couple of settlements at the south end of the bay— Bellingham and Fairhaven—were gaining footholds. Fairhaven, as legend would have it, was founded by one Dan Harris, better known as Dirty Dan Harris.

Born on Long Island, Dan Harris left home as a teen to travel the world on whaling ships. At about the same time Roeder and Peabody were helping settle the north end of Bellingham Bay, Harris showed up on a beach about 2.5 miles south. He rowed some 50 miles from Victoria to get there, having just jumped ship (or been kicked off; details are sketchy) shortly after his ship returned from China.

Once on Bellingham Bay, he made good. For the next 25 years or so, Harris made his living as a smuggler and in real estate. A big man, he rowed frequently to Victoria and smuggled liquor into Fairhaven, the South Side town he would eventually found. Harris was somewhat of a loner, living by himself in a cabin on the bay. A true character, he was known for his unkempt appearance and uncouth manner—thus his nickname, Dirty Dan. Over time, however, he proved he was more than just some odd recluse with a high odoriferous content. He was a wheeler and dealer and knew how to make a buck, especially in real estate. He platted streets, built Fairhaven's first hotel, and become the town's eccentric real estate tycoon, owning more than 200 acres there.

Bellingham, just north of Fairhaven, was the fourth town on the bay. It was founded in 1871 and quickly boomed. It

ℹ️ *Fairhaven: artsy-historic today, tarty and rough-and-tumble then. This South Side neighborhood that everyone flocks to for its cafes, shops, massage therapists, and yoga classes has a somewhat checkered past. Some accounts say that in 1889 Fairhaven boasted 31 saloons and "sporting houses"—i.e., brothels—in 1 square block.*

merged with Fairhaven, and together they had high hopes that their fine city would become the West Coast terminal for the Northern Pacific Railroad and become the Chicago of the west, as it were. But Seattle got the call instead, and Fairhaven and Bellingham quickly busted.

Though gold and railroad fever spurred and then stalled the area's economic growth, the area's natural resources were so plentiful that it couldn't help but grow and succeed over time. (This, despite the fact that the Roeder mill, which was never a huge success anyway, burned down in 1873 and Sehome's first coal mill closed down in 1878, the result of cave-ins, floods, and fires.) Investors from other parts of the United States—Washington territory was not yet a state—were flooding in, putting their money in docks, land, mines, and mills.

Like many cities in the Northwest, one of Bellingham's growing pains manifested itself in the less-than-sparkling manner in which it dealt with certain groups of immigrants. With mills, mines, and railroads burgeoning, there was a need for plentiful cheap labor, and many Chinese immigrants

ℹ️ *For a vivid portrayal of Bellingham life during its pioneer days, read* The Living, *by Pulitzer Prize–winning author Annie Dillard. Be forewarned, however, that more than one reader has commented that the gritty novel should be more aptly titled* The Dying.

flocked to the area in the early days of settlement. But given the area's economic ups and downs, anti-Chinese resentment was never far away. The Chinese Exclusion Act of 1882 prevented any more Chinese from entering, and in 1885 they were actually kicked out. Loaded up on boats and unceremoniously shipped out, their expulsion was celebrated with a torchlight parade.

An 1893 real estate ad to lure newcomers to town reads almost like something out of *Blazing Saddles:* "The foreign population are nearly all Norwegians, Swedes, and Canadian . . . there are no Chinese, no Hungarians, and few Italians." Of course, just a few years later when the canneries began to boom and cheap labor was again needed, the Chinese were lured back. In 1890 there was just a single Chinese person in Whatcom County; 10 years later there were almost 900.

Bellingham's early behavior with local Native Americans wasn't always the best, either. Along with confining the local Lummis to a peninsula of land about 12 miles west of town, Lummi children were forced to leave their families and attend white-run, English-speaking-only boarding schools in Lynden, or even faraway places such as Oregon and Idaho. It was part of the U.S. program requiring Native Americans to attend federal Indian boarding schools.

As the 1904 commissioner of Indian Affairs wrote, the goal was "To educate the Indian in the ways of civilized life . . . is to preserve him from extinction, not as an Indian, but as a human being. As a separate entity he cannot exist . . . in the body of this great nation." The consequences were horrific, and in 2000 the assistant secretary of Indian Affairs apologized for this sad chapter in America's history.

Though Bellingham didn't get the Northern Pacific Railroad terminus, by the early 1890s three other railroads connected the area to markets down the West Coast and across the continent, and the timber industry took off. By 1900, Whatcom County had nearly 70 shingle mills.

Fairhaven's Puget Sound Sawmills & Timber Company was the largest shingle mill in the world, turning out 135,000 shingles a year (1901) by itself. By 1907, Bellingham Bay Lumber Company was turning out almost a quarter-million shingles each year. At one time, there were more than 70 sawmills and 100 shingle mills in the Bellingham Bay area. Fishing boomed, too. By 1901, 12 bayside fish canneries were operating, employing some 5,000 workers, including almost 1,000 Chinese immigrants.

ROAD TO MOUNT BAKER

Meanwhile, some folks were heading farther inland toward the Cascade Mountains. In the later half of the 19th century, miners, loggers, homesteaders, and others began arriving and founding settlements along the Nooksack River closer to the mountains. As road-building improved in the 1870s and 1880s there was a push to build a road that would one day span the North Cascades into eastern Washington. (That wouldn't become a reality for almost 100 years. Highway 20, the North Cascades Highway, opened in 1972 and crosses the Cascades about 30 miles south of where civic leaders hoped it would.)

By 1896 a road extended all the way from Bellingham Bay to the now-defunct mining townsite of Shuksan, about 50 miles away at the base of Mount Baker. (It's near the present-day Silver Fir campground, about milepost 46 on the Mount Baker Highway.) And that's as far as it went until the mid-1920s when some Bellingham developers formed the Mount Baker Development Company. They made an agreement with the federal government to build a lodge in return for a 9-mile road that would climb 2,000 winding feet, to a selected site at about 4,500 feet.

In 1927 the highway to the posh Mount Baker Lodge, located near the present-day ski area and Heather Meadows, opened to great fanfare. Each of the lodge's 100 rooms had hot- and cold-running water and a telephone, which is more than can be said of the spot today. (Even today there is no landline phone service at the Mount Baker Ski Area, the area's only present-day concession.) Many of the trails in the area—around Table Mountain, Bagley Lakes, etc.—were completed at this time for guests to enjoy. The highway's final 3 miles to Artist Point were completed in 1929.

Oddly, given the area's present-day reputation as a winter wonderland and one of snowboarding's places of origin, the lodge was a summer resort only. It opened in June and closed just after Labor Day.

The lavish lodge offered miniature golf, sightseeing, boating, swimming, hiking, fishing, and guided mountain climbing. Unfortunately, in 1931 it burned to the ground in an electrical fire. But with its good road built high into a spectacular subalpine setting, Heather Meadows and Artist Point grew in reputation as a regional tourist destination spot.

CONSOLIDATION

In 1889 Washington became the 42nd state in the union. A year later Bellingham and Fairhaven merged as Fairhaven. The next year, Whatcom and Sehome became New Whatcom. (Ten years later, New Whatcom changed its name to Whatcom.) With industries established and new ones burgeoning all the time and a population

Today a five-minute drive along State Street and the Boulevard is all that separates Fairhaven from downtown. A little more than 100 years ago, however, the roads were so rough and forest still so thick that most people traveled between the two by steamship. Most roads in those days were wood planks laid atop dirt, which, given the area's high precip levels, inevitably turned to muck and mud.

Mount Baker Marathon—Ski to Sea

In the early 1900s, before the road to Heather Meadows and the Mount Baker Lodge was built, civic leaders in Bellingham made a push for the Mount Baker Area to be designated as a National Park. The Mount Baker Club, a group of Whatcom County outdoor recreation-minded business leaders, formed with the hope that with the lure of a national park in its backyard, Bellingham and Whatcom County would become a real tourist destination. They were encouraged by what happened to local communities near Mount Rainier after it became a national park in 1899. (The club still exists today though with a different focus; it's called the Mount Baker Hiking Club.)

To publicize the idea, the Mount Baker Club came up with the idea for the Mount Baker Marathon, a race from Bellingham to the top of Mount Baker and back in which competitors were allowed to use any mode of conveyance that they wished. To get from Bellingham to the trails leading to the mountain, racers chose between the 44-mile Bellingham Bay and British Columbia Railroad ride to the town of Glacier (from there it was 14 miles one-way up wooded trail and glacier; a 28-mile run-hike-climb round-trip) or driving 26 miles to a local ranch just west of the mountain (from there it has a run-hike-climb of 16 miles; a 32 mile round-trip through forest and glaciers).

Given that the upper 5,000 feet or so of Mount Baker is heavily glaciated (much of it riddled with crevasses) not to mention prone to avalanche, it's not surprising that this race was held only three times before being discontinued for safety reasons. In the 1913 race, a racer fell 40 feet into a crevasse and almost froze to death as he waited some six hours to be rescued. The Mount Baker Marathon was never held again.

In 1973, however, a spirit of the race was revived with the initiation of the now-annual Ski to Sea relay race. Held Memorial Day weekend, Ski to Sea is the centerpiece of Bellingham and Whatcom County's biggest community event. Instead of individuals racing to and from Mount Baker's summit, more than 300 8-person relay teams cross-country ski, downhill ski, run, road bike, canoe, mountain bike, and kayak an 80-mile course from the Mount Baker Ski Area to Marine Park on Bellingham Bay. Along with almost 2,500 race participants, more than 100,000 people converge on the area for a weeklong celebration featuring fairs, concerts, art shows, and more.

The early Mount Baker Marathons brought publicity to the area, but they didn't bring the mountain or the area national park status. Concerns over the mining and logging restrictions that would be imposed were it to become a national park stalled the movement, as did encroaching World War I. The area remained under the jurisdiction of the national forest.

In 1968, however, 684,000-acre North Cascades National Park was signed into law. It included Mount Shuksan but oddly not Mount Baker. Lobbying by area conservationists paid off in 1984, however,

Mount Baker. WWW.PHOTOS.COM

when 117,500 acres of national forest in the Mount Baker area—including most of Mount Baker itself—much of it bordering the national park to the west, was proclaimed the Mount Baker Wilderness Area. The goal of a wilderness area is to manage human use so it doesn't alter natural processes. No logging or mining can take place, and motorized vehicles are not allowed into the backcountry.

In conjunction with the wilderness act, the Mount Baker National Recreation Area was also created in 1984 so winter snowmobile use could legally continue on the south side of Mount Baker in the Schreibers Meadow area.

As you walk throughout Fairhaven, take a moment to look down. Historical markers point out sites of the neighborhood's colorful and sometimes notorious past. There's Dirty Dan's cabin site (Padden Creek trail); the Unknown Dead, expired bodies in need of ID-ing (10th Street and Harris Avenue); Counterfeiters' Hideout (11th Street and Mill Avenue); and lots more.

that was growing, residents turned their attention to the future. In 1903 consolidation as one bayside city was proposed.

At first, both support for and in opposition of such a move was vocal. At the north end of the bay, Whatcom residents saw the advantages in increased government services and a legitimacy and prosperity that would come with becoming Washington's fourth-largest city. They believed it would be better to face the future as a single city rather than two small towns. Down in Fairhaven, the fear was that only those large landowners in Whatcom would prosper, businesses would bolt from the South Side, and in no time, Fairhaven would become a ghost town. In the end the consolidation election wasn't even close: It passed by more than a 3 to 1 margin.

But now, there was the pesky matter of a name—should it be Fairhaven? Whatcom? Or, as was even suggested by one of the town's newspapers, Whathaven? Townsfolk compromised by choosing Bellingham, the former name of one of the townsites as well as the bay. On December 28, 1903, Bellingham was officially born. Its population was roughly 22,000, and another 10,000 would move in over the next decade.

THE OLD CITY HALL

One of today's most prominent Bellingham icons, the distinct red Victorian brick and Chuckanut sandstone City Hall building (now the Whatcom Museum of History and Art) hails from those formative years. Built in 1892 atop a bluff above Whatcom Creek—and thus overlooking where Roeder and Peabody first went ashore and built their mill—the buildings four red cupolas and four-sided clock tower are visible from much of Bellingham.

When it opened as New Whatcom's city hall, one of the first orders of business was enacting a law banning cows from wandering the streets at night. The town's mayor was subsequently arrested for illegally entering the pound and busting out his cow, which had been guilty of nighttime street roaming. But the mayor was found innocent after pleading that he'd done no such thing. Rather, the cow had merely spotted him outside the pen and become so overcome with longing that it just followed the mayor home.

Back in those days, prostitution was a viable industry as well. Local lady of the night Lizzie Rose had her house of ill repute listed in the city directory. Her occupation: madam. There was even "The Sporting House and Club directory for Whatcom and Fairhaven." In time, as the towns consolidated and Bellingham was moving forward as a legitimate city, the sporting houses were abolished in 1910. But not without a little reluctance on the part of the town's fathers. Of the city's $150,000 budget at the time, $17,000 of it came from fines related to prostitution. Cutting out that fine money meant the city would have to miss out on two fire trucks it had planned to buy.

20TH CENTURY

Throughout the 20th century, Bellingham and the surrounding county grew as industries such as agriculture, fishing, timber, and others became further established. Fairhaven-based Pacific American Fisheries, which operated out of Bellingham through the mid-1960s, was once the largest salmon cannery in the world,

A historic look at the Mount Baker Highway. BELLINGHAM WHATCOM COUNTY TOURISM

Hollywood and Mount Baker

Once the paved road to Heather Meadows was completed in 1927, it wasn't long before Hollywood productions came calling, drawn by this new, relatively easy high-mountain access. First, there was *Wolf Fangs* in 1927, a feature about a dog named Thunder who left his human family for the lure of the wilderness. For the shoot, more than 500 sheep and 30 dogs were transported to the meadows.

Next was *The Call of the Wild* in 1934, starring Clark Gable and Loretta Young. Based on the classic Jack London adventure novel set in Alaska (and once again focusing on a dog), the film was one of Hollywood's biggest budget movies. Filming took place at the Heather Meadows Area and along the Nooksack River. Because it was a winter shoot, the road to Heather Meadows was plowed through the winter for the first time ever.

In 1937, Heather Meadows once again stood in for Alaska when the gold-rush pic *The Barrier* was filmed there. In contrast to *The Call of the Wild,* this was a summertime shoot, and the crew had to shoot around the summertime sightseers and picnickers, many of whom were curious and tended to get in the way of shooting.

The area became a movie set once again in the late 1970s when scenes from *The Deer Hunter* were shot here. Scenes were also shot high on Glacier Creek Road. Oddly enough, the location was supposed to be depicting western Pennsylvania.

employing more than 1,000 people at its Fairhaven plant.

The timber industry boomed—the Puget Sound Saw Mill and Shingle Company was the largest shingle maker in the world—and businesses such as shipping, canning, fish salting, ship making, box making, and others that met the needs of established industries provided employment as well. Coal mining had its ups and downs, with mines being established (and eventually being closed) on the south end of Lake Whatcom (Blue Canyon) and at the north end of Bellingham near today's Birchwood neighborhood.

As homesteaders in outlying areas cleared more and more forest, Whatcom County became a major agricultural force, too. Early crops included potatoes, lettuce, celery, hops, flax, and sugar beets. Dairy and poultry farms were big, too. The area's mild climate—not especially hot, not especially cold, usually pretty damp—was conducive to horticulture, which also took off. Tulips became so popular and such big business that in 1920 the first Tulip Time Festival—featuring its own Tulip Queen—was held. The following year, more than

ℹ *Two-time Oscar winner Hilary Swank hails from the Bellingham area. She grew up on Lake Samish, just south of Bellingham, and honed her acting chops on stages at Sehome High School and the Bellingham Theatre Guild.*

100,000 bulbs were planted. (The festival was the forerunner to today's annual Ski to Sea Festival.) Bulb production continued to blossom until severe freezes in the late 1920s killed thousands of bulbs, forcing the industry to move 25 miles south to Skagit County. (The annual Skagit Tulip Festival is that community's largest event.)

These days, along with being the largest raspberry producer in the United States, Whatcom County is Washington State's biggest dairy producer, and one of the top 12 in the country.

PIPELINE DISASTER

In 1999 Bellingham made the national news as a result of one of the saddest chapters in its history, the Olympic Pipe Line disaster, which killed three youths. On June 10, a pipeline that carried gasoline, diesel fuel, and jet fuel from refineries near Ferndale ruptured in Whatcom Falls Park and spilled 276,000 gallons of gasoline into Whatcom Creek. Ninety minutes after the pipeline broke, the gas ignited and shot a gasoline fireball along the creek and through the park, which killed two 10-year old boys and an 18 year old man and injured eight others.

A thick plume of black smoke rose 6 miles into the sky, and many residents who remembered Mount St. Helens' 1980 eruption wondered if Mount Baker had blown

In 1949 Bellingham had the world's tallest Christmas tree. The 153-foot tree was decorated with lights and put up downtown on Railroad Avenue. During a national radio broadcast from New York, Edward R. Murrow, who grew up about 10 miles south of Bellingham, flipped a switch and turned on the lights.

🛈

its top. Property damage was estimated at $50 million. For its negligence, Olympic Pipe Line was fined $36 million and forced to pay $75 million to the families of those who died.

TODAY

In 2003 Bellingham celebrated its 100-year anniversary. In the past 20 years, its reputation as one of the most sought-out places to live, noted for recreational opportunities on land and sea as well as its colleges, city parks, public schools, and cultural events, has grown significantly. It's a city—and part of a county—that's poised for the future, intent on maintaining its unique character as well as honoring its role as caretaker of one of the most spec-tacular natural settings in the country.

ACCOMMODATIONS 🛏

Visitors to Bellingham and the Mount Baker area have a vast array of accommodation choices. Along with most of the major mid- and economy-price chain motels that have a presence here, Bellingham is also served by some unique accommodations, several of which take advantage of the city's waterfront setting and surrounding scenic beauty. History too, is served, as B&Bs set in charming Victorian homes recall the city's early days as a turn-of-the-20th-century seaport.

Closer to Mount Baker, a number of lodges, cabins, B&Bs, and the like offer places to stay. Take note, however, that the nearest accommodations to the Mount Baker Ski Area and Artist Point are in and around the small town of Glacier, at least 17 miles away. That's because the last stretch of the Mount Baker Highway passes through National Forest where there are no private lodging facilities. (Glacier is 33 miles east of Bellingham.)

Until about 2000, most Bellingham offerings in the lodgings department were fairly unspectacular. But within mere months, it seemed, three luxury boutique hotels opened along the waterfront—not crammed next to each other but not far from each other, either—two with their own spas and upscale seaside eatery. With amenities and ambience heretofore unknown in the City of Subdued Excitement, the Fairhaven Village Inn, the Hotel Bellwether, and the Chrysalis Inn have raised the bar on Bellingham's lodging options. And this being Bellingham and not, say, Scottsdale, the overwhelming majority of rooms in these hotels can be had for less than $200. (That is, except for the Bellwether's three-story Lighthouse Suite, which has its own observation deck.)

Looking forward, in 2006 and 2007, both the Silver Reef Casino and Nooksack River Casino plan to open brand-new hotels. With 105 and 200 rooms, respectively, they would be among the largest hotels in the area. And sometime in the near future, the 24-room Mount Baker Trailhead Lodge, a 23,000-square-foot lodge and conference center, is planned in the woods near Glacier.

Generally, Bellingham lodging rates are cheaper from about October to May. In Bellingham, in-season is considered from about mid-May to the end of September. In local parlance, that would be from Ski to Sea to back-to-school at Western Washington University. A good source for off-season deals is WashingtonRes.com (888–261–7795; www.washingtonres.com), which works with local accommodations and convention and visitors bureaus to offer good deals.

Closer to Mount Baker, many places have two in-seasons: a summer one from Independence Day to Labor Day when the hills and valleys and mountains are crawling with hikers, climbers, and sightseers and a winter one—Christmas till sometime in March, depending on what kind of snow year it is—geared for the skiers, snowboarders, and snowshoers. Expect some places to offer reduced rates from September to November and April to June.

Several motels are located off the Samish Way exit of Interstate 5, which is the closest exit to Western Washington University and is convenient to Fairhaven, too. Exits close to the airport and Bellis Fair Mall also have their share of places to stay, and these make for easy springboards to Vancouver, Whistler, and points north. But of course the whole area is small enough that pretty much anyplace is convenient—i.e., less than a 20-minute schlep—to anyplace else in town.

All establishments accept credit cards and offer non-smoking rooms. They're in accordance with ADA regulations, and though most places don't accept pets, a surprising number do. Those are noted.

The chapter is organized as follows: Bellingham hotels and motels first, followed by B&Bs. Following that are the Mount Baker–area lodging choices, treated separately because most of these are at least 30 miles outside of Bellingham.

PRICE CODE

$	Less than $75
$$	$76 to $125
$$$	$126 to $175
$$$$	More than $176

HOTELS AND MOTELS

Airport/Mall

Best Western Heritage Inn   **$$**
151 East McLeod Road
(360) 647-1912, (800) 780-7234
www.bestwestern.com/heritageinn bellingham

This is a Northwest Best Western with a twist—a New England theme is present in its Cape Cod architecture, colonial furniture, and floral quilts. Of course this is the 21st century, so along with all the services and amenities one expects from Best Western—clean, comfortable rooms, free *USA Today* newspaper, cable TV with HBO, conference rooms, etc.—this smoke-free, professionally run hotel offers free high-speed Internet service and a heated swimming pool with a Jacuzzi spa. Though the 90-room hotel has no restaurant, its free continental breakfast is quite hearty, offering waffles to ham to hard-boiled eggs. Many restaurants are nearby: i.e., Denny's, Mi Mexico, Thai House, Red Robin, a gourmet burger restaurant, and more. Located just off I-5 exit 256, the hotel is across the Guide Meridian from Bellis Fair Mall, thus shopping and movie-going opportunities are plentiful.

Comfort Inn   **$$**
4282 Meridian Street
(360) 738-1100, (877) 424-6423
www.choicehotels.com

Conveniently located to I-5, Bellis Fair Mall, Whatcom Community College, and Bellingham International Airport, this 85-room motel features an indoor pool, a hot tub and sauna, and an exercise room. Though it has no restaurant, an Olive Garden and other chain eateries are close by, as well as Costco, Wal-Mart, and Bellingham's biggest mall. Most rooms are of the one-king or two-double-bed variety, though more posh suites are available as well. Options include the Whirlpool Suite, which comes with a two-person Jacuzzi tub, and the Presidential Suite, which has a full kitchen and separate living area. For business travelers, the motel offers a meeting space that can accommodate 24 people. All Comfort Inn guests may also partake in a deluxe complimentary breakfast, which includes Belgian waffles, fruit, muffins and breads, yogurt, and more. Other amenities include a free *USA Today* and free in-room Internet access.

Hampton Inn Bellingham Airport   **$$**
3985 Bennett Drive
(360) 676-7700, (800) HAMPTON
www.hamptoninn-bellingham.com

As hinted at in the name, this Hampton Inn is the nearest hotel to Bellingham International Airport. And because the airport is small, the noisy associations one might have with staying near runways is not applicable at all. Instead, this clean, 132-room well-appointed hotel makes a great choice for those flying into Bellingham or planning day trips or getaways to Vancouver or Seattle. The Hampton offers free *USA Today* daily, Starbucks coffee and cookies at night, an outdoor swimming pool, an on-site fitness center, and shuttle service to the airport and train-ferry-bus station. It's also noted for its free 21-item breakfast buffet, which boasts pancakes, waffles, fruits, cereals, and the buffet headliner, homemade pecan-caramel cinnamon rolls. Rooms feature either king-size or two queen-size beds, and some come with jetted tubs. For event planners, the Hampton is also the site of Fox Hall, a state-of-the-art meeting facility. The 3,700-square-foot ballroom can be divided into a couple of large meeting rooms or even a 350-seat theater.

Holiday Inn Express $$
4160 Meridian Street
(360) 671-4800, (800) HOLIDAY
www.ichotelsgroup.com
Located on the Guide Meridian just off I-5 exit 256, this fresh, clean hotel in the popular chain is conveniently located near a number of Bellingham's shopping destinations and just across the street from Whatcom Community College. Bellis Fair Mall (with its Regal Bellis Fair Cinema) is a half-mile away, with Costco, Wal-Mart, Home Depot, and like emporiums, not to mention like dining options—Olive Garden, Wendy's, Taco Bell, etc.—less than half that far. The hotel, noted for its ultra-accommodating staff, features 101 rooms, including 90 non-smoking ones, high-speed Internet access, an indoor pool and Jacuzzi, and a mega-deluxe complimentary breakfast bar that'll keep you stuffed into the afternoon. Shuttle service is free to Bellingham International Airport, which is 2 miles down the road, as well as to the Amtrack/Greyhound station in Fairhaven, about 5 miles away. Pets are welcome.

Quality Inn Baron Suites $$
100 East Kellogg Road
(360) 647-8000, (800) 900-4661
www.choicehotels.com
Perhaps a little more upscale than the nearby Comfort Inn (both members of the Choice Hotels chain), though not a lot more expensive, the Baron Suites offers amenities such as free 24-hour shuttle service to nearby Bellingham International Airport and state-of-the-art meeting facilities for up to 100 people. Rooms are a tad larger and perhaps better appointed than the Comfort Inn, and some feature bal-

conies. Larger suites come with kitchens, entertainment centers, and whirlpool tubs. The heated outdoor pool and hot tub are glorious during the summer months, and families needn't fret about leaving Fido at home; this is a pet-friendly hotel. The free continental breakfast features a make-your-own waffle bar.

Fairhaven

The Chrysalis Inn & Spa $$$$
804 10th Street
(360) 756-1005, (888) 808-0005
www.thechrysalisinn.com
One of Bellingham's three luxury boutique hotels, the Chrysalis is located right on the bay, just above the newly built Taylor Avenue Dock, which has quickly become the city's favorite bayside promenade. Along with 34 deluxe rooms that boast gas fireplaces, two-person tubs, window seats, and Internet access, guests at the Chrysalis can choose from nine luxury suites. These up the ante on the amenities scale with such comforts as two-person Jacuzzi tubs and separate living rooms with wet bar. All rooms are appointed in a classic Northwest style—lots of wood and windows that open to island and sunset views. Conveniently located (trails less than a half-mile long lead to Fairhaven in the south and Boulevard Park in the north) the Chrysalis is also renowned for its day spa, The Spa at the Chrysalis Inn, and the Fino Wine Bar, its upscale restaurant, which boasts waterfront views. Note: Train noise can sometimes be a problem.

Fairhaven Village Inn $$$
1200 10th Street
(360) 733-1311, (877) 733-1100
www.fairhavenvillageinn.com
Though built less than a decade ago, the Village Inn fits in perfectly with Fairhaven's historic turn-of-the-20th-century feel. Located just a few blocks from Bellingham Bay—as everything in Fairhaven is—this small boutique hotel (just 22 rooms) boasts period window

The Chrysalis Inn, adjacent to Taylor Avenue Dock. MIKE MCQUAIDE

treatments, signs, and lighting, and ornate molding work. Just inside, the library's dark wood, stuffed bookshelves, and welcoming fireplace round out the picture, as does the cashier's cage at the front desk, like something from an old Western. Rooms are spacious and tastefully appointed, with bayside rooms featuring fireplaces and balconies opening to bay and island views. (To be truthful, several rooftop views, too.) The Fairhaven is perhaps Bellingham's most conveniently located hotel for visitors without a car, or for those who like to drive as little as possible. It's just up the street from the ferry/train/bus station and within walking distance of every Fairhaven and downtown attraction—shopping, parks, trails, etc. (The front door opens to the South Bay–Boulevard Park Trail, which traces the

waterfront for about 2 miles on its way downtown. Also just outside is the Fairhaven Village Green, home to a Wednesday farmers' market and numerous festivals and performances throughout the year, including an outdoor cinema in summer.) A full continental breakfast is included with a night's stay, and kids younger than age 12 stay free in the parents' room. Pets are welcome.

Lakeway

Best Western Lakeway Inn $$
714 Lakeway Drive
(360) 671-1011, (800) 671-1011,
(800) 780-7234
www.bellingham-hotel.com
With clean, comfortable Best Western

rooms, a good-size conference center containing more than 11,000 square feet, and a Grand Ballroom that can accommodate 500 guests, the Lakeway Inn has hosted many a New Year's Eve and Halloween party over the years. Along with an indoor pool and hot tub, the Lakeway has a restaurant and bar, Poppe's Bistro and Lounge, which has live entertainment on weekends. Its location, just off I–5 exit 253 close to downtown and Western Washington University, make it a popular lodging spot for parents dropping off, visiting, or picking up their college-going progeny. Also nearby are a Fred Meyer Shopping Center and a number of storefront shops and restaurants.

Val-U Inn Motel $
805 Lakeway Drive
(360) 671-9600, (800) 443-7777
www.bellinghamvaluinn.com
Located across Lakeway Drive from Best Western Lakeway, Val-U Inn is right off the freeway, so it's easy to find and convenient to Western Washington University and downtown. With 82 rooms, Val-U Inn is smaller than the Lakeway. It's also less expensive, though it has, perhaps, fewer amenities. But as its name suggests, it's a decent value for the money. Rooms are clean and have one queen- or king-size bed (or two queen-size), a coffeemaker, and HBO. Guests also receive a free *USA Today,* a continental breakfast, and, on weekday evenings, homemade cookies. The motel offers free shuttle service to Bellingham International Airport as well as to the train/bus/ferry station in Fairhaven. It's also a pick-up and drop-off point for the Airporter Shuttle to and from Seattle's Sea-Tac Airport.

Samish Way

Ramada Inn Bellingham $$
215 Samish Way
(360) 734-8830, (800) 272-6232
www.ramada.com

Recently remodeled, this Bellingham link in the popular hotel chain is conveniently located near Western Washington University and, outdoor enthusiasts will be happy to know, a large REI store. All rooms have HBO, radio, hair dryer, and iron and ironing board, and some have microwave ovens. Most feature queen-size beds, though some have king-size beds and walk-out balconies. Continental breakfast is free and available in the lobby. The large outdoor heated swimming pool is open from May to September and, for taking in the rays (or just taking it easy) features a large sundeck. Located on Samish Way, it's within walking distance of grocery shopping, movie theaters, various dining establishments including Lemon Grass and On Rice (both Thai), Black Angus (steak house), and the usual suspects in the fast-food establishments.

Squalicum Waterfront

Hotel Bellwether $$$$
One Bellwether Way
(360) 392-3100, (877) 411-1200
www.hotelbellwether.com
There's posh and then there's the Hotel Bellwether, Bellingham's only four-star hotel and one of only three in the Northwest. Situated at the end of a spit jutting out into Bellingham Bay, the $16 million Bellwether, which opened in 2000, is a small boutique hotel with 66 rooms, all boasting jetted tubs (with separate shower—nice touch), marble and granite countertops, furniture imported from Italy, gas fireplaces, high-speed Internet access, CD/DVD players, and balconies with either a water view to the sunset and San Juan Islands or a city perspective against the backdrop of Mount Baker. Some rooms feature both. The Bellwether's true highlight, however, is the Lighthouse Suite, a three-story building with kitchenette, "Ultra-masseur tub," and a private observation deck with 360-degree views. Three floors with two spiral staircases offer

views of water, islands, mountain, and city. Wanna really splurge? Go for the private butler, champagne, and caviar option.

With its sweeping views and renowned reputation in hospitality circles, the Bellwether is popular for weddings, graduations, and the like (it has more than 13,000 square feet of event space) and the hotel, as well as the upscale Harborside Restaurant, go all out to help create memories that will last a lifetime. About 10 minutes from Bellingham International Airport, the Bellwether also has a 220-foot dock for those arriving by boat or seaplane. Along with the upscale Harborside Restaurant, the Bellwether has a fitness center and a world-class spa, and with its location at the end of the spit, it's adjacent to shops, galleries, and restaurants. Just outside a paved walking path weaves along the waterfront to Squalicum Harbor, one of Puget Sound's largest, with more than 1,800 commercial and pleasure boats.

Nearby

Semiahmoo Resort $$$$
9565 Semiahmoo Parkway, Blaine
(360) 318-2000, (800) 770-7992
These are true luxury accommodations on a mostly undeveloped spit of land jutting into Semiahmoo Bay just south of the U.S.–Canada border, about 25 miles northwest of Bellingham. Along with boasting two of the state's top three golf courses (one designed by Arnold Palmer), Semiahmoo features a deluxe spa, several dining options, and 198 luxurious rooms, including 28 suites. And with its location on a spit with tidewater on its sides, spectacular sunsets are a given. (Sunrises too, if you happen to be up that early.) As are views of Mount Baker and San Juan Island. The spacious Northwest-appointed rooms (i.e., lots of rich dark and honey-colored woods) take full advantage of those views with patios or walk-out balconies. Rooms range from single rooms with one king-size or two queen-size beds to executive

king suites with spacious living rooms and wood-burning fireplaces. All have in-room phones with voice mail, high-speed Internet connection, and coffeemakers, and guests receive free daily newspapers.

The spa and salon offer all manner of massages, facials, and various nail and hair treatments. Likewise, at the fitness center, guests can enjoy not only yoga and aerobics sessions but also fitness evaluations and personal training. The golf courses, Loomis Trail (rated number one in Washington State) and Semiahmoo Golf Club (number three), are not actually on-site but located within 3 miles of the resort property. The resort is located at the end of a 1.5-mile-long spit, much of which is county park. A paved trail follows the length of the spit and offers great walking and biking.

Skagit Valley Casino Resort $$–$$$
5984 North Darrk Lane, Bow
(360) 724-7777, (877) 275-2448
www.theskagit.com
Located about 20 minutes south of Bellingham, the Skagit offers a little bit of Las Vegas in the Northwest. There's a casino with table games and more than 650 slot machines, live entertainment, restaurants, a buffet that stays open until all hours of the night, and a 103-room hotel. All that's missing is the desert and the triple-digit temperatures. (And the traffic and crime too, but that's another story.) The Skagit is just off the freeway between Bellingham and Mount Vernon. The hotel's clean comfortable rooms have a 25-inch television with on-demand movies, Internet access, Sony Playstations, coffeemakers, and hair dryers. For a little more money than a standard room, the Skagit's 29 suites come with a two-way fireplace visible from both the living room and bedroom and two-person jetted tubs. Also nice are the indoor heated pool with retractable roof, fitness center, and hot tub and dry spa available to all guests. Continental breakfast also comes with a stay at the Skagit.

The Willows Inn $$$
2579 West Shore Drive, Lummi Island
(360) 758-2620, (888) 294-2620
www.willows-inn.com

Not all the San Juan Islands are hours from Bellingham. Lummi Island, that close-by forested hill out there in the middle of the water and visible from most points in Bellingham, is only a six-minute ferry ride from Gooseberry Point, which is only about 20 minutes from downtown Belling-ham. Rural Lummi is where you'll find the Willows Inn, a charming eight-room inn that dates from 1910. Rooms are homelike and comfortable, and several offer gas fireplaces and views of the surrounding water and islands. Besides a private cottage for those ultra-romantic times, the Willows rents a beautiful guesthouse with full kitchen, fireplace, and two-person Jacuzzi tub. The inn is a true getaway, for the pace on Lummi is *slooow,* and the Willows takes full advantage of it. Inn activities include playing bocce, birding, bicycling, walking the surrounding country roads, and soaking in the hot tub that overlooks Rosario Strait and Orcas Island. Sunday is movie night with films screened on the in-house theater. Full breakfasts, which can be anything from organic eggs to fresh-baked breads and muffins to local breakfast meats and organic produce, are also included with a stay at the Willows. Speaking of food, the Willows has a terrific restaurant that specializes in North-west cuisine, much of it homegrown (the Willows' owners also own the organic farm next door) and home-caught in surrounding waters. Another dining (and/or sipping) option is the inn's Taproot Café, which serves a full range of coffee and espresso drinks as well as soups, sandwiches, and quiches.

BED & BREAKFASTS

Western Washington University

North Garden Inn $$
1014 North Garden Street
(360) 671-7828, (800) 922-6414
www.northgardeninn.com

Perhaps Bellingham's most popular B & B, the North Garden Inn is, at 4 blocks away, also the closest available lodgings to Western Washington University. And downtown is just a few blocks down the hill in the other direction. But it's got a heck of a lot more going for it than just location, location, location. Set on the side of a hill overlooking Bellingham Bay and the old GP plant—soon to be Bellingham's emerging waterfront—the North Garden Inn is a striking Queen Anne Victorian house built in 1897 by Robert Morse, one of Bellingham's earliest and most success-ful businessmen. (Morse Steel Service is in business to this day, headquartered at the same State Street address as 120 years ago.) The expansive inn offers 10 rooms, each with varying price ranges and a dif-ferent theme—the Renaissance Room has majestic 10-foot ceilings and appropriate touches like period oil paintings, and the Blue Room features French doors that open to a private deck with sweeping bay and island views. Or, if you're having a family reunion or business retreat, you can rent out the whole inn. Breakfasts are scrumptious and feature homemade breads and muffins, waffles with raspberry sauce, and various fruits depending on the season. Main breakfast entrees rotate throughout the year and feature dishes such as Vegetarian Marinated Artichoke Heart Frittata with Proscuitto Ham and Roasted Red Potatoes. Rooms offer free wi-fi, too.

Lake Whatcom

Schnauzer Crossing Bed and Breakfast Inn $$$
4421 Lakeway Drive
(360) 734-2808, (360) 733-0055,
or (800) 562-2808
www.schnauzercrossing.com

Along with schnauzers crossing your path (the owners have three), you're likely to come across a deer or two at this charming bed-and-breakfast above Lake Whatcom. Located in a quiet neighborhood about 3 miles east of I-5's Lakeway exit, Schnauzer Crossing has three lodging options. Nestled among 100-foot cedars, the Cottage is a stand-alone structure with a romantic oversize bedroom with a king-size bed. With its wraparound deck opening to terrific lake views, not to mention the Jacuzzi, it has the feel of a luxurious tree house. The Garden Suite, so called because the property's extensive gardens surround it on all sides, boasts a Jacuzzi as well as a wood fireplace. The Queen Room, though the smallest, has its own charm, including lake views and a private bath. The inn's bountiful breakfast fare includes everything from homemade quiche to blueberry bran muffins to fresh-picked berries to tasty fruit parfaits.

South Bay Bed and Breakfast $$$
4095 South Bay Drive
Lake Whatcom
Sedro-Woolley
(360) 595-2086, (877) 595-2086
www.southbaybb.com

At the far southern tip of Lake Whatcom, where the foothills rise high on all sides and it looks like some primordial Scottish loch, sits South Bay bed-and-breakfast, a secluded retreat that's a true slice of heaven. Nestled at the edge of an old-growth cedar forest, the inn offers four rooms with lake views, each with bay window seats and private decks from which to bask in the sunset, private baths with huge jetted tubs, and way-cush, way-comfy Euro-Flex Luxury Beds. (Rubber duckies are available upon request, too, for bath-time fun.) Visitors can borrow a canoe or kayak to paddle the lake or borrow a mountain bike to go for a spin or explore the five-acre grove that's often visited by hawks, eagles, owls, and hummingbirds. Then again, an afternoon doze in the hammock or chatting with fellow guests on the huge wraparound patio-deck overlooking the lake aren't bad ideas, either. The hearty breakfast is served in the conservatory-slash-sunroom, which has lots of glass with wood trim and, of course, those lake and forest views. Fall visits, with the leaves changing colors, are especially spectacular.

Squalicum Lake Cottage $$$
Squalicum Lake Road
(360) 592-1102
www.sqlakecottage.com

This secluded guesthouse is the perfect romantic getaway. Overlooking a lake a few miles outside Bellingham, this cottage for two nestled among the trees features a bedroom, living room, bathroom, fully equipped kitchen, and skylights galore. Fragrant, colorful perennial gardens surround the cottage, and if you're in the mood for a peaceful paddle—what the owners call the "Walden Experience"—a rowboat is available for plying the tranquil lake's waters. Keep an eye out for eagles, herons, hawks, and kingfishers—along with the deer, they're just about your only neighbors. The cottage also features satellite TV and radio, wi-fi access, and, with advance appointment, massage therapy with a licensed practitioner. Breakfast, which can be anything from waffles to eggs to blueberry pancakes, is left at the doorstep of the cottage's private porch entrance, a nice touch for those romantically inclined.

The Olympic Mountains. WWW.PHOTOS.COM

Eldridge Avenue

DeCann House Bed and Breakfast $$
2610 Eldridge Avenue
(360) 734-9172
www.decannhouse.com
One of Bellingham's only B&Bs in a residential neighborhood, the DeCann House offers a choice of two rooms, each with a private bath. Located in a turn-of-the-20th-century home in the Eldridge neighborhood—one of the city's oldest—the house boasts views to Bellingham Bay, the San Juan Islands, and, when the clouds are few, the Olympic Mountains. Antique furniture and stained glass adorn the house, and the richly wooded common room boasts an antique pool table, available to guests. Breakfasts are real treats and feature anything from omelets to blintzes, muffins to pancakes. Nearby Elizabeth Park in one direction and the Bay to Baker Trail in the other make for great walking destinations.

Mount Baker Area

Duck Inn Bed & Breakfast $$
6960 Baker Circle, Glacier
(360) 599-9944
www.duckinnbb.com

Located in the Snowline condominium community, this small, two-room inn offers a few things other local lodgings don't— namely access to an indoor heated swimming pool, a small fishing pond, tennis courts, and, if you can't get enough of the outdoors, picnic tables with barbecue pits. Located at the edge of the Mount Baker–Snoqualmie National Forest, the inn is one of the closest places to stay near Mount Baker. It's close to trails and eateries such as Graham's and Milano's in Glacier, about a mile away. The inn boasts two cozy comfortable rooms (one shared bath) as well as outdoor hot tub, patio dining, satellite television, and lots and lots of windows that afford views of Church Mountain. Hearty breakfast offerings include eggs, pancakes, sausage, omelets, and homemade baked goods, too—owners Steve and Dee Sarich are hard-core outdoor enthusiasts so along with pointing you where to go for your outdoor endeavors, there's no way they let you leave the house hungry. Kids are welcome; however, pets are not allowed.

Glacier Creek Lodge $$–$$$
10036 Mount Baker Highway, Glacier
(360) 599-2991, (800) 719-1414
www.glaciercreeklodge.com
Probably the closest thing to a motel this far out the Mount Baker Highway, the Glacier Creek Lodge offers clean comfortable cabins and rooms pretty much smack-dab in downtown Glacier. (As much as there is a downtown, that is.) Mount Baker, with its myriad ski, snowboard, and hiking trails, is less than 20 miles away up the road. The lodge features 12 one- and two-room cabins, all with kitchens or kitchenettes and some with separate dining area. The 10 motel rooms, located in the centralized lodge building, do not have cooking facilities. Rooms are fairly basic and might inspire a sense of déjà vu; except for details such as compact TVs and VCRs, the wood-paneled interiors probably don't look much different than they did in the 1970s. The prices are good and there's an outdoor hot tub for all to

enjoy after a strenuous day on the slopes, so what difference does it make? Complimentary continental breakfast is available from 8:30 to 10:30 A.M. Despite Glacier's small size, the Glacier Creek Lodge is adjacent to a couple of fine restaurants, such as Milano's and Graham's.

Inn at Mount Baker $$–$$$
8174 Mount Baker Highway, Maple Falls
(360) 599-1776
www.theinnatmtbaker.com
Most B&Bs are located in houses that were originally family homes for decades and generations until one day, someone realizes that hey, wouldn't this place make the perfect bed-and-breakfast? The Inn at Mt. Baker, about 30 miles east of Bellingham between Maple Falls and Glacier, has a different lineage. It started with the view. In the late 1990s owners Bill Snyder and Carole MacDonald came across an undeveloped hillside with a stunning vista of Mount Baker rising from the Nooksack River Valley. They bought 40 acres, built a 6,000-square-foot house with five guest bedrooms (each with its own bath) facing that view, and filled it with comforts and amenities such as 6-foot bathtubs with pillow rests, feather beds, rocking chairs, a patio hot tub with umbrella for when the rain flies, and more. The result was the Inn at Mt. Baker. For breakfast, the owners serve gourmet choices such as upside-down peach and potato pancakes, eggs Benedict, organic coffee, and homemade granola and muffins. The bed-and-breakfast has been highly praised and featured in *Sunset* magazine, among other publications. The Inn is about 23 miles from the Mount Baker Ski Area and is an adult-only establishment.

Mt. Baker Lodging $–$$$$
7463 Mount Baker Highway
Maple Falls
(360) 599-2453, (800) 709-7669
www.mtbakerlodging.com
If all you know is that you want to stay somewhere near Mount Baker but you don't know the area at all, Mount Baker

Lodging is a great place to start. It's a one-stop reservations agency with access to up to 75 cabins, condos, and chalets, as well as to rather upscale vacation rentals in and around the towns of Maple Falls and Glacier, the last two towns on the Mount Baker Highway. All are privately owned and range from cozy cabins for romantic getaways to spacious chalets perfect for extended-stay group ski trips. Some have hot tubs and saunas, some allow pets, some have kitchenettes, some have fireplaces and complimentary breakfasts, but none of them could be described as roughing it. All are near either Maple Falls or Glacier (the towns are only 7 miles apart) and thus close to services and a gas station. Prices range from $50 to $235 per night. Call or visit the lodging office on the Mount Baker Highway in Maple Falls, or you may contact them via their Web site.

RESTAURANTS 🍴

Time was, there wasn't a whole lot of variety to Bellingham cuisine. It was mostly a college town populated with inexpensive Mexican, Asian, and pizza joints with maybe a couple of nice upscale dining establishments.

Boy, has that changed. As Bellingham has grown over the past couple decades so has the diversity of its menu choices as well as the level of sophistication. These days there are terrific Indian, Thai, Japanese, Northwest, Greek, Vietnamese-French, Southwest, and other eateries throughout the city, not to mention French bakeries, breweries, wine bars, alehouses, and even, as of late 2005, a meadery, one of only four in Washington State. (Remember mead from your high school days studying Beowulf?) Of course, pizza is still popular, but these days Bellingham abounds in pizza of the gourmet variety. One place wood-fires it—but not with just any wood; it's gotta be apple wood from orchards in the Yakima Valley. Another offers more than 40 different toppings. And some of the Mexican-themed eateries are surely not "joints" but nice, family sit-down restaurants.

Upscale dining options have multiplied too, with many restaurants specializing in homegrown Northwest cuisine. Which is one way of saying that they offer an eclectic menu with a little bit of everything with an emphasis on sea creatures caught just outside the restaurant's window in the waters off, and nearby, Puget Sound, such as salmon, scallops, oysters, and Dungeness crab. And several of the upscale dining spots take full advantage of Bellingham's seaside, mountain-, and forest-view setting. Nimbus is at the top of Bellingham Towers, the highest building in the city; the Cliff House and Anthony's are at water's edge; the Oyster Creek Inn is perched atop a stream seemingly in the middle of the woods.

This being the Pacific Northwest, eating organic and the like is a high priority of many diners. Local restaurants understand this, and many places offer dishes specifically for vegans, vegetarians, and others who closely watch where their food comes from.

As a college town, and one located just 90 miles from Seattle, Bellingham is a hotbed of coffee and the whole cafe culture. And as with its diversity of restaurants, its collection of coffee establishments cover the range as well, some offering drive-thru service, some offering food in the soup-and-sandwich vein, some with live music and poetry readings, and some with free wi-fi. Almost all of them are terrific places to just sit, sip, and pass the hours. Bellingham's cafe's names are quite entertaining too—Brewed Awakening, Jake and the Bean Stop, Mug Shots, etc.

Bellingham is blessed when it comes to the natural-surroundings department, so many places offer outdoor seating. In summer, deck, sidewalk, and waterfront seating can be quite nice, because the temperature rarely hits 80, and from July through September, rainfall is minimal.

Bellingham, too, is casual with a capital C. Laid-back with a capital L. (Or would that be "L-B?") Shorts, Teva sandals, and a fleece vest are appropriate for just about all occasions including dinner at one of Bellingham's most upscale establishments and an orchestra performance at the Mount Baker Theatre. Many diners have spent the day boating or golfing or snowboarding, so they're not expected to get gussied up for dinner.

Closer to Mount Baker, dining options are few, but then again the people are, too. There's only one road—the Mount Baker Highway—and the last 24 miles are nothing but national forest and wilderness. That said, the small town of Glacier, which is the last town before the forest boundary, is served by two good restaurants, Milano's and Graham's. Both know how to take care of folks who've been skiing or snowboarding or hiking all day. Next door to the restaurant, Graham's Store is a great place to pick up a sandwich or some snacks for a sightseeing trip to Mount Baker.

Most of Bellingham's upscale restaurants take reservations. On Friday and Saturday nights (and sometimes Thursday nights in summer) at most other eateries throughout the city, you can expect to wait a few minutes for a table. Especially in late May, because of Ski to Sea and the myriad related events; throughout June, because of Western Washington University and area high school graduations, and mid- to late-September, too, because of students starting and returning to Western. On weekends expect a bit of a wait at popular downtown and Fairhaven eateries that serve breakfast.

Just about all restaurants are wheelchair accessible, and as of late 2005, smoking is banned in all public workplaces, which includes restaurants, lounges, and outdoor patio areas.

Restaurants in this guide are listed alphabetically by cuisine. Chain restaurants are not included because an Olive Garden in Bellingham is not really any different from one in Orlando or Chicago. Most restaurants accept major credit cards. Those that don't are noted.

PRICE CODE

The dollar sign found in each listing represents the approximate price for a meal for two including an entree and nonalcoholic beverage as well as an appetizer and dessert. Please keep in mind that some restaurants have a wide range of prices.

$	Less than $20
$$	$20 to $40
$$$	$41 to $60
$$$$	More than $60

AMERICAN/NORTHWEST

Bayside Café $$-$$$
1801 Roeder Avenue
(360) 715-0975
This Squalicum Harbor all-day eatery (breakfast, lunch, and dinner) is set at water's edge and, with its open, many-windowed feel, has among the best maritime views of any Bellingham restaurant. The harbor is home to almost 2,000 boats, most of which you'll swear you can see from pretty much any booth or table in the house. You'll find views of the San Juan Islands and Western Washington University, too. As befitting a restaurant that serves a wide range of people not only getting their pleasure but also making their livings from the sea, the menu includes omelets and waffles; burgers, soups, and sandwiches; as well as seafood, steaks, and pasta.

Boundary Bay Brewery
and Bistro $$-$$$
1107 Railroad Avenue
(360) 671-5897
www.bbaybrewery.com
A Bellingham institution since 1995, Boundary Bay is one of those very popular places that seems to fire on numerous cylinders—it's an award-winning brewery; an all-ages bistro serving everything from nachos to veggie wraps to the Great Northwest Pizza (basil, smoked salmon, roasted garlic, and chevre cheese) to New York steak; a popular nightspot renowned for its beer garden and outdoor stage featuring live music most nights of the week; and, given its prime downtown location adjacent to the Farmer's Market, it's pretty much a B'ham place that's not to be missed. With its faux-industrial gray-block exterior, Boundary Bay is easy to find; if in doubt, just look for the place with cars parked out front with roof racks sporting kayaks and/or mountain bikes. As for its beer: Boundary Bay regularly cleans up at the North American Beer Awards and its brews are not only served in-house but at more than 100 pubs, taverns, and restau-

rants throughout Washington State. Reservations are accepted and are a good idea on weekends.

Chiribin's $$-$$$
113 Magnolia Street
(360) 734-0817
The story goes that when owner Michael D'Anna was a boy, his auntie from the Old Country had a rooster who used to jump up and down on the keys when she'd play the piano. Chiribin was the rooster's name, an Americanization of *Ciribiribin,* the Italian waltz tune that D'Anna's auntie would play on the piano. That's the name. As for the food, well, Michael D'Anna also owns D'Anna's Café, one of Bellingham's most beloved restaurants, so that gives you an idea of the quality though the two eateries' menus couldn't be anymore different. Chiribin's offers gourmet burgers, steaks, and seafood—decidedly American fare—as well as ribs and pork chops. Open for lunch and dinner throughout the week, Chiribin's serves dinner only on weekends and offers live music on certain nights throughout the week. Outdoor seating is available. Local art hangs from the walls, which, like many of downtown Bellingham's eateries, are composed of charming turn-of-the-20th-century brick. Up front the large south-facing windows let in plenty of natural light, while in back you'll more than likely take note of the huge, colorful wall-size mural of Chiribin playing the piano.

Graham's Restaurant $$-$$$
9989 Mount Baker Highway, Glacier
(360) 599-1964
www.grahamsrestaurant.com
There's casual and then there's Graham's Restaurant, right there on Main Street (Mount Baker Highway) in downtown Glacier. This is kind of a little-bit-of-everything eatery—burgers to burritos to Thai dishes to T-Bone steak. Graham's menu good-naturedly warns that "you get what's coming to you" and to "be ready for a long wait—our cooks are slow in the morning." Speaking of cooks, a couple

years ago they served no breakfast over Labor Day weekend because the chef was away at Burning Man. "Yeah, we're bummed too," read the Web site. But the food is good and tasty and seems even more so if you've spent the day hiking or snowboarding the mountain, as much of the trending-toward-noisy clientele has. Graham's serves lunch and dinner daily and breakfast on weekends and is a popular nightspot with live music a couple nights a week. Its bar "closes when the last person leaves." The building, which also houses Graham Store right next door, was built in 1902 as a general store for area coal miners. The imposing solid mahogany bar has its own fascinating history—the story goes that it was constructed in 1827 and spent time in the Yukon and San Francisco before finally arriving at its present location after the 'Frisco earthquake and fire of 1906.

Harris Avenue Café $$
1101 Harris Avenue
(360) 738-0802
Though it's been in existence for less than a decade, the Harris Avenue Café, like its historic Terminal Building mate, Tony's, has become a Fairhaven institution. It's got the same big windows, the same big sunny (and drizzly) views of Fairhaven's comings and goings, and, because there's a wide-open doorway allowing easy indoor access between the two establishments, a lot of the same clientele. With its yummy breakfast and lunch menu, the Harris Avenue Café shares a perfectly symbiotic relationship with Tony's. In fact you can sit in Tony's and order food from next door, and vice versa. Harris's breakfast offers all the typical breakfast favorites, many with playful names such as the Belling Ham Omelet: eggs (or tofu) and ham with smoked mozzarella, gruyère, pepperjack, or cheddar cheese; and the Chubby Checker's Choice Taters: ham, caramelized onions with Slackey's Southern Comfort Barbeque Sauce topped with pepperjack cheese and two eggs. Lunch is an array of soups, salads,

sandwiches, burgers, etc., along with what they call their "Hoighty Toighty" offerings: Kelang Chicken Salad (with sesame, ginger, cilantro, garlic and coconut), Pavia Pollo Panini (chicken breast with smoked mozzarella and basil aioli on grilled focaccia), and others. The cafe is open seven days a week. Here's a tip: If you make plans to meet someone at Tony's and when you get there, they don't seem to have arrived yet, poke your head in the doorway and see if they're at the Harris.

Jacci's Fish and Chips $-$$
1020 Harris Avenue, Fairhaven
(360) 733-5021

Jacci's is easy to spot—it's the only big red double-decker bus parked at the corner of 12th Street and Harris Avenue in Fairhaven. (Actually, it's the only red double-decker bus parked anywhere in B'ham.) Specializing in yummy fish 'n' chips—halibut, cod, or king salmon, all in a light beer batter—Jacci's plays on the British double-decker motif and serves its food in newspaper. Besides fish, Jacci's serves chicken strips, clam chowder, and similar fare. Sit outside and watch the comings and goings of downtown Fairhaven or, when the weather's not good, sit in the little gazebo-like building next to the bus. As for the bus, it was built in 1948 and imported from England, and word is it was once used in a film about the Kennedys.

Shrimp Shack $$
1200 Cornwall Avenue, Downtown
(360) 752-9100

The old Shrimp Shack was located in a low-slung, dilapidated building on the banks of Whatcom Creek, but it had just about the best fish 'n' chips in town, and the shrimp was out of this world. After closing in the late 1990s for five years only to reopen a couple years ago in a spiffy new downtown spot, guess what—they still serve just about the best fish 'n' chips in town and the shrimp is still out of this world. The clam strips, scallops, and oysters are world class as well. This is casual

dining in a comfortable setting. The nautical decor features hanging sharks and swordfish, a giant fish tank (much to the delight of children), and a huge mural behind the counter of the San Juan Islands, which you can just about see through the many windows of this corner-spot eatery. It's also kid-friendly, with outdoor seating when the weather's right.

Skylark's Hidden Cafe & Wine Parlor $$-$$$
1308 11th Street, Fairhaven
(360) 715-3642

Before its 2005 expansion, Fairhaven's Skylark's really was a hidden cafe—its only entrance was an alley that was easy as heck to miss. But it wasn't just any alley. It was a charming shaded cobblestone one that, because Skylark's offered patio seating out there, could seemingly transport you to some Old Country cafe for a couple hours. Well, the patio seating is still there, but since the recent remodel gave Skylark's 1,300 more square feet and a storefront entrance on 11th Street, it's no longer hidden. The restaurant serves breakfast, lunch, and dinner and, as suggested by the phrase *wine parlor,* offers full bar service (which it didn't before), including more than 30 varieties of wine. Skylark's has always been renowned for its made-from-scratch breakfasts, which include favorites such as pancakes, hash browns, and omelets, as well as more eclectic offerings such as Mediterranean frittatas. The lunch and dinner menus focus on Northwest seafood and pasta offerings. They include favorites such as bay scallops au gratin, baked salmon dijon, beef stroganoff, and butternut squash lasagna and sandwiches such as focaccia turkey Caesar and the Lumberjack Club—ham, roast beef, bacon, Swiss and other cheeses, and condiments galore. A late-night tapas menu is also available. With its rich dark wood, exposed brick, imposing antique bar, and elegant appointments, Skylark's expanded front room looks like something from Fairhaven's early days. And thankfully, you still have the option of patio seating in the alley. Skylark's is open from 7:00 A.M. to 9:00 P.M. Sunday through Thursday and until midnight on Friday and Saturday.

Swan Café and Deli $-$$
1220 North Forest Street, Downtown
(360) 734-8158
www.communityfoodcoop.com

Beloved by Whatcom County vegetarians everywhere, there's more to this Community Food Co-op establishment than spelt-breaded tofu cutlets and roasted asparagus with almonds. A casual, airy place with many windows, it's a great spot to meet with friends, grab an organic juice or espresso drink, a cup of soup and/or a salad, and while away the hours chatting and watching Bellinghamsters pass by. As for the menu, the Swan features local organic ingredients as much as possible and serves a wide variety of meat, seafood, vegetarian, and vegan dishes. Salad offerings include everything from the above-mentioned roasted asparagus to Tuscan white bean and tuna; entrees from tofu cutlets to fig-stuffed Beeler's pork loin and chipotle catfish. Also a deli, all dishes are available to take home. Desserts range from crème brûlée to peanut butter chocolate pie. At the Swan's juice bar, you can create your own smoothie, getting as eclectic and creative as you'd like. Add shots of wheatgrass or go for the Mocha Monkey: banana, milk, ice, chocolate, peanut butter, and espresso—yum.

ASIAN

House of Orient $$-$$$
115 East Holly Street
(360) 738-4009

Recently moved next door to the busiest intersection downtown, hoppin' House of Orient offers terrific Vietnamese and Thai dishes in an upscale, understated atmosphere featuring gentle lighting, hardwood floors, and exposed brick. The wide-ranging menu serves up more than ample portions of all your favorite Asian dishes and offers them in vegetarian, seafood, or various meat options. Popular with the business crowd, House of Orient couldn't be more conveniently located, with a spacious Starbuck's right across the street. (Or Avellino, about half a block away for those who'd rather buy local.) House of Orient is popular also for its take-out menu. At night, House of Orient undergoes somewhat of a transformation. There's karaoke in the back—and I think we all know what happens when the liquor flows and people who think they can sing are handed a microphone. 'Nuff sed.

La Patisserie
3098 Northwest Avenue
(360) 671-3671

From its unassuming storefront in a Northwest Avenue strip mall that's seen better days, La Patisserie delights and surprises. Half-Vietnamese eatery, half-French bakery (which makes sense when you consider that the French occupied Vietnam in the 1950s), this small, sunny establishment serves up some yummy pasta and noodle dishes, as well as terrific pastries, croissants, and cakes.

Oriento Grill & BBQ $$
2500 Meridian Street
(360) 733-3322

Terrific Chinese food at great prices—those are the calling cards of this popular Fountain District eatery located between downtown Bellingham and the mall sprawl section of Meridian Street. Spacious and comfortable inside, perhaps even a tad more elegant than one would expect, Oriento offers generous portions of everything from egg rolls to egg foo yung to Mongolian beef to Kung Pao Chicken to Moo Shu Pork. If you like your Chinese spicy, try the General Tso's Chicken. Just make sure you've ordered plenty of Chinese beer to wash it down. Oriento is open seven days a week for lunch and dinner and offers take-out dining also.

Osaka $$$
3207 Northwest Avenue
(360) 676-6268
Northwest Avenue, between Yeager's and
the gas stations and strip malls of the
Birchwood neighborhood, might not be
the last place you'd expect to find a slice
of The Land of the Rising Sun, but it'd be
awfully darn close. But there the sprawl is,
surrounding Osaka Japanese restaurant, a
full-on Japanese garden with pond and
gurgling waterfalls, bamboo, rock, statues,
and outdoor art all entered via a wood
bridge. Serenity arrives now. Inside Osaka,
the peaceful mood continues with light
wood, plants, bamboo, and, of course, a
small tatami room. Along with its tranquil
setting, the restaurant is renowned for its
sushi, which comes in a variety of combinations from Nigiri sushi to assorted
sashimi. Teriyaki options are big, too, and
come with everything from salmon to
beef to chicken to tofu. Other offerings
from the wide-ranging menu include tem-
pura, sukiyaki, spicy stir fry, and Yokisoba
and Donburi. Portions are huge, but fret
not. Take a couple turns around the garden to work off your meal. A kid's menu is
available, and Osaka is open for lunch.

Supon's Thai Cuisine $$
1213 Dupont Street
(360) 734-6838
Located in a kind of not-quite-commercial
but not-quite-residential section of Bellingham that's not quite downtown but also
not quite North Bellingham, Supon's is a
delightful surprise that offers sumptuous
lunches and dinners at prices that folks in
a college town love. The decor at this tiny
bistro is simple but tasteful—cushy, high-
backed chairs, an ornate gold screen
standing by the entrance, an oversize
Asian fan mounted on the wall. A broad
range of Thai dishes are offered—pud Thai,
cashew nut chicken, fried rice—and come
with a choice of chicken, beef, pork, or
tofu. Vegetarian dishes such as Pud Thai
Jay are available as well. Garlic prawns,
Plalard Plig, and spicy squid are among the
plentiful seafood offerings. In keeping with

its casual, low-cost atmosphere, Supon's
offers counter seating for that diner feel.
For dessert, try the Coconut Ice Cream or
Black Sticky Rice. It's darn near impossible
to go wrong ordering anything here.

BREAKFAST

Arlis's Restaurant $
1525 Cornwall Avenue
(360) 647-1788
There's nothing fancy about this eatery at
the north end of downtown, just good,
solid breakfast food and plenty of it. Eggs,
bacon, pancakes, chicken-fried steak, pancakes—straightforward breakfast fare in a
nice sunny corner space. Truly a favorite
of old- and long-timers who wouldn't
think of starting their day without their
eggs Benedict and a steaming cup of coffee. (Get the daily trivia question right,
and the coffee's free!) Truly a family affair,
Arlis's was recently purchased by Ryan
Callier, a 20-something lifelong Bellinghamster, whose first job was as a busboy
at Arlis's when he was age 14. His mother,
Denise, has been a waitress here for
almost 15 years. Arlis's serves lunch, too.

Diamond Jim's $
1906 North State Street
(360) 734-8687
Hungry? I mean really hungry? For gut-
busting breakfasts that won't bust your
wallet, head for the little pink triangle-
shaped building amid the car lots and
light industry on James Street. Inside it's
small, as in tiny, thus it always feels a little
crowded, but portions of all your hearty
breakfast faves—pancakes, waffles, bis-
cuits 'n' gravy, any omelet you can come
up with—are huge and will keep you sated
till dinnertime. Size-wise, breakfast is
brunch whether you were planning on it
or not. Diamond Jim's also serves lunch.

Little Cheerful $-$$
133 East Holly Street
(360) 738-8824
One of the most popular, if not *the* most

popular downtown breakfast eateries, the aptly named Little Cheerful has much to offer. Heaping portions of great all-American breakfast food (lunch too), a bustling atmosphere both inside and out—situated as it is at the corner of Railroad Avenue and Holly Street, it couldn't be more centrally located unless it was in the middle of the intersection—and their famous hash browns. (Veggie browns for the veggie set.) Entertainment inside this sunny open restaurant is provided in spades by the grill cooks, who build your breakfast on just the other side of the counter. Outside seating is available, but be forewarned that, though mostly plenty safe, Railroad Avenue is perhaps Bellingham's most, uh, colorful. On weekend mornings, expect to wait for a table.

Old Town Café   **$–$$**
316 West Holly Street
(360) 671-4431
Head down West Holly Street any Saturday or Sunday morning and without fail you'll see a line of people waiting for a table outside this Bellingham breakfast icon. This is the hippy-granola end of the Bellingham spectrum; all that means is that you're getting a terrific hearty breakfast made from scratch with largely organic and/or locally grown ingredients. And that a dreadlocked guitarist may show up and ask to sing and play for his breakfast, and he'll be allowed to. You can get all your breakfast favorites here, including omelets stuffed with everything from turkey to sausage to green peppers to sour cream, and have them garnished with corn tortillas, beans, and herbed potatoes. The walls feature works from local artists, and the large sunny dining room even had a little play area for the young ones. As for the line on weekend mornings—Old Town Café is beloved by locals, so unless you get there fairly early, expect to wait for a table. But it's worth it. Something about the place that's ultra cool—for more than 30 years the cafe has been serving free Thanksgiving dinners to the less fortunate.

Drive down Holly Street any Friday or Saturday morning and you'll see a line waiting to get into the Little Cheerful and Old Town Café. Here are a couple tips: Go on a weekday or early, just after the restaurant opens. Bellinghamsters are late risers; you know what they say: The early breakfast bird gets the table.

CAFES

Avellino   **$**
1329 Railroad Avenue
(360) 715-1005
This Railroad Avenue hole-in-the-wall between a secondhand clothes store and a shoe repair shop serves some delectable treats and munchies as well as some darn fine espresso drinks from its imposing old-school hand-pump espresso machine. Crème puffs and carrot cake cupcakes, quiche Lorraine, and gluten-free apricot almond scones are just a few of the eats available at this ultra-casual, ultra-local, ultra-comfortable cafe. Read from the stack of community newspapers and paperbacks or just relax in one of the overstuffed chairs. This is a place made for just whiling away the hours.

Bean Blossom Coffee Company   **$**
Corner of Broadway and Elm Street
(360) 647-1643
For sure, Bellingham has its share of drive-thru espresso joints as well as sit-down wi-fi-accessible cafes. The Bean Blossom combines the two, as well as being a pleasant eatery that serves bodacious breakfast bagels and hearty lunchtime sandwiches and wraps. And of course, any place that serves Cool Coffee Creams— vanilla ice cream with blended espresso and chocolate—is a winner. Small but more than pleasant on the inside (pegboard games for the kiddies, lots of window tables, a shelf full of paperbacks to peruse), the Bean Blossom has a couple of outdoor seats, too. It's located just across from a firehouse (don't be alarmed

if your reverie is broken by a wailing siren) and around the corner from Elizabeth Park, one of the oldest and, with its huge leafy trees, perhaps most stately park in town. The Bean Blossom also takes phone orders; phone it in and they'll have it ready by the time you swing by.

The Black Drop $
300 West Champion Street
(360) 738-3767
www.theblackdrop.com
Wanna feel like a local? The Black Drop is just far enough off the downtown beaten path (but not really at all) to be a place that maybe not every out-of-towner will find. Free wi-fi, comfy-if-well-worn couches and chairs, and chess sets—what else could one want in a cafe? Oh right, good coffee. The Black Spot has that by the tankful. All the espresso, coffee, tea, and Italian soda drinks are here, as well as interesting specialties such as Monkey in a Tree, which boasts espresso, chocolate, coconut, and banana; Gingersnap Macchiatos, and something called Stephanie's French Toast Latte. Also served are various munchies and treats, including cinnamon rolls, breakfast cookies, biscotti, and pizza bagels. The Black Drop has great atmosphere, and along with being close to bookstores where you could spend hours browsing, it's within a couple blocks of the Whatcom Museum of History and Art, the Mount Baker Theatre, and the Railroad and Radio museums.

Colophon Café is housed in the distinct brick masonry Knights of Pythias building, which was built in 1891 and served as a meeting place for a number of Fairhaven's secret societies. It has housed a number of stores and even a speakeasy during Prohibition. Until 2004 it was the home of Village Books, which moved next door to a brand-new building.

Colophon Café $-$$
1208 11th Street, Fairhaven
(360) 647-0092
www.colophoncafe.com
Since 1985 this Fairhaven favorite has been serving some of the best homemade soups in town, along with terrific sandwiches and desserts that can only be described as decadent. Upstairs has a casual diner/deli feel—order at the counter, get your number, and pick a booth. Downstairs, which is still casual like most everything in Bellingham, has sit-down table service in a dark but comfy space dominated by exposed sandstone walls and pillars and an antique hand-operated elevator for transporting items up and down the stairs. As for the award-winning soups, which are offered on a rotating basis, the African peanut, Mexican corn and bean, honey chicken chili, and Thai ginger chicken are just the tip of the soup iceberg. Take a look at the posted soup calendar to find out what's on tap. Take note, too, of a certain cow theme that persists—Holstein imagery is everywhere from lights to a large upstairs mural to menus to T-shirts that are for sale. There's outdoor café-style seating at both the upstairs entrance on 11th Street and downstairs, which opens to the Fairhaven Village Green. Grab a table and take in the Wednesday Farmer's Market or the Monday-afternoon bocce-ball tournaments.

Tony's Coffees $
1101 Harris Avenue
(360) 738-4710
To many folks, Tony's *is* Fairhaven. Occupying a prime corner spot in the old brick Terminal Building (circa 1888) smack in the heart of Fairhaven since 1971, it's been the place for locals to meet, to quaff, to nibble a munchie, and/or to solve the problems of the world. Many's the perfect afternoon that's been whiled away at one of Tony's tables or window seats reading, picking at a snickerdoodle, and looking up every once in a while to check out the wide variety of folks who make their way through the door and past the front win-

Fairhaven's Colophon Café. BELLINGHAM WHATCOM TOURISM/TAIMI GORMAN

dows. Tony's is a place that's truly favored by both locals and out-of-towners (easy to spot since they're the ones wearing dress shoes, not Tevas or hiking boots). College students meet here to "study," cyclists—both human and motor-powered—congregate here before and after rides, and environmentalists and local politicos meet here to plan, harangue, or just throw up their hands. Along with a wide selection of espresso, coffees, and teas (lattes and mochas and chais, etc.—oh my!), Tony's also offers various pastries. You can also order food from the Harris Avenue Café next door.

CONTINENTAL

Le Chat Noir   **$$$**
1200 Harris Avenue
Third floor of Sycamore Square
(360) 733-6136
Situated on the third floor of Fairhaven's historic Sycamore Square building, Le Chat Noir offers one of Bellingham's unique dining experiences. (Find the location by looking up at Fairhaven's main intersection—the window sign features a black cat, which is what Le Chat Noir means in French.) That third-floor location ensures terrific island and sunset views, along with a birds-eye view of Fairhaven, and it is complimented nicely with an interior of exposed brick, high ceilings, and touches reminiscent of a Parisian streetscape. When the sun goes down, the light stays low, ensuring a romantic evening.

Open for dinner only, the casual-yet-sophisticated restaurant and lounge offers a French-slash-Mediterranean menu. Appetizers can be everything from bacon-wrapped water chestnuts to prawn skewers with aioli and cocktail sauce to Northwest oysters. Entrees offer a little bit of everything, from gourmet pizzettes to ravioli to pot roast, as well as a variety of chicken, pepper steak, and pasta dishes. And of course, what's a French restaurant without onion soup, vichyssoise, and crepes, and Le Chat Noir excels in all

three. It's interesting—almost no one I've spoken to is lukewarm about the restaurant. Either they love it and rave about every little detail, or they rant about poor service or (before the statewide smoking ban) excessive smoke from the bar. One thing both groups seem to agree on is the high quality of the food.

ICE CREAM

Mallard's Ice Cream   **$**
1323 Railroad Avenue
(360) 734-3884
This downtown business has a couple things going for it that Bellinghamsters love: it's locally owned and offers seriously yummy homemade ice cream that has more than half its ingredients coming from local food producers. The old place on Holly Street had high ceilings that tended to let the sound of delighted, squealing children dissipate a bit and the new spot, just around the corner, is just as kid and family friendly. (Crayons, board games, and other toys were always available.) Mallard's offers 28 ice-cream flavors at a time—their vitae lists more than 300—with some trending toward the, uh, unusual, such as chai tea, cucumber, and pepper. Milk shakes, sundaes, coffee, espresso, and the like are also available. Mallard's is another one of those Bellingham institutions that's not to be missed.

INDIAN

India Grill Restaurant & Lounge   **$$**
1215-½ Cornwall Avenue
(360) 714-0314
First known to Bellingham folk through its stand at the Bellingham Farmer's Market, downtown's India Grill injects some much needed diversity into the city's gastronomic offerings. Authentic Eastern Indian dishes such as Chicken Tikka Masala (boneless chicken chunks in tomato sauce with coriander, garlic, ginger, cardamom, and cinnamon) and Aloo Baingan (egg-

plant and potatoes) are served under a colorful hanging canvas which, along with various hanging tapestries of rural Indian life, transport you from a little storefront on Cornwall Avenue to some exotic location thousands of miles away. Along with offering a variety of lamb dishes (the Lamb Kadahi, with cumin, cinnamon, and coriander, is popular), India Grill is a favorite of the vegetarian set. It's popular with bargain hunters, too, as its lunchtime special is an all-you-can-eat buffet for about $6.00. The restaurant features a full bar as well as a kids' menu and is open for lunch and dinner.

ITALIAN/MEDITERRANEAN

Book Fare $$
1200 11th Street
(360) 734-3434

A couple years ago, when Village Books built its impressive new home on the corner of 11th and Knox Streets, they knew they wanted a small cafe on the third floor with sunset views of the San Juan Islands. At about the same time, the owner of Pastazza, a popular Italian eatery in Barkley Village, was looking to open a small satellite eatery. Lucky for us, they bumped into each other—just like peanut butter and chocolate from the old Reese's Peanut Butter Cups commercials—and the result can be experienced on Village Books' top floor. It's small and casual but very tasteful with wood floors, local art on the walls, and, with plenty of windows, views of the water, the sunset, and the islands. You can also see the Village Green down below, which has the ambience of a European marketplace. And the food is great, too. Specializing in lunch and dinner, Book Fare offers everything from lighter fare such as soups, salads, and panini sandwiches to such heartier dinners as chicken parmigiana, roasted vegetable quiche, and Pastazza Mac & Cheese, a big-people version of the kiddie's fave with Parmesan, pecorino, romano, and Gorgonzola. Daily specials are usually a

lasagna dish. But maybe you're here mostly for the books, and that's okay, too. Book Fare is the perfect nook to crawl into with a good read and a good latte and perhaps something from the dessert menu, like the white chocolate pot de crème, or fruit crisp, or carrot cake, or . . . As the menu says, "Eat, drink, and be literary."

Café Akroteri $$
1219 Cornwall Avenue
(360) 676-5554

Let's face it: Sometimes the Northwest winter rains can make things seem a little bleak and you find yourself pining for warmer, sunnier climes, like, say, Greece. When that's the case—or if you just want a terrific Greek dining experience—head to Café Akroteri, just a couple blocks from the Mount Baker Theatre. In an atmosphere of openness and light, with Old World paintings and charm adorning the walls, Café Akroteri serves authentic Greek dishes such as beef, chicken, lamb, or vegetarian gyros stuffed with feta cheese and zatziki sauce; grape leaf rolls stuffed with rice, beef (or vegetables), and spices; deep-fried calamari, and the like. And of course, dessert selection includes baklava, which is baked on-site daily and stuffed with walnuts and almonds and coated with honey. The restaurant is open for lunch daily except on Sunday and open every day for dinner.

D'Anna's Café Italiano $$-$$$
1317 North State Street, Downtown
(360) 714-0188

On the East Coast, where Italian restaurants and pizzerias are as prevalent as Mexican and Thai restaurants are on the West, restaurantgoers expect a certain high standard when it comes to their Italian fare. D'Anna's, which specializes in homemade Sicilian dishes, meets that East Coast standard and surpasses it. Their fresh, made-on-the-premises pasta is perhaps best sampled in their ravioli (filled with cheese, spinach, or chard and meat), which has become so yum-yum renowned that Seattle restaurants buy D'Anna's pasta in bulk. Local grocers sell D'Anna's sausage, too. Diners will find all their favorite Italian dishes on the menu—spaghetti, chicken parmesan, lasagnas—as well as seafood dishes. Try the puttanesca. As the menu tells it, it's a dish favored by Sicilian ladies of the night. Oversize Fellini posters and grainy black-and-white photos of relatives from the Old Country on the walls, not to mention the piped-in mandolin-heavy music, might just make you think you're in Little Italy on the set of a Scorsese movie. D'Anna's is also open for lunch.

Manninos $$$
1007 Harris Avenue, Fairhaven
(360) 671-7955

This sophisticated Fairhaven eatery offers a truly special upscale Italian dining experience. With outdoor seating, indoor patio seating around a heated fireplace, or just plain-old indoor seating in a spacious interior with lots of natural lighting, Manninos' seating options run the gamut, just like its menu. Changed often, Manninos' menu features entrees from throughout Italy and offers dishes such as braised lamb ravioli, housemade marche-style lasagne with wild mushroom cream, and Sicilian roasted game hen. A neat feature here is a tasting menu that changes monthly and includes small portions of several entrees along with cheeses (e.g., Danish Blue with walnuts), antipasti (prosciutto di Parma), and dessert. Manninos is open for lunch and dinner, and reservations are recommended.

Milano's Market and Deli $$$
9990 Mount Baker Highway, Glacier
(360) 599-2863

After a day spent skiing or snowboarding at Mount Baker or hiking the myriad trails across its flanks—and in the process working up a Mount Baker–size appetite—nothing quite hits the spot like a steaming plate of Milano's seafood linguini featuring clams, mussels, prawns, and calamari. 'Cept maybe the spinach ravioli with walnut cream sauce. Or perhaps the pasta

puttanesca with a nice bottle of wine from Milano's well-stocked wine cellar. Point is, you simply can't go wrong with anything on Milano's menu, which features fresh-made pasta, appetizers, sandwiches (hence, the imposing deli counter), and daily specials. There's a great lunch menu, too. If the weather permits, grab a table outside and peer up at Church Mountain, rising about 5,000 feet overhead. Don't worry about your attire: Depending on the season, half the clientele is either in ski pants or hiking shorts.

Pastazza $$-$$$
2945 Newmarket Street, Suite 101
Barkley Village
(360) 714-1168
www.pastazza.com

Years ago one of the most popular Mediterranean fine-dining experiences to be had was at Innisfree, which was located in the foothills some 30 miles east of Bellingham near the entrance to the Mount Baker-Snoqualmie Forest. As if answering the prayers of its devoted patrons who lived in Bellingham, owners Fred and Lynn Berman closed that restaurant in 1997 and opened Pastazza in Barkley Village, at Bellingham's northeast corner. Fresh is the word at Pastazza, as all pastas and sauces—from the Pastazza red to the Pastazza pesto and about a half-dozen others, from the seafood linguini to the ravioli of the day—are made from scratch using local, organically-grown ingredients as much as possible. All water, whether it's used for boiling pasta or making tea or coffee, is filtered through an advanced, state-of-the-art water filtration system. Pastazza serves lunch and dinner, with lunch featuring a variety of soups, salads, grilled panini sandwiches, and lunch-size portions of the dinner offerings. Along with a nice wine list, the eatery boasts mucho dessert offerings, all made from scratch and all mega tasty. The honey crème caramel and the chocolate almondbutter pie are just a couple that will transport your tongue to heights of otherworldly delight. Lots of windows let in plenty of natural light, the better through which to watch the comings and goings of Barkley Village, one of Bellingham's mixed-use neighborhoods that was developed in the late 1990s as an urban village. Pastazza was one of Barkley Village's first tenants.

Pizzazza $
1501 12th Street, Fairhaven
(360) 756-9322

Bellingham's dining scene is full of pleasant surprises. For example, from the outside, the Exxon service station in Fairhaven at the corner of 12th and Larrabee Streets looks like any other gas station and mini-mart in America. Except for the neon Pizzazza sign in the window. Pizzazza sound suspiciously like Pastazza, the yummy Italian eatery over in Barkley Village, and with good reason—they're owned by the same people. Pizzazza is kind of a satellite venue, and once you step inside, you realize this isn't your typical gas and go joint. At a take-out counter to the left, you can order yummy slices of gourmet pizza as well as light, yummy pasta dishes. There's even a couple tables. The gas station/gourmet pizza stop is unique also in that, while yes, it does sell mini-mart standbys such as candy bars, beer, anti-freeze, and hot rod motorcycle magazines, it boasts a surprisingly well-rounded wine selection.

Zephyr Bistro $$-$$$
11 Bellwether Way
(360) 671-3767

Located just outside the Hotel Bellwether at the end of the spit that is Bellwether Way, Zephyr's is a terrific little Italian gourmet deli that serves breakfast, lunch, and dinner.

Sandwiches are of the hero variety—Italian, hot Reuben, roast beef and cheddar, etc.—as well as grilled paninis of the Vincenso (meatballs, marinara, and mozzarella) and Paisano (prosciutto, basil, mozzarella, and pesto) variety. Desserts are super, if not exactly light on the calories: New York cheesecake, tiramisu, black forest cake, and the like. Zephyr's interior is charming, with posters and maps of Italy and shelves stuffed with bottles of its extensive wine collection. But with its setting at the end of the spit, it's difficult not to want to get your food to go, find a place to sit just outside on Tom Glenn Common, and watch the boats sail by or the leaves change color on Sehome Hill. A unique touch is Zephyr's Friday-night wine-tasting that's held from 5:00 to 8:00 P.M. and has a different theme each week.

LOCAL DRIVE-INS

Boomer's Drive-In $
310 North Samish Way
(360) 647-2666

If Burger Me boasts a 1950s interior, then Boomer's Drive-In has dibs on the 1950s exterior. Pull up to the curb, check the menu and its wide selection of burgers, World-Class waffle fries, fish 'n' chips, and the like, decide what you're in the mood for, then turn on your lights. Seconds later one of the waitstaff approaches your car to take your order, re-emerging minutes later with a steaming tray of tasty food they'll hang on your window. Enjoy. For the true 1950s experience, maybe you'll be here on one of the nights the local vintage car club gathers. Munching your french fries and sipping your shake while parked amid '57 Chevys and '32 Deuce Coupes and '46 Roadsters, you'll feel like you're in a scene from *American Graffiti*. Limited indoor seating is available, and it's especially nice on colder evenings when the dining room's imposing fireplace will chase any chill from your bones. Boomer's is often voted as having the best burger in town by the local press. It also has peanut butter milk shakes to die for.

Burger Me $
1220 Lakeway Drive
(360) 715-1843

Step into Burger Me and you kinda feel like you've walked into some local burger joint from the 1950s. (Not in an overwhelming, kitschy way, mind you.) That feeling is because of the black-and-white tile floor and checked walls, the retro 1950s clock with colored neon, the padded red booths and chrome lines, and the fact that the counter help isn't wearing headsets and ball caps like they do at all the national chains. Good, standard, nothing-fancy food (burgers 'n' fries) is offered at locally-owned Burger Me, all at a great price. The fresh-cut fries are the kind that some people go gaga over. For dessert, try a to-die-for Blast Me, a frozen custard mixed with your favorite toppings—i.e., Reese's peanut butter cups, butter pecans, Oreos, etc., for something every bit as good as ice cream but with less fat. Its location, with Little League fields directly across Lakeway, adds a nice touch. It makes for a true Americana evening—burgers and fries and kids playing baseball. Burger Me also has a drive-thru.

Win's Drive-In $
1315 12th Street, Fairhaven
(360) 734-5226

Newcomers to Bellingham and visitors to Fairhaven often wonder what those folks are doing standing around in the parking lot between the Fairhaven Market and the Sycamore Square building. Why, they're waiting for their takeout—yummy burgers, crunchy french fries, and a peanut butter milk shake, no doubt. Or perhaps their turkey burger or fishwich or French dip, made as they have been since 1964 when Winnefred Easterly opened this Southside burger joint. It's Fairhaven's oldest eatery and a great spot for a good, solid inexpensive meal. Indoor seating is available, but because this is Fairhaven and thus there are many great places to walk, lots of people get their food to go.

MEXICAN/SOUTHWEST

Bandito's Burritos $
120 West Holly Street
(360) 738-8488
www.banditosburritos.com

If salsa is your thing, then Bandito's Burritos is for you. This cozy downtown eatery prides itself on having more varieties of salsa than anywhere this side of Seattle, with a dozen flavors from Mango Tango, Garlic Lover, and Green Apple Burn and almost as many flavors, from XXX Hot to Wild to simply Mild. Not just a typical burrito stand, Bandito's prides itself on using low-fat beans, skinless chicken, high-fiber brown rice, and the like. As the menu states, "Deep-fat frying and grilling are *not* an option at Bandito Burritos." Menu items cover the whole burrito-taco-quesadilla spectrum and most are available with beef, chicken, or pork. Veggie items, including potato burritos, are available, too. Outside seating is an option when the weather permits, and for those who'd prefer to eat at home or the office, Bandito's Burrito has free lunchtime delivery.

Casa Que Pasa $
1415 Railroad Avenue
(360) 738-8226

This place is kind of like the Bagelry with a liquor license. (And of course, a Southwest/Mexican menu.) By that I mean good, inexpensive food, a colorful, varied clientele that draws locals of all stripes, and giant windows through which downtown Bellingham provides entertainment. There's lots of local flavor here, from the "art" on the walls done by local "artists" to a nonchalant waitstaff who sometimes act like they'd rather be doing just about anything than taking your order. But the food is top-notch and ridiculously inexpensive. Standbys such as quesadillas, chimichangas, fajitas, and soups are all winners, but it's the potato burrito that Casa Que Pasa claims is world famous. And rightfully so; it is to *die* for. As for that liquor license, the sign out front brags that Casa Que Pasa is the home of the Tequila Research Institute, where you can choose from 80 varieties of tequila, hopefully not all in one night. The eatery's large, front room with its high ceiling is great for families. It's loud and informal, and nobody will notice if little Jake or Maya has a meltdown.

Pepper Sisters　　　　　　**$$-$$$**
1055 N. State Street
(360) 671-3414

For tasty and interesting Southwest-slash-Mexican fare with its own unique Bellingham flair, Pepper Sisters is definitely the place. High-ceilinged, brick-walled, and many-windowed with views to the bay, Pepper Sisters has that laid-back, Bellingham Texas 'n' fleece-vest atmosphere. Menu-wise, it's definitely got its own thing going. Options include spicy roasted potato and garlic enchilada, chicken elote enchiladas, blue corn rellenos, spicy eggplant tostadas, as well as simple fare such as black bean burritos. Pepper Sisters also has a great downtown location on State Street, close to the Farmers' Market and the Boulevard Trail to Fairhaven.

Super Mario's Food　　　　　　**$**
1422 North Forest Street
(360) 920-4330

Known affectionately as the Taco Truck—to those, that is, who even know about it—Super Mario's is perhaps one of the best food deals around for the money. It's certainly the best food deal on wheels. For Super Mario's cooks and serves its fine Salvadorian food from a UPS-size truck parked near the edge of downtown in front of the perhaps less-than-inspiring Cigarette Mart. The menu offers up yummy and hugely ample tacos, burritos, quesadillas, and tamales with a choice of asada (grilled steak), chicken, pork, or tongue. Combo plates and chicken fajitas are available, too. Outdoor seating is basically lawn chairs around an old service-station gas-pump island, but hey, you're here for the food, right? Super Mario's is a fave of college students and those looking for a ridiculously cheap and ridiculously tasty lunch.

Taco Lobo　　　　　　**$$**
117 West Magnolia Street
(360) 756-0711
www.tacolobo.com

Offering handmade tortillas made from the wood tortilla press behind the counter and food made from the freshest ingredients,

Taco Lobo is the downtown spot for authentic Mexican food. Just within blocks of downtown destinations such as the Mount Baker Theatre and the Whatcom Museum of History and Art, the restaurant's interior can transport you to Mexico. Sun-themed art (i.e., oversize medallions) hangs from walls painted sunlike reds and golds, and a giant three-dimensional desert scene, complete with cacti and coyotes, dominates one wall. (Sidewalk cafe seating is available just outside when the weather permits.) Then there's the menu, which may have you standing at the counter for a bit trying to decide what to order. (There's no table service at this casual eatery.) Along with typical Mexican fare, such as burritos, enchiladas, and four types of nachos, the menu also offers more unusual dishes such as tortas, French rolls filled with pork, sirloin, chicken, or sausage. Most menu items are available with those four meats, and vegetarian and seafood dishes are offered as well.

Taco Lobo, which is closed on Sunday, serves a wide selection of imported beers, many of them Mexican.

PIZZA

Cascade Pizza & Italian Cuisine
No. 1　　　　　　**$$**
2431 Meridian Street
(360) 671-0999

This large casual Meridian Street institution is a favorite of families, groups such as local soccer and softball teams, and, from the looks of the parking lot, local law enforcement. (They're there to eat, not round up troublemakers.) Located just north of downtown in the mostly residential Fountain district, Cascade Pizza specializes not only in pizza but also a variety of baked pasta dishes (the pepperoni lasagna is a favorite), sandwiches (meatball, ham, etc.), and salads. Desserts are of the delectable variety, with cheesecake among the offerings. Prices are seriously reasonable here: A large pepperoni pizza goes for about $10. There's plenty of seating with booths downstairs and open tables upstairs. The eatery has somewhat of a throwback feel since it's been locally owned since the late 1970s by Nikolas and Nikitas Tsoulouhas and many of the staff have worked here forever, and there's a feel of casual familiarity you don't get from the chain eateries. The Tsoulouhas brothers also own Cascade Pizza & Italian Cuisine No. 2, which is in Mount Vernon.

La Fiamma $$–$$$
200 East Chestnut Street
Downtown
(360) 647-0060
www.lafiamma.com

A perennial winner in local best pizza polls, La Fiamma serves Bellingham's finest gourmet pizza and is one of the city's most popular eateries. Gourmet means this ain't pizza of the lotsa grease and flimsy-crust variety. It's wood fired, and pizza toppings run the length and breadth of the word eclectic—the Spuddy is a baked potato pizza, the BBQ Chicken features, guess what, barbequed chicken, the Grecian Formula has everything from spinach to peppers to flank steak to Kalamata olives to feta and more. La Fiamma also serves a few pasta dishes and paninis (sandwiches on homemade rosemary focaccia bread) made from, as the menu says, "our super-duper fancy Italian sandwich squisher." Choose from the wide wine and microbrew selection and save room for dessert—the Wood Fire S'more will bring back campfire memories, and the Brownie Sundae is, well, a toffee and peanut butter brownie topped with vanilla ice cream and fudge. Can't go wrong there. La Fiamma's welcoming interior is kind of retro cool—exposed brick and faux industrial with wood and steel beams. Outside seating is available, too.

Rudy's Pizzeria $$
1230 North State Street
(360) 647-7547

Rudy's takes the phrase "the choice is yours" seriously. Sure, lots of pizza places offer a variety of toppings, but more than 40? Everything from avocado to zucchini, potatoes to sunflower seeds, with veganrella and Kalamatas in between. Then there's the cheese choice—feta? Bleu? Soy? Mozzarella? Oy! Can't decide? Pick Cheeze Rudy, five cheeses and extra garlic. Or Taco Rudy, with refried beans and salsa. Needless to say, you can get pretty much anything you want at Rudy's, and best yet, all the pizzas—which are available with white or whole wheat crust, in regular thickness or thin—all terrific. Extras include salads, breadsticks, and apple turnovers. And if all that isn't enough, Rudy's has free delivery, too. But go there. The ambience, with its former brick exterior wall and wood floors, is Bellingham funky and cool.

Stanello's Italian Restaurant $$–$$$
1514 12th Street
(360) 676-1304
www.stanellos.com

This Fairhaven eatery, a South Side staple since 1974, has a split personality—one-half family pizza and pasta restaurant and one-half a raucous sports bar (smoke-free) stuffed with fans whenever the Seahawks play and whenever the Sonics and Mariners make the playoffs. Thankfully, a wall divides the two, so family dinners are not disturbed whenever a Sonic slam dunks or a Mariner goes deep. All manner of pizza and pasta are available, with gourmet pizzas such as the chicken and sundried tomato pesto, the barbequed chicken, and the Venus Royal, which is covered with pepperoni, Canadian bacon, and about half a dozen other toppings, being among the most inviting. Regular pizzas come with a choice of five sauces—from white to pink to pesto to barbecue—and 30 different toppings. The spacious dining room boasts exposed brick and oversize historic black-and-white photographs from Fairhaven's early days. West-facing, it also boasts stunning views west toward the San Juan Island sunsets, especially from the outdoor seating section.

Along with serving the same menu as the dining room, the sports bar has its own menu, which includes mega-plates of nachos with more than 25 toppings to choose from. A nice touch: All pizza and Italian dinners are 20 percent off during Seahawk games.

UPSCALE

Anthony's at Squalicum Harbor $$$-$$$$
25 Bellwether Way
(360) 647–5588
www.anthonys.com

Before heading to Anthony's, strike all negative connotations you might have of the phrase chain restaurant from your mind. Sure, Anthony's is a chain, albeit a regional one with its restaurants taking up space on some of the region's finest waterfront parcels. Other than the fact that they serve food and expect to be paid for it, Anthony's has nothing in common with the whole Mc-Wendy-Taco-King spectrum of speedy eateries. There are 23 Anthony's from Bellingham to Bend, Oregon, and like all of them, Bellingham's restaurant specializes in seafood with a capital S, as in they own their own seafood company, thus freshness and quality are not issues. Ambience-wise, Anthony's is tough to beat. Located right on the harbor, the restaurant's huge windows open to the stunning water-island-sunset views, while inside the exposed-beam ceiling, chrome accents, and salmon motif lend an air of casual sophistication. For starters, try the Anthony's Baker's Bowl and Caesar salad, which features the award-winning clam chowder (lauded by everyone from *Evening Magazine* to the *Seattle Times*) served in a toasted loaf of sourdough. Other appetizers include Hawaiian Ahi Nachos, Pan-Fried Willapa Bay Oysters, Crispy Coconut Prawns, and more. Entrees run the gamut of fresh fish (Alder Planked Salmon), prawns (Roasted Garlic), shellfish (the Fishermen's Cioppino has Northwest mussels, Manila clams, lingcod, and salmon), and for the nonfish eater, New York steak and filet mignon. Anthony's also offers a Sunday Crabfeed (all-you-can-eat Dungeness crab), and Monday through Friday Sunset Dinners, a four-course dinner including appetizer, chowder or salad, entree, and dessert, are offered at a reduced price.

Cliff House Restaurant $$$$
331 North State Street
(360) 734–8660
www.bellinghamcliffhouse.com

With its west-facing views overlooking downtown and Bellingham Bay, the Cliff House is one of the top in-town spots for that upscale dining-and-sunset combo. Conversation about the Cliff House usually begins with the thick, creamy homemade Whiskey Crab Soup, which *is* definitely something to write home about. Located a couple blocks down the hill from Western Washington University, the Cliff House specializes in seafood, steaks, pasta, and combinations thereof. Regular specials include items such as Kuhiku Prawns (prawns rolled in coconut) and Seafood Pasta (clams, mussels, and prawns with linguine). Among the steak and seafood favorites offered are garlic tenderloin and New Zealand rack of lamb, with king salmon fillet and a seafood medley being some of the favorites from the sea. For dessert, just as the Whiskey Crab Soup more than likely made you weak in the knees, the homemade peanut butter pie will make you reach for something to keep from falling. If peanut butter's not your thing, a variety of other desserts (including homemade Bailey's Irish cheesecake) are available that deliver a similar effect.

Dirty Dan's $$$$
1211 11th Street
(360) 676–1011
www.dirtydanharris.com

It's perhaps the irony of ironies that one of Fairhaven's upscale restaurants is named for a man whose sobriquet reflects his high less-than-hygienic, more-than-odoriferous quotient. Because Dirty Dan's—named for the former rum smuggler and all-around rapscallion who founded this South side neighborhood in the 1880s—is Fairhaven dining at its finest. Though set within an expansive space in a turn-of-the-20th-century historic building, Dirty Dan's low lighting, dark wood, and exposed brick create an intimate setting, perfect for special-occasion dining or sharing an intimate evening with a loved one. Historical art and photographs on the walls complement the setting. This is hearty seafood, steaks, and prime rib country, and the menu features all the greatest hits you'd expect and some surprises—Alaskan king crab, local pan-fried oysters, filet mignon, New York strip, rack of Australian lamb, all served with baked potato or garlic potatoes and seasonal vegetables. Also nice is a two-page wine list that contains all the best selections from Northwest and California vineyards. Someone graduating from Western Washington University or you just wanna splurge a little? Dirty Dan Harris's is a great choice.

Fino Wine Bar and Fine Food $$$$
804 10th Street
(360) 676-WINE
www.finowinebar.com
Located on the ground floor of Fairhaven's Chrysalis Inn and Spa, the Fino Wine Bar lays claim to one of the most impressive settings in town. And with a sophisticated, understated ambience— linen tablecloths, fireside seating, cool jazz music, light wood that enhances the stunning waterfront and sunset vista—not to mention a rotating wine list that appears to be as long as the 6.5-mile Interurban Trail, the Fino could be intimidating to some. As if to counteract that, however, the menu states up front: "Forget pretense, ceremony and puffery—this is a place for wine drinkers, not wine snobs." Though noted for its wine, Fino, named for a renowned dry sherry from Southern Spain, serves a full menu specializing in Northwest and European specialties. Main entrees include offerings such as seafood linguini with prawns, scallops, salmon, and

mussels and Spanish-style rack of lamb with garlic-bean puree. The "Grazing Menu" offers appetizers, tapas, hors d'oeuvres, and antipasti, as well as soups and sandwiches, such as the pesto-roasted pork loin panini with mozzarella. As for that wine list—wow! Along with a wide selection of aperitifs and wine cocktails, Fino offers sparkling wines and reds and whites from all over—Spain, Portugal, Hungary, Austria, Germany, Italy, and France, as well as California, Oregon, and Washington. Wines are available by the "taste" (three ounces), the glass (six ounces), or the bottle.

Nimbus $$$$
119 North Commercial Street, 14th Floor
(360) 676-1307
www.nimbus.to
Of all the Bellingham restaurants with sunset views, aptly named Nimbus, which is located in the clouds 14 stories above street level at the top of the Bellingham Towers building, might just have the most jaw-dropping. (You can see it for yourself on the restaurant's Web site, which posts sunset photos that are taken every Thursday.) Thankfully, the restaurant's menu and cool sophisticated atmosphere live up to those views. The restaurant opened in 2002, and owner Frederick Hilyard, who studied Environmental Science at Western Washington University, is intent on using fire, water, earth, and air as his guiding principles. It's reflected not only in the name and view but also in the warm shades of orange and gold inside the restaurant. Hilyard changes the menu four times each year, at the solstices and equinoxes, and it generally centers around Northwest cuisine. Past appetizers have included blue corn nachos with avocado salsa and white cheddar and Dungeness crab salad with green curry coconut vinaigrette; entrees have ranged from linguini primavera to rack of lamb to sesame grilled ahi tuna. Nimbus opens at 4:00 P.M.—it serves dinner only—and closes at midnight Monday through Wednesday and 1:00 A.M. on Thursday through Satur-

day. It's closed on Sunday. Nimbus is also a popular and romantic nightspot. With those views, how could it not be?

The Oyster Bar
on Chuckanut Drive $$$$
2578 Chuckanut Drive, Bow
(360) 766-6185
www.theoysterbaronchuckanutdrive.com
Located about 10 miles south of Bellingham's Fairhaven neighborhood, the Oyster Bar is famous for being one of the top destination dining spots in the area, if not *the* top. Set at the edge of a forest above Samish Bay, the west-facing dining room enjoys stunning water views of the San Juan Islands and nightly sunsets that turn the sky all manner of reds and purples and oranges and golds. Serving lunch and dinner. Oysters certainly are a feature of the menu—the oyster tasting menu offers five different varieties including Samish Bay, from just outside the restaurant—but are no means the only highlight. Tantalizing seafood specialties include Australian lobster, Alaskan king salmon, and California abalone along with some more decidedly inland entrees, such as New Zealand filet mignon and wild South Dakota buffalo. The extensive wine list is not so much a list as it is a book—25 pages kept together in a heavy binder. Wine is big at the Oyster Bar and, in fact, the restaurant has won *Wine Spectator* magazine's prestigious Best of Award of Excellence. Desserts are equally as enticing, with offerings such as chocolate espresso mousse cake, cappuccino crème brûlée, and key lime pie. The restaurant got its start in the 1920s as the Rockpoint Oyster Company on Samish Bay. They sold oysters to travelers on Chuckanut Drive and eventually put in a lunch counter where people could sit and eat. Over the years and through several changes of ownership, it transformed into the Oyster Bar, one of the top dining destinations in the region. In 2000 the restaurant was renovated and given somewhat of a lodge feel, perfect for its setting at the edge of a for-

est high above the water. The Oyster Bar is pricey, but for special occasions you're hard-pressed to find a more special place.

Oyster Creek Inn $$$$
2190 Chuckanut Drive, Bow
(360) 766-6179
www.oystercreekinn.com
For a unique, as well as thoroughly can't-go-wrong, satisfying dining experience, head south from Fairhaven along the bay via Chuckanut Drive. Where the road becomes so winding that you're focusing almost all your attention on the next curve instead of the water and islands to your right, you've just about reached your destination: Oyster Creek Inn. Beloved for decades by connoisseurs of fine food and drink throughout the region, the Oyster Creek Inn is perched like a tree house over a creek at Chuckanut Drive's sharpest hairpin turn. (More on that in a sec.) The restaurant's interior, one of simple sophisticated elegance, takes perfect advantage of its idyllic hillside setting in the woods. So what about the food? The contemporary Northwest menu features local oysters (local, as in from outside on Samish Bay), prawns, Dungeness crab, Alaskan halibut and salmon, as well as New York steak, filet mignon, and New Zealand rack of lamb. The extensive wine list features labels from all over the entire West Coast as well as Europe, and the sumptuous dessert menu changes frequently but usually includes delectables such as dark chocolate mousse and crème brûlée. Regarding that creekside setting: A few years ago it was determined that the circa-1920s building that houses the restaurant was slipping down the creek and would eventually find itself floating in Samish Bay. So the restaurant closed for about two years while 650 tons of concrete and steel were sunk into the 70-foot-deep bedrock to secure it in place. Now it ain't goin' nowhere. The Oyster Creek Inn is also open for lunch, and dinner reservations are recommended.

Pacific Café $$$$
100 North Commercial Street
Downtown
(360) 647-0800

This is one of Bellingham's most intimate, romantic, and beloved restaurants, and when there's something shaking at the Mount Baker Theatre (it's housed in the same building), it's darn near impossible to get a table without reservations. Everything is tasteful (no pun intended) at the Pacific Café—from the understated semi-Asian interior accented with light wood and downtown's exposed brick to elegant table settings to the waitstaff's quiet unrushed manner. Then there's the food, a mix of Asian, Northwest, and a touch of the Mediterranean, which is tasteful indeed. Entree choices include Thai chicken Panang coconut curry with bamboo shoots and straw mushrooms; Pacific seafood linguine Parmesan with prawns, clams, and fish, and standbys such as prime beef tenderloin. As for desserts . . . yes, well, with tempting delectables such as Belgian chocolate torte, crème caramel courvoisier (a baked custard), and almond chocolate praline to choose from, perhaps it's best to throw away the calorie counter for the evening. The Pacific Café serves both lunch and dinner, and it's closed on Sunday.

BAKERY/DELI

Avenue Bread and Cafe $
1313 Railroad Avenue
(360) 676-9274

1135 11th Street, Fairhaven
(360) 676-1809

Like the Bagelry, just two doors down from Avenue's downtown location, Avenue Bread is one of those local, casual eateries that specializes in inexpensive but high-quality breakfast or lunch. It's a grab a section or two from the stack of read-while-you're-here newspapers kind of place, somewhere you can amuse yourself and learn a little about the community by reading the thumbtacked flyers announc-ing upcoming shows and concerts or the newest yoga or meditation. It's also just a place to sit by the window and watch the Bellingham morning or afternoon pass by. Avenue offers 16 specialty sandwiches as well as standbys such as ham, roast beef, and turkey, soups, and, of course breads, including focaccia, sourdough, and pane rustica. In late 2005 Avenue Bread opened a Fairhaven location.

The Bagelry $
1319 Railroad Avenue
Downtown
(360) 676-5288

Wanna kill two birds with one stone by grabbing some breakfast or lunch and getting in some people watching? Go to the Bagelry, which features terrific bagels, soups, and all manner of foods to put on bagels, but also floor-to-ceiling windows through which you can watch seemingly all of Bellingham pass by. The fresh, baked-in-the-back bagels and bialys (a type of bagel without a hole; they are not boiled before they are baked the way that bagels are) come in a rainbow of flavors (poppy, sesame, pumpernickel, salt, garlic, blueberry, whole wheat, everything, etc.) and make for great sandwiches or the foundation for a variety of cream cheeses, spreads, and lox. Also a popular breakfast spot, the Bagelry serves a wide variety of omelets, all on a bagel, of course. One thing, don't ask to have your bagel toasted—they have no toaster. Nor does the Bagelry take plastic—cash or check only.

Lafeens Family Pride Donuts And Ice Cream $
1466 Electric Avenue
(360) 647-1703

Sometimes the inner doughnut lover in all of us must be served. And when that's the case, there's no better place in town than Lafeens. Beloved by locals, as business- and postcard-covered walls attest, Lafeens bakes and doles out glazed-, cake-, and old-fashioned doughnuts by the hundreds, twists and maple bar and well, you know where I'm going with this. But wait, there's more. Lafeens offers up croissants, scones, and muffins, too, as well as ice cream, coffee, espresso, and the like. It's open seemingly all hours too—from 5:00 A.M. to midnight most days, which is unusual for a locally owned bakery. Lafeens is conveniently located across from the Electric Avenue entrance to Whatcom Falls Park. So start the morning with a walk, and end it with a maple bar. Or with an apple fritter the size of your head. Or with a cheese Danish. Or . . .

La Vie En Rose French Bakery and Pastry Shop $-$$
111 West Holly Street, Downtown
(360) 715-1839
www.laviebakery.com

La Vie En Rose means life is a rose. Which is all well and good, but sometimes you might want a little more. Like say, peanut butter chocolate chip bars, lemon ginger or apricot honey scones, or perhaps something lighter like a French *batard* or *Pan de Mie.* If so, put this way-versatile downtown bakery/eatery on your things-to-do/places-to-go list. Why versatile? Well, along with its more-than-yummy breads, croissants, cakes, and other offerings baked and made daily at La Vie En Rose's other outlet in Anacortes, the Bellingham establishment serves pizza on a homemade sourdough crust. Pizza choices change daily but usually include toppings along the lines of Kalamata olives and sun-dried tomato pesto. Sandwiches, casseroles, and lasagna are also served. Seating is available, or you can order food to take home or back to the office to eat. Like many downtown establishments, La Vie En Rose is closed on Sunday.

Mount Bakery & Creperie $-$$
308C West Champion Street, Downtown
(360) 715-2195
www.mountbakery.com

Located at street level in the Mount Baker Apartment building, this popular downtown cafe serves terrific breakfasts and lunches as well as pastries and desserts of suitably decadent and delectable character. Sunny (at least when the sun is out), downtown, and beloved by locals, Mount Bakery makes everything from scratch and uses organic ingredients wherever possible, and it's a member of the Fourth Corner Slow Food, a local advocacy group that champions local farmers' markets, sustainable agriculture, and the like. Along with various omelets, crepes, homemade granolas, and yogurts, breakfast options include Shirred Eggs: baked eggs cooked atop a French "triple cream," d'Affinois cheese, shallots, and Swiss Emmental. Lunches are quiches, cold sandwiches (the veggie with roasted zucchini and the prosciutto with provolone are a couple) and various hot sandwiches, also called croques. Croque Monsieur has prosciutto, provolone, and red onion; the veggie croque has roasted zucchini, red pepper, red onion, Swiss Emmental, and Kalamata olive tapenade. Also on tap are sweet crepes such as Belgian chocolate with vanilla bean pastry cream and, of course, crepe Suzette. The Mount Bakery is closed on Monday and closes at 3:00 P.M. most days and at 4:00 P.M. on Sunday.

PARKS AND TRAILS 🌳

There are myriad reasons Bellingham forever seems to be popping up on some magazine or organization's list of 10 best outdoor or adventure towns in the United States. Its location, at the edge of Puget Sound about an hour from the North Cascade Mountains, is key: Where else can you spend the morning skiing or snowboarding through deep powder and the afternoon sea kayaking in an intertidal waterway? Bellingham also has a terrific city park and world-class trail system. In fact, Bellingham is tops in the country when it comes to the amount of green space available: 16 percent of the city's total land area is park, trail, or natural reserve. That means that one of every seven acres is somewhere to play or just go for a nice walk.

More than 20 parks dot the city, with 50-plus miles of trails winding and wending their way throughout the city limits. An impressive amount considering that the city itself is just more than 20 square miles. And that doesn't even include Larrabee State Park and the Chuckanut Mountain Parklands, just south of the city, which together add another 5,000-plus acres of public wilderness and more than 40 miles of trails.

PARKS

The diversity of Bellingham's city parks is mind-boggling. Cornwall Park boasts dense, dark forest with giant western red cedars hundreds of years old. Boulevard Park has open, bayfront views to the San Juan Islands and the North Coast Mountains above Vancouver, B.C. Arroyo Park features a rugged rock- and snag-choked gorge where thousands of salmon return to spawn in the fall. Big Rock Garden Park is a showcase of Japanese-style gardens and permanent outdoor sculptures. And that's just the tip of the Bellingham park iceberg.

Almost all the parks share one thing in common: water. (Which, given the Northwest's propensity for rain and other things wet, perhaps isn't surprising.) Be it a lake, a bay, a creek, or a pond, nearly every Bellingham park offers some body of water that invites contemplation, swimming, fishing, or rock skipping.

Here's a rundown of Bellingham (and nearby) parks that offer the gamut of wilderness experiences. Many also offer basketball courts, horseshoe pits, barbecue pits, restrooms, etc. Admission to all parks is free. For more Bellingham park information, check out www.cob.org/parks/source/html/facilities.htm on the Internet.

Arroyo Park
Old Samish Drive and Chuckanut Drive
(360) 676–6985
A walk through Arroyo Park is like a walk through a gorge in a mini–rain forest. Heavy timber dims whatever sun there is outside, and the tangle of hanging limbs, lichens, and swordferns add to an otherworldly atmosphere. Chuckanut Creek rushes down the middle and in late fall is asplash with hundreds of salmon rounding third and heading for home. (And their graves.)

Trail mileage is actually rather sparse in Arroyo Park (maybe three-quarters of a mile) but given that it's bisected by the popular Interurban Trail and is the northern terminus of the Lost Lake Trail, it's often visited by folks on their way to other places. As only a semideveloped park, Arroyo offers no amenities other than parking lots and a porta-potty off Chuckanut Drive.

Big Rock Garden Park
Sylvan Street and Illinois Lane
(360) 676-6985

Art meets nature in this unique 2.5-acre neighborhood park just above Lake Whatcom. Meander along the wooded gravel paths and you'll find yourself face to face with one of more than 35 works of steel, brick, granite, cedar, bronze, and similar media that are permanently on display at the park. *Lipchitziana* is a striking 9-foot-tall mélange of cerulean steel shapes and lines by the Mexican artist Sebastian. *Kwakiutal Sun Mask* is a totemic 7-foot-wide cedar carving by British Columbian First Nations artist Jimmy Joseph. And so on, with pieces by both local and international artists. Throughout the summer the park's collection is expanded by an additional 10 to 20 pieces during the International Sculpture Exhibit.

Also adding to the Big Rock Garden experience is the brilliant springtime blooming of the park's rhododendrons and azaleas, and each September, the more than 100 varieties of maples signal that fall is on the way. With assistance, the park is wheelchair accessible.

Bloedel Donovan Park
2214 Electric Avenue
(360) 676-6985

This 18-acre lakefront park boasts one of Bellingham's most popular swimming beaches. Though, to be frank, at some point during almost every summer, the city closes it down because of E. coli and/or fears of high fecal coliform levels. That's because the lake is at least as popular with the Canadian geese population as it is with humans, if you catch my drift. Still, its setting on vast Lake Whatcom against the forested (if a bit clear-cut up) folds and ridges of Stewart Mountain make this one of Bellingham's most scenic parks.

A developed park, Bloedel has all the picnicking, barbecuing, volleyballing, basketballing, and playground amenities that one would expect, as well as an indoor meeting space and gymnasium. In season the park's open grassy fields see plenty of

soccer and softball action. There's even an in-season snack bar, boat rentals, and a miniature golf course. Boating enthusiasts can take advantage of the lake's only public boat launch within city limits, though canoeists, kayakers, and those seeking a bit of peace and quiet when they ply the water might want to choose somewhere else to paddle. On warm summer weekends, motorized boats and Jet Skis on the lake can make it sound like a NASCAR speedway.

Boulevard Park
South State Street and Bayview Drive
(360) 676-6985

What this waterfront park might lack in size, it more than makes up for with its views and its trail access to downtown Bellingham and, now via the Taylor Street Dock, Fairhaven. Basically it's a narrow, 14-acre strip of grassland between Bellingham Bay and the Burlington Northern railway, but upon that grassland are some of the best picnicking, barbecuing, volleyballing, sunbathing, and, every Independence Day, fireworks-watching spots in town. Views extend far into the San Juan

On Saturday summer nights, grab a picnic dinner and blanket and head for the park for outdoor cinema night. Classic movies (and classic wannabes) are shown on an inflatable screen at various park venues throughout town, usually preceded with a live music performance. Check www.whatcomfilm.org and click on "Traveling Pickford Show" for schedule.

and Gulf Islands and Canada's Coast Mountain Range. A true walker's park, Boulevard Park is 1 mile south of downtown Bellingham and 0.75 of a mile north of Fairhaven via the South Bay Trail. In summer, Boulevard Park is the site of various festivals as well as a popular concerts-in-the park series.

Cornwall Park
2800 Cornwall Avenue and
3242 Meridian Street
(360) 676-6985

Established in 1909, a year after Whatcom Falls Park, 66-acre Cornwall Park is like a smaller version of that park, with lots of big trees, multipurpose fields, a prominent creek with a tumbling waterfall, and some great trails (about 3 miles' worth). There's just less of all of it than at Whatcom Falls Park. But with its brand-new (2004) kids spray park and spiffy, kind of new playground equipment, as well as a covered picnic shelter, Cornwall Park is an extremely popular place for those with little ones. One unique feature of the park is a disc golf course set in the middle of the woods, which draws tie-dyed and dreadlocked folks from all over. Other features include tennis courts, horseshoe pits, a picnic area, and fragrant rose garden.

Elizabeth Park is named after Elizabeth Roeder, wife of Henry Roeder, one of Bellingham's first settlers. The Roeder Home, today used for music performances and the like, was the former home of Victor Roeder, one of Henry Roeder's sons.

Elizabeth Park
Madison Street and Elizabeth Street
(360) 676-6985

The Columbia neighborhood is about as close as you'll get in Bellingham to some imagined idealized 1950s neighborhood of picket fences, kids' lemonade stands, and hot apple pies warming on windowsills. Elizabeth Park, the city's oldest neighborhood park, embodies that time, especially in summer. From June to August, free Thursday evening concerts draw huge crowds, many of whom spread their dinners out on blankets and cross their fingers that the dozens of children dancing and running around don't knock over the potato salad. A non-advertised Fourth of July celebration features sack races, pie-eating contests, and of course a parade, the route of which seems to be made up at the time by whatever 8- or 10-year-old is in front.

The park is shaded by dozens of massive trees, but not the evergreens that you'd expect in a park in the Northwest. These are walnuts, chestnuts, maples, and the like—mostly deciduous, thus making Elizabeth Park popular with those drawn to fall colors as well as smaller folk who like to build and destroy leaf piles. Turn-of-the-20th-century lights and a restored water fountain add to the park's character. Also of note are a couple tennis courts and a play structure that gets lots of use.

Fairhaven Park
107 Chuckanut Drive
(360) 676-6985

Fairhaven, a nice, open all-around park (tennis and basketball courts, newish kids' play structure, multiuse fields, rose garden), is one of the city's oldest. A new (2004) spray park has made it popular with those of single-digit age and their folks. Several sheltered areas offer meeting and party spaces, and, like most Bellingham parks, easy access to a major trail (in this case, the Interurban Trail) makes getting here on foot or bicycle a snap. In late fall, the park's Padden Creek often becomes choked with salmon returning on their spawn-and-die cycle.

Fairhaven Village Green
Corner of Mill Avenue and 10th Street

Not too many years ago, this was just a

A free concert at Elizabeth Park. MIKE MCQUAIDE

muddy field behind Village Books that no one seemed to know what to do with. Then in the early 2000s some local folks calling themselves the Fairhaven Village Green Committee raised about a third of a million dollars and, together with the city park's department, turned this formerly nondescript one-acre plot into an inviting village square reminiscent of a European marketplace. Centrally located, the park is surrounded by popular shops, restaurants, cafes, and Fairhaven Village Inn, a charming 22-room lodge. Main features of the park itself include a wood-and-glass pergola, brick walkways, and an outdoor performance space. Also a focal point is the life-size sculpture of Dirty Dan Harris, one

of Fairhaven's founders but never a man to be confused with a bouquet of roses (thus his sobriquet).

The park hosts various fairs and festivals throughout the year, eclectic events such as bocce ball tournaments, live theatrical and musical performances, and, in summers, an outdoor cinema. The park has restrooms and a drinking fountain. For those who'd rather not deal with parking or driving hassles, Fairhaven Village Green is easily accessed from downtown Bellingham via the South Bay Trail. For those from the South Side, the Interurban Trail passes within 2 blocks of the Village Green.

Lake Padden Park
4882 Samish Way
(360) 676-6985

Along with being the biggest park in Bellingham city limits, Lake Padden is perhaps the most well-rounded park, offering something (and more than likely three or four things) for everyone. Do you like to walk, hike, run, or otherwise perambulate? A wide, partly open, partly forested 2.6-mile gravel trail circles the lake and is one of the best places for residents (and visitors) to get in their morning (or afternoon or evening) constitutionals. Like to get off the beaten path a bit, perhaps on a mountain bike or a horse? Another 5 miles of rugged, densely forested and often muddy trails can be found just south and east of the lake.

Like to swim? Like to fish? Like to canoe, kayak, or windsurf? The park's namesake—Lake Padden—features beaches and boat launches and plenty of room to paddle around. (Motorized boats and Jet Skis are prohibited.) Like to play softball, throw a Frisbee, or play basketball? Like to sunbathe or picnic? Padden Park hosts all of these things too, as well as several popular annual events, including the Junior Ski to Sea race, the Lake Padden Triathlon, and the Padden Mountain Pedal, a mountain bike festival. The park also features an expansive dog off-leash area. The available changing rooms with showers are also nice. And if you're a golfer, just next door, the Lake Padden Golf Course is one of the best and most inexpensive municipal golf courses that you'll find anywhere.

Larrabee State Park
245 Chuckanut Drive
(360) 676-2093

Unfortunately, the dictionary is a bit scant when it comes to supplying sufficient superlatives for this park. Spectacular, splendiferous, breathtaking, awesome, really cool, and the like just don't do it justice. Located 6 miles south of Bellingham city limits (but easily accessed by foot, bike tire, or horse hoof via the wonderful Interurban Trail; or by car via Chuckanut Drive), Larrabee became Washington's first state park in 1915. It remains one of the state's largest parks, boasting about 2,600 acres of wilderness forest crisscrossed by about 15 miles of trails, more than 1.5 miles of saltwater shoreline, and an 80-site campground.

Though the waters of Puget Sound are cold year-round, the park's shallow tidepools provide endless beachcombing fun. So does the park's characteristic Chuckanut sandstone, with swoops and swirls perfect for scrambling up and down. Tame paths past smooth-barked madrona trees meander down to along the water's edge, while across Chuckanut Drive, tougher stuff awaits. A 2-mile trail heads to peaceful, rock- and forest-rimmed Fragrance Lake, climbing about 1,000 feet on the way. About halfway up, a short, signed jaunt leads to a stunning viewpoint west toward dotted islands, mountains far into Canada, and Bellingham Bay far below. At the park's south end, Clayton Beach is a tucked-away oasis, a sandy beach where the water's a little warmer, the sun seems a little hotter, and the fun is perhaps a little funner.

Little Squalicum Beach Park
Marine Drive and Lindberg Avenue
(360) 676-6985

Sometimes all you want from a park is a place to watch the water, skip some stones, and maybe find an interesting seashell or two. Little Squalicum Beach is that park. Nothing fancy here. There's nothing to sit on but the ubiquitous driftwood of Bellingham Bay. There's no playground equipment for the kids—just a creek to dam up, divert, then dam up again, then divert, and so on. In other words, hours of sloppy fun.

Views from the roughly half-mile of very strollable, sand-stone-and-shell beach are super, with all of south Bellingham laid out before you. There's Western Washington University up on the hill; Fairhaven, the Taylor Avenue Dock, and the Alaska Ferry Terminal against a

Chuckanut Mountain backdrop; and, farther to the south, islands and mountains
that stretch to infinity.

The park is conveniently located on the
Bay to Baker Trail, which offers easy off-
road access to Squalicum Parkway, not far
from Cornwall Park. It also provides access
to a proposed, yet-to-be-named, yet-to-
be-built park and sports complex just
north of the Columbia neighborhood. With
the recent port of Bellingham acquisition
of prime waterfront property from Georgia
Pacific, proposed plans for the redevel-
oped waterfront include potential trail
and/or parkland from Little Squalicum
Beach all the way to Fairhaven.

Marine Park
West end of Harris Avenue
(360) 676-2500
This barely an acre large, narrow slice of
lawn has no playground, no soccer fields,
no big ancient trees, or anything like that
to recommend it. It has just three very
important things: location, location, location. Situated as it is at pretty much the
westernmost tip of Fairhaven, the only
thing between park visitors and Lummi
Island is about 6 miles of Bellingham Bay.
That's it. Nothing, save for a buoy here or
there and a dive-bombing cormorant, to
block the spectacular views. Marine Park
is about beachcombing, boat and bird-
watching, and island counting, but mostly
it's about taking it easy, gazing at the
water, and watching for the fiery skies of
sunset. Compared to other city parks,
there might not seem to be much to draw
folks, but if you're a sunset-and-water
gazer, this is your place.

Maritime Heritage Park
1800 C Street
(360) 676-6985
Downtown Bellingham's biggest park,
Maritime Heritage Park has recently
undergone several upgrades, including a
spectacular hillside amphitheater with
views to the San Juans, re-vamped trails
with a boardwalk promenade, and an
Environmental Learning Center so visitors

can learn about salmon and other wildlife
that make this corner of the world their
home. Trails lead to the mouth of Whatcom Creek, where in the early 1850s settlers set up the first area sawmill. The park
is conveniently located near the Whatcom
Museum of History and Art, and the
Whatcom Children's Museum.

Samish Park
673 North Lake Samish Drive
(360) 733-2362
Located about 3 miles southeast of
Bellingham, this 39-acre county park is
one of the area's most popular swimming
holes, and with good reason. The swimming area's southern exposure ensures
that the lake water warms up (and stays
warm) a little earlier in the season than
other lakes and, perhaps even more key,
for whatever reason, geese and ducks
don't seem to gather here in as great
numbers as at other nearby lakes. Thus
there seem to be fewer cases of the
dreaded swimmer's itch and other such
nasties.

Samish Park also rents canoes, kayaks,
and paddle boats, and it boasts a fishing
dock as well as picnic and playground
equipment. The park is free for Whatcom
County residents, though nonresidents
must pay a $4.00 per-car day-use fee.

Sehome Hill Arboretum
25th Street and Sehome Hill
(360) 676-6985
Imagine, if you will, that in a scenic seaside town like Bellingham, there was one
prominent hill pretty much smack-dab in
the middle of everything that had the
best views not only of the city itself but
also of the outlying area, including countless islands, mountains, and distant cities
in a foreign land. And that this prominent,
view-rich hill was not gated off by developers for homes that only the wealthy
could afford, but was open to everyone.
That, my friend, is Sehome Hill Arboretum. Rising like a bent knee under a blanket, Sehome Hill, the backdrop against
which Western Washington University is

set, rises 650 feet into the air between downtown Bellingham and Fairhaven. At the top, an observation tower offers the best city, bay, and western Whatcom County views you'll find in the city. Though a paved road leads to a small parking lot at the top, for the true experience, follow some of the 6 miles of trails that wind their way up and down the mini mountain.

Much of this hill was logged and burned in the late 1800s, but efforts in the 1920s turned toward making it into a park. With its well established ferns and hanging moss and overgrown second-growth forest, these days Sehome Hill has a real wilderness feel, which is remarkable since it's mere yards from the university and its nearly 13,000 students. Classified as semi-developed by the city, Sehome definitely offers a back-to-nature experience with no restrooms, picnic tables, playground, or similar amenities. The arboretum is conveniently located next to scenic Western Washington, itself worthy of an afternoon's meander, especially with its renowned outdoor sculpture collection.

Taylor Avenue Dock
Taylor Avenue and 10th Street
(360) 676-6985
Located just south of Boulevard Park, this newly refurbished dock and boardwalk has quickly become the most popular promenade in the city. And with good reason. The roughly one-third-mile over-the-water pedestrian walkway extends out over Bellingham Bay, affording not only impressive 360-degree water-island-and-South-Hill-home views but look-sees down below, too. Amid the sea stars and waterfowl, harbor seals are often seen poking their heads up and looking about as if wondering what all the fuss is about. On a sunny Saturday or Sunday afternoon, there's almost no finer place in Bellingham to be, and you almost always see someone here you know. The original dock was built in the late 1800s and used for various commercial enterprises, one of which was a salmon cannery.

Whatcom Falls Park
1401 Electric Avenue
(360) 676-6985
Established in 1908, this 210-acre gem might just be the crown jewel of Bellingham parks. Heavily forested with giant Douglas firs and western red cedars, this park also features about 5 miles of trails. And of course, there are the falls. A wide mini-Niagara greets visitors as they make their way into the park via the way-impressive circa-1939 WPA (Works Progress Administration, a Depression-era jobs program) stone bridge. Farther on, trails meander creekside as the stream snakes its way through woods and squeezes between house-size boulders on its way to Bellingham Bay. A number of wide bends where the creeks pools invite wading, swimming, and, at one popular spot, cliff jumping.

The park features tennis and basketball courts, a playground, multipurpose fields, and a picnic area. There's also a trout hatchery with interpretive displays and a children's fishing pond. Trails at the north end of the park lead to Bloedel Donovan Park and Lake Whatcom. Whatcom Falls Park is easily accessed via the Railroad Trail, and it's also just a few blocks from Galbraith Mountain, making it a popular meeting spot for mountain bikers and hikers.

Zuanich Point Park
Harbor Loop Drive
(360) 676-2500
If someone tells you to go fly a kite, don't be offended, just go here. You won't be sorry. This waterfront park's ubiquitous southern winds and wide-open fields are perfect for getting (and keeping) a kite airborne. Points throughout the park overlook Bellingham Bay and most of the city's waterfront, with impressive views up to Sehome Hill and Western Washington University. A 2-mile paved path (with quarter-mile markers) is popular with walkers, runners, and in-line skaters and winds its way through the park, nearby Squalicum Harbor, and adjacent Bell-

wether Way. This will hopefully someday be part of a terrific 6- to 8-mile-long waterfront park and trail network that will stretch from Little Squalicum Beach to Fairhaven.

Zuanich Point Park also features a playground, Squalicum Boathouse (a popular meeting facility with floor-to-ceiling picture windows), and Fishers Memorial, a touching tribute to fisherman who've lost their lives at sea.

Parks to come. . .

As of press time, ground had yet to be broken on an as-yet-not-named park off Squalicum Parkway just north of the Columbia neighborhood. Along with picnic and playground equipment, the park would feature several soccer and baseball-softball fields.

And in what is perhaps the biggest undertaking in Bellingham history, in 2005 the port of Bellingham took over 137 acres of prime waterfront property from Georgia-Pacific West Inc., who ran a mill for decades at the site. The port receives the land for free with the stipulation that they pay the estimated $60 million cleanup costs, mostly from years of mercury contamination.

A 10- to 20-year redevelopment project includes a waterfront neighborhood with residences, retail and office space, parks, and likely an extension of the waterfront South Bay Trail so that it extends approximately 6 to 8 miles from Little Squalicum Beach to Fairhaven and beyond.

WALKING/HIKING (AND RUNNING/BIKING TOO)

As if Bellingham's wealth of parks weren't enough, the city's trail system is perhaps second to none. In the mid 1990s, the American Hiking Society named Bellingham Trail Town USA, the only town in

If you're ever at Elizabeth Park and the wind is from the south (which it almost always is), don't be surprised if you hear the sound of far-off barking. The culprit? Sea lions basking and barking on the docks down by Zuanich Point Park, about half a mile away.

Washington or Oregon to receive the designation. More than 50 miles of off-road paths wag, wend, wind, and crisscross the city's 22 square miles. And if you consider Chuckanut Mountain, there's another 40 miles just south of town.

Some trails snake through deep dark woods that are homes to great horned owls, pileated woodpeckers, and a host of other critters. Others follow creeks where each fall, hordes of salmon can be seen enacting their annual fight-the-current, spawn-and-die drama. Waterfront trails trace the Bellingham Bay shoreline and offer opportunities for kayak, sailboat, and, occasionally, whale-gazing. Other trails are merely downtown alternatives for getting from point A to point B without having to drive.

Thus, with so many miles, Bellingham's hikers, bikers, pedestrians, equestrians, and anyone else who likes to put foot, tire, or hoof to dirt are a happy lot. Here are some of Bellingham's most popular and unique trails. (Unless noted, trails are open to all user groups.)

For maps and more detailed descriptions of these trails, visit www.cob.org/parks/parks_trails/trail_guide.htm.

Bellingham Trails

Bay to Baker/Little Squalicum Beach This wide, gently graded 1.2-mile (one-way) old rail bed parallels Squalicum Parkway from Little Squalicum Beach almost all the way to Cornwall Park. Stop for water (or to swing on the monkey bars) at Birchwood Park. This trail will eventually offer access

Hikers along the Mount Baker Highway. BELLINGHAM WHATCOM COUNTY TOURISM/JIM POTH

to a new park being planned at the south end of Squalicum Parkway.

Civic Field Trails This still-emerging 1.2-mile loop offers a nice walk after a session at one of the Civic Field Complex's facilities, which include the Sportsplex's ice rink and indoor soccer fields, Arnie Hanna Aquatic Center, Civic Field Stadium's track and soccer fields, Frank Geri softball fields, and the recently added skateboard and bike parks. Start by the Sportsplex, head north through the forest, bypass a few softball fields, and, after another forest foray, emerge by the track. Eventually the trails will link to Salmon Park and Whatcom Creek Trails.

Connelly Creek Trail This peaceful 1-mile forested path follows Connelly Creek as it snakes its way through wetlands near the Happy Valley neighborhood. It's a key connector trail that offers easy access to Sehome Arboretum to the north and Happy Valley Park and the Interurban Trail to the south.

Interurban Trail Way back when, folks hoped that Bellingham, not Seattle, would become the major Northwest port city. It never happened. But these days, Bellinghamsters are blessed with the 6.6-mile Interurban Trail from Fairhaven to Larrabee State Park, which follows a wide, mostly flat, old rail bed from those heady times. Half-mile markers along the way let you know how far you've gone (or still have to go). The official Fairhaven terminus is at 10th Street and Donovan Avenue, but there are numerous access points.

Lake Whatcom Trail This flat, shaded, 3.1-mile (one-way) lakeside trail follows the old Blue Canyon Mine railroad along the northern shore of Lake Whatcom. Check out the cool waterfall at about the 1-mile mark. (Half-mile markers let you know how far you've gone.) The trail has plenty of spots for you to stop, dangle your feet in the water, and pretend you're Huck Finn. The trailhead is located near the end of North Shore Drive, about 8 miles outside of town.

Mud Bay Beach Walk While the name of this 1-mile (depending on the tide) trail might not be pretty, a walk or run on the beach here sure is. Eagles, herons, and osprey soar the skies and pick at critters in the sand; at lower tides, sandstone boulders invite exploration. (Not suitable for bikes.)

Padden Creek Trail (Larrabee Trail) This gravel, behind-the-scenes 0.4-mile path winds through a south Fairhaven neighborhood, passes behind various businesses, and follows Padden Creek near its outlet into Padden Lagoon. This is Dirty Dan Harris's old stompin' grounds. The west trailhead features bay and island views near the . . . um, sewage plant.

Railroad Trail This amazing old 3.2-mile (one-way) rail bed is best described by listing all it connects and accesses: Sunnyland neighborhood to Barkley Village to St. Clair Pond to Alabama Street Overpass to Bloedel Donovan and Whatcom Falls Parks. And from there the only thing separating Whatcom Falls Park from the Lake Padden end of the world is a little thing called Galbraith Mountain, aka mountain-bike mecca.

South Bay Trail/Boulevard Park Running from Maple Street in downtown Bellingham to Fairhaven Village Green behind Village Books, this 2.3-mile one-way major trail thoroughfare follows the waterfront with spectacular bay, island, and sunset views. About a mile south of downtown Bellingham, the trail enters Boulevard Park, and just south of the park, it meets the popular Taylor Avenue Dock.

Stimpson Nature Reserve A 3-mile loop located off Lake Louise Road, this newish park and conservation area includes deep, dark forest, squishy marshland, and a peaceful lake. As you follow the trail, look and listen for herons and kingfishers, woodpeckers and waxwings, ospreys and eagles. But please leave Fido at home. This being a conservation area, dogs (and bicycles) are not permitted.

Miles and miles of great trails can also be found in the following parks: Cornwall Park, Whatcom Falls Park, Sehome Arboretum, Lake Padden Park, Larrabee State Park, Zuanich Point Park, and Squalicum Harbor.

Canyon Lake Creek Community Forest

For a trip to more than 1,000 years ago, head out the Mount Baker Highway to the Canyon Lake Creek Community Forest. Until about 150 years ago, this pocket in the foothills about 25 miles east of Bellingham was just a big, forested canyon with a creek snaking through the bottom. But in the mid-1800s an earthquake caused much of the canyon's west wall to collapse and, with its attendant forest, slide into the creek, creating a natural dam in the process. Thus was Canyon Lake born, and today evidence of the slide can be seen in the hundreds of cedar snags that poke up through the lake's surface like raised hands in a classroom. Eventually the creek will erode down through the landslide and drain the lake, but not for many hundreds of years.

In the early 1990s, the Whatcom County development firm that owned the land planned to log a 700-acre stand of old-growth trees about 3 miles up the Canyon Lake watershed. Before they did, however, the Whatcom Land Trust, a local conservation group, arranged for a forest ecologist to determine the age of the forest, which was made up of mostly Alaska yellow cedar, hemlock, and Pacific silver fir. It was presumed that the trees were about 400 to 500 years old, the age of most Northwest old-growth forests. Core samples, however, revealed them to be at least 800 years old, with some more than 1,000 years of age.

As the ecologist's report read: "The Canyon Lake Old Growth parcel is one of the oldest forest stands known in the Pacific Northwest and one of the largest intact stands of its age."

Logging plans were halted, and the scramble was on to find the $3.6 million needed to purchase the watershed so that the forest could be preserved. Eventually, through private and public donations—half of it coming from the Paul Allen Foundation—the funding came through and Canyon Lake, the ancient forest, and 1,500 acres of rejuvenating forest opened to the public in 2001. Whatcom County Parks, Western Washington University, and the Whatcom Land Trust manage the land jointly.

To reach the ancient trees from Canyon Lake requires a 3-mile hike on a retired logging road with a gentle grade. Ever-expanding Nooksack Valley views and the chance to spot palm-frond fossils

Chuckanut Mountain Trails

Chuckanut Ridge Trail For trail lovers who like a challenge, this 3.0-mile (one-way) trail is quite possibly the top of the food chain. Roller-coaster ups and downs snake along Chuckanut Mountain's densely wooded spine and offer occasional views to Mount Baker and the San Juan Islands—what's not to love? To get there, head south on Chuckanut Drive for about 4 miles to Hiline Road, which soon becomes Cleator Road, and turn left. Follow Cleator Road for 3.6 miles to the Lost Lake Overlook sign at a bend in the road.

in the Chuckanut sandstone rock faces along the trail help pass the time.

Much of this old road passes through forest logged 20 to 30 years ago and, truth be told, right now it's got a bit of that post-logging wasteland feel to it. In time the young forest should blend in well with the ancient forest. Speaking of that ancient forest, after about 3 miles, go right onto the newly constructed trail that quickly ducks into the old, old growth. Things get dark in a hurry.

The 1.2-mile, needle-strewn dirt trail snakes through trees that were just getting their start in life at about the time Leif Eriksson bumped into North America. Because of the relatively high elevation of the forest—about 3,800 feet—the wonderfully gnarled trees, despite their age, are not the giants one might expect. Still, they're stately, grand, and super tenacious—they've had dibs on this place for a thousand years.

So, to recap: Canyon Lake Creek Community Forest boasts a peaceful, tree- and waterfall-rimmed lake with some recent natural history to it and an ancient forest with some of the oldest trees in all the Pacific Northwest. It's only shortcoming would seem to be its lack of a mountain vista. Not so fast, I'm getting to that.

Once you reach the end of the ancient forest trail, you pop out onto a ridge at 4,500 feet, which offers spectacular front-row views of Mount Baker (only 10 air miles away), the Twin Sisters Range, and all three forks of the Nooksack River.

After ogling the views, return via the forest trail, or consider taking the retired logging road down. Views north include the Nooksack Valley and eventually Canyon Lake. That is, until the creek erodes the landslide and drains the lake away. But that shouldn't happen for a few hundred years.

To get to Canyon Lake Creek Community Forest, head east on the Mount Baker Highway to milepost 16.8 and turn right onto Mosquito Lake Road. Follow this road for 1.7 miles and turn left onto gravel Canyon Lake Road, following the sign for Canyon Lake Creek Community Forest. Continue following signs and green arrows for 6.7 miles to the road-end parking lot. (At about 6.1 miles bear to the right at an unmarked intersection.) The parking lot elevation is 2,350 feet.

To get to the old-growth forest and the ridge with mountain views, go left from the parking lot and follow the retired logging road trail for about 3 miles to the old-growth trail; it's 4 miles to the ridge.

Fragrance Lake Trail This is a very popular, rain foresty–feeling 4.2-mile-round-trip trail that's a great introduction to Chuckanut Mountain. You'll find big leafy ferns, big coniferous trees, and big-time San Juan Island views. Then there's the lake, a rock-rimmed jewel that's fun to frolic in or around. It's all here and it's all good. From Fairhaven, go south on Chuckanut Drive for about 5 miles to the trailhead parking area on the left. It's directly across from the main entrance to Larrabee State Park. Bicycles and horses are not allowed on Fragrance Lake Trail.

Hemlock Trail This 3.5-mile (one-way) main east-west arterial trail of the Chuck-

(Q) **CLOSE-UP**

Nooksack Falls

On the way to Mount Baker, consider a quick stop at Nooksack Falls. About 40 miles east of Bellingham and less than 15 miles before the Mount Baker Ski Area, two threads of the mighty Nooksack River lose their battle with gravity and plunge 90 feet to a jumble of boulders below. The explosion of water is quite thrilling, especially during the winter and spring when the river is at its highest flow. Kids (and waterfall lovers in general) go nuts at Nooksack Falls, though it's also a place that can be dangerous and that has a history of tragedy.

Because of the high splash content, it's very misty and the rocks can be extremely slippery. Chain-link fences keep visitors from the slipperiest, most potentially dangerous viewing spots. Unfortunately, because the fencing partially blocks some of the views, some waterfall lovers have made bad choices in attempts to get a better look. In June of both 1998 and 1999 individuals ignored the multiple warning signs posted in the area and climbed past the safety fence, only to slip on moss-covered rocks and plunge to their deaths. So, stay behind the fence. As a reminder, before heading down to the falls, read the interpretive signage across from the parking lot, which includes warnings and the names of eight individuals who've plunged to their deaths during the past 60 years.

About half a mile past milepost 40, turn right onto Wells Creek Road (Forest Service Road 33) and continue for another half-mile to a parking lot just before a bridge. Follow your ears to the falls, which are 25 yards away on the opposite side of the road from the parking lot.

anut Mountain trail system connects the Arroyo Park/Lost Lake/Interurban trails sphere with the Pine and Cedar Lakes end of the world. From Arroyo Park, follow the signs for Lost Lake Trail, and you'll reach the Hemlock Trail intersection in a little less than a mile.

North Lost Lake Trail Here's the best route into the heart of Chuckanut Mountain with the least amount of driving. The at-times-challenging (read: *steep*) trail, which is 4.6 miles one-way from Arroyo Park to the north end of the lake, follows an old roadbed to a hidden lake. Along the way, it also connects to the Pine, Cedar Lakes, and Chuckanut Ridge Trails. Pick up the trail at Arroyo Park near the top of the hill on the south side of Chuckanut Creek and follow the signs for Lost Lake. This trail can also be accessed from the south via Fragrance Lake Road in Larrabee State Park.

Oyster Dome Trail Find here what most people call the Bat Caves, a jumble of boulders at the foot of a 300-foot rock face on Blanchard Mountain. In those caves live some bats, Townsend's Big-Eared Bats to be exact. And apparently skunks, too. So enter at your own risk. A rugged trail leads to the top of the rock wall and rewards you with spectacular views spanning seemingly all of northern Puget Sound. From Fairhaven, go south on Chuckanut Drive for about 10 miles to milepost 10. Park on the right; the trailhead for this 7-mile round-trip trail is on the left.

Pine and Cedar Lakes Trail Among the steepest trails around (there are more than 1,300 feet of climbing in first 1.5 miles), this trail on Chuckanut Mountain's north flank leads to a couple of otherworldly, forest- and rock-lined ponds. Just before Cedar Lake, the trail intersects with the Hemlock Trail, which accesses the Lost Lake and Arroyo Park trails. The Pine Trail is 4.5 miles (round-trip), and the Cedar Lakes Trail is 4 miles (round-trip).

Teddy Bear Cove Short and steep but a real gem, this 3-mile round-trip forested trail snakes seemingly straight downhill from Chuckanut Drive to a protected pocket beach just south of Bellingham perfect for combing and roaming. From the North Chuckanut Mountain Trailhead parking lot, follow the Interurban Trail for about 0.5 mile to the Teddy Bear Cove intersection. Turn right, being careful as you cross Chuckanut Drive. (Trail is not suitable for horses or bikes.)

Mount Baker and Heather Meadows

And then there are the mountains. If you think the city's parks and trails are great, wait till you step out and experience these. There are alpine vistas stretching to infinity; heather- and blueberry- and wildflower-meadows you'll never want to leave; and contemplative lakes strewn with icebergs, even in August—all dominated by a couple spectacular peaks that couldn't be more different. Mount Baker (10,781 feet) is an icy volcano in the classic, what-you-think-of-when-you-think-of-a-volcano sense, like an impression left from a giant funnel full of vanilla cake frosting left upside down. Mount Shuksan

is a nonvolcanic mélange of jagged rocks, pointy peaks, and ice-blue hanging glaciers—an absolute Picasso of a mountain thrust from deep within the earth some 150 million years ago.

Aptly named **Heather Meadows,** at the end of the Mount Baker Highway, places you smack in the middle of both, and is a terrific place to ogle, stare, gape in wonder, and just take it all in. There's everything here from barrier-free paved paths, perfect for the casual sightseer and those with small children, to more rugged trails leading deep into the wilderness and right up to the toes of the big peaks.

While there, visit the Heather Meadows Visitor Center and Austin Pass Picnic Area. Perched on a rock ledge looking out at the Bagley Lakes basin and flat-topped Table Mountain, this picnic area makes for a super munching spot on a Picture Lake–Artist Point day. (Artist Point is just 2 miles *up* the road, and Picture Lake is 2 miles *down* the road.) Twenty-plus picnic tables ensure that there's plenty of room for everyone. Visit the Heather Meadows Visitor Center, which was built in 1940 by the Civilian Conservation Corps as a warming hut for interpretive displays on the area's flora, fauna, geology, and history. The visitor center is open during summer only.

What follows are some of the easier hikes and walks at the Heather Meadows area. Many of these trails were built in the late 1920s when the Mount Baker Lodge, a posh 100-room resort, was located here. Several of the short loops connect back to the main parking lots.

Call the Glacier Public Service Center (360-599-2714) for the latest conditions and to find out how far the Mount Baker Highway is open. In general the last 3 miles of the highway don't open until sometime in July, and they close sometime in October. Often the road is plowed as far as the Heather Meadows Visitor Center—about a mile past the ski area's upper lodge—for a couple weeks before and after those dates. All of these trails are accessed from the last 4 miles of the Mount Baker Highway.

Mount Baker from Artist Point. DEBORAH CASSO

Parking at Heather Meadows requires a Northwest Forest Day ($5.00) or Season Pass ($30.00). They're available at the Glacier Public Service Center, on the east end of the small town of Glacier, near milepost 33 on the Mount Baker Highway.

At the Glacier Public Service Center, pick up a copy of *North Cascades Challenger,* the free visitor information guide, which includes a trail map. Another good map is Green Trails Mount Shuksan 14.

Artist Ridge If you're pressed for time, make this easy 1-mile round-trip trail the one hike you do on your Heather Meadows visit. You start at the top—at the Artist Point parking lot at the end of the road—where everything is laid out before you, including countless Cascade peaks

and valleys, subalpine meadows, snowfields for silly August snowball fights, and close-up views of both Mount Baker and Mount Shuksan. Look up for Mount Baker and its icy, crevasse-riddled glaciers; look down for Baker Lake, almost 10,000 feet below, at the terminus of countless evergreen folds and ridges. Mount Shuksan's icy rock face is just 4 air miles away. To reach the trail, go to the end of the road and follow the Mount Baker Highway east for 57 miles to the Artist Point parking lot at road-end.

Bagley Lakes–Lower Wild Goose Trail Follow the trail sign down into the narrow Bagley Creek gorge, which many moons ago was the site of a hydroelectric power plant for the long-gone posh resort that was the Mount Baker Lodge. (It burned down in 1931.) With flat-topped Table Mountain looming straight ahead to the south, follow this gentle lake- and creek-side 1.5-mile round-trip path as it wends its way between Mount Herman on your right and the ski area's Panorama Dome on your left. Take note of the columnar andesite on your left. About 300,000 years ago, this basin was awash in lava. When it cooled, its did so quickly and formed into very distinct six-sided columns that fit together like pieces in puzzle. These columnar joints can be seen at places throughout Heather Meadows. Drive the Mount Baker Highway to milepost 54.6 and the upper parking lot for the Mount Baker Ski Area Heather Meadows Day Lodge, and follow the sign for Bagley Lakes to reach the trail.

Fire and Ice This wide, 0.5-mile round-trip, mostly paved, barrier-free and completely easy-to-follow trail winds its way through open meadow and open forest populated by ancient hemlocks. Interpretive signs tell why the trees are not especially huge—they're at 4,400 feet here and most of the year they're covered in snow and have a short growing season. Flat-topped Table Mountain looms almost straight overhead; Bagley Lake is at the bottom of the basin to your right. Find the trailhead just to the left of the Heather Meadows Visitor Center, at about milepost 55.2.

Picture Lake Path This is a 0.5-mile round-trip, paved and barrier free path. A great place to start your Heather Meadows exploration—big-time views of Mount Shuksan reflecting in Picture Lake, an image that's graced more postcards and coffee table books than you'd care to

Mount Shuksan from across Picture Lake. DEBORAH CASSO

count. There're picnic tables here, so pack a lunch; a mini dock extends partway into the lake for further exploration. In winter, Mirror Lake's and next door's Highwood Lake's bowls fill with snow, making for terrific sledding and snow tubing. This is a gem, and, best yet, because it's so short, you can jump back in the car and continue up the road to other trails. Picture Lake Path is located at Mount Baker Highway to milepost 54.1, just below the Mount Baker Ski Area Heather Meadows Day Lodge. You'll have reached the lake when you come to the one-way loop that follows Picture Lake's shoreline. Park on the wide shoulder.

Upper Wild Goose Trail At 0.8 mile one-way, this is mostly a connector trail that steeply climbs heathery hillocks and wildflower meadows—sometimes almost straight up—from the Heather Meadows Visitor Center to Artist Point. Steep, yes— it climbs 600 feet in about three-quarters of a mile—but at least it's short, and the alpine views are more than grand the entire way. The trailhead is just to the left of the Heather Meadows Visitor Center.

Longer Mount Baker-Heather Meadows Day Hikes

Chain Lakes Loop This popular 7-mile round-trip loop trail includes everything you could possibly want in a North Cascades hike. There are big mountains— both Mounts Baker and Shuksan loom ultralarge—plus wildflower and blueberry meadows, lava cliffs, a high-alpine traverse, permanent snowfields, and, of course, the peaceful, contemplative lakes for which the trail is named. In the too-short era of the Mount Baker Lodge (1927 to 1931) packhorses would follow this loop as they took visitors on fishing excursions to the Chain Lakes. Start this trail from either the Heather Meadows parking lot at the end of the Mount Baker Highway or

the Heather Meadows Visitor Center. If you do a car shuttle, start at Artist Point and end at the visitor center, cutting off about a mile and getting rid of about 600 feet of elevation gain.

Lake Ann Trail If the Picture Lake view of Mount Shuksan inspires you—the one you see on countless postcards—this view is one that'll stick with you for the rest of your life. The lake itself is an otherworldly pool of azure blue, set at the very foot of Mount Shuksan, which rumbles and grumbles as avalanches and icy blocks tumble down its flanks. You're looking seemingly straight up at hanging glaciers thousands of feet overhead. (But don't worry, the lake is far enough away that you won't get plunked by falling ice.) The 8.2-mile round-trip trail also features some of the youngest granite you'll find on the face of the earth, just 2.2 million years old or so— piping fresh, right out of the oven, you might say. Go east on the Mount Baker Highway for 56 miles to the Lake Ann trailhead, which is less than a mile above the Heather Meadows Visitor Center.

Ptarmigan Ridge This high alpine ridge walk is almost entirely above the tree line and boasts spectacular unobstructed Cascade views the whole way. It's 11 miles round-trip, depending on the snow level. On the way out, you feel like you're about to crawl right up the spine of Mount Baker; on the way back, you're drawn by stunning views of Mount Shuksan, which is in your sight all the way back to Artist Point. While not an especially steep trail, it does pose a potential for danger. Starting at 5,100 feet and climbing to more than 6,400 feet, this trail's snow melts later than on any other trail in this book. In fact, the trail's couple of permanent snowfields make carrying an ice ax, and being able to use it, a good idea. Plus, the weather can change quickly out here. Find the trail by following the signs from the Artist Point parking lot for the Chain Lakes/Ptarmigan Ridge Trail.

Table Mountain The flat-topped mountain to the west there is Table Mountain, and this extremely popular trail that's been blasted into the side of an almost vertical wall of lava gets you to the top in a hurry. The 2.5-mile round-trip trail is short and easy to get to, and the 360-degree views are spectacular; on weekends you'll never be lonely up here. This flat-topped massif is what remains of a massively thick lava flow that occurred about 300,000 years ago, long before Mount Baker ever existed. The steep drop-offs on all sides of Table Mountain were caused by erosion from streams and glaciers. To reach the mountains, go to Artist Point at the end of the Mount Baker Highway and look up to the anvil-shaped peak that looks close enough to touch. Go there.

OTHER OUTDOOR RECREATION 🚲

Here are myriad other recreation opportunities that await those visiting or planning to relocate to Bellingham or the Whatcom County area. From golf to bicycling, river rafting to running and more, the area offers an incredible bounty of outdoor fun.

CAMPING

Near Bellingham

Larrabee State Park
245 Chuckanut Drive
(360) 676-2093
About 7 miles south of Bellingham, Larrabee State Park boasts a picturesque 85-site campground high atop the bluffs above Chuckanut Bay. The oldest of Washington's state parks (established in 1915), Larrabee boasts beach and tidepool access (more than 8,100 feet of saltwater shoreline), a kids play area, miles and miles of hiking trails, and an amphitheater. It also has restrooms with showers, an RV dump station, and a coin-operated laundry. Sound dreamy? It is, mostly, except for the active train track that passes between the campground and the water that can sometimes make for fitful sleep.

Reserve a campsite by calling (888) CAMPOUT or (888) 226-7688, or go online to www.parks.wa.gov and click on "Reservations."

Closer to Mount Baker

Douglas Fir Campground
(877) 444-6777
www.reserveusa.com

Located just off the Mount Baker Highway at about milepost 36, this forested 28-site (tent or trailer) campground is situated right on the North Fork of the Nooksack River (gurgle-gurgle) and makes a great place for sleeping. Eighteen of the sites can be reserved. The rest are available on a first-come basis. This campground, which is open from May to October, also features pit toilets, running water, and three wheelchair-accessible sites. To get here, go east on the Mount Baker Highway to milepost 35.3. The campground is on the left, just past a Nooksack River bridge and across the road from the Horseshoe Bend Trailhead.

If you're looking for something to do while camping here, the gentle, river-hugging Horseshoe Bend Trail is just across the Mount Baker Highway and the village of Glacier, with its general store, fine restaurants, and ski and snowboard shops, is a couple miles west. Call or visit the Web site to reserve a spot.

Excelsior Group Campground
(877) 444-6777
www.reserveusa.com
Also on the Nooksack River near the site of an old turn-of-the-20th-century mine, this forested group campground offers two sites that each accommodate up to 50 campers. Reservations are required. Open from May to October, the campground features pit toilets but no water; you must bring your own. To get here, go east on the Mount Baker Highway to milepost 39.8; the campground is on the right. Nooksack Falls and the Excelsior Pass trailhead are about a mile east of the campground. Call or visit the Web site to reserve a spot.

Silver Fir Campground
(877) 444-6777
www.reserveusa.com

Located at the bend in the road (near milepost 46) at the base of the Mount Baker Highway's final 10-mile, 3,000-foot ascent to Artist Point, this is the closest campground to the Heather Meadows Area and North Cascades National Park. Situated on the Nooksack River, the campground is at the former townsite of Shuksan, which sprang up in 1898 when gold was discovered near Twin Lakes at the Lone Jack site about 5 miles northeast of here.

There are 20 forested tent-trailer sites, of which 13 can be reserved. Along with pit toilets, running water, and three barrier-free sites, the campground offers a day-use picnic shelter. To get here, go east on the Mount Baker Highway to milepost 46.9, and the campground is on the right. Twin Lakes Road and Hannegan Road, both of which lead to hiking trails with world-class views, are less than a mile from Silver Fir Campground. Call or visit the Web site to reserve a spot.

Silver Lake Park
9006 Silver Lake Road, Maple Falls
(360) 599-2776
www.co.whatcom.wa.us/parks/index.jsp

Along with 80 tent/trailer campsites (many with partial water and electricity hookups), this 400-plus-acre park about 30 miles east of Bellingham features a lake for swimming and fishing, restrooms with showers and flush toilets, canoe rentals, a group picnic area, horse trails and a horse-camp area, and rental cabins that include an eight-person overnight lodge. There's also one wheelchair-accessible campsite available.

To get to Silver Lake Park, head east on the Mount Baker Highway to Maple Falls (about milepost 28) and the intersection with Silver Lake Road. Turn left and follow Silver Lake Road for about 3 miles to the park, which is on your right. Call to reserve a site.

EAGLE VIEWING

Each November about 200 bald eagles converge on a stretch of the Nooksack River near Deming (about 17 miles east of Bellingham) to dine on spawning and dying salmon. They usually stay through February.

You'll see some slowly soaring overhead, others perched regally in trees while contemplating their next move, and still others by the river's edge and gravel bar, picking and clawing at tasty chum salmon morsels. Please don't approach or otherwise disturb the eagles, even if they're incredibly close and seem oblivious to you. Eagles need to conserve their energy as much as possible; they waste it if they have to flee overcurious humans wanting to get a closer look.

Two of the best eagle-spotting places are along Mosquito Lake Road and the Deming Homestead Eagle Park. To reach Mosquito Lake Road, head east on the Mount Baker Highway to just before milepost 17 and Mosquito Lake Road. Turn right and follow Mosquito Lake Road for 0.75 mile to a bridge over the Nooksack River. Park just ahead on the side of the road, but do not park at the fire station. Scan the sky and river for the eagles' white heads and tails from the bridge. Another pull-out spot can be found a mile down North Fork Road, a quarter-mile past the Nooksack River bridge on the left. (When parking at either of these spots, be sure to respect private property.)

To reach Deming Homestead Eagle Park, go east on the Mount Baker Highway for 15 miles to Truck Road, just past the Highway 9 intersection in Deming. Turn right onto Truck Road and follow it for half a mile; the well-marked park is on your right. This park has about one-third mile of riverfront access with about the same distance of level, easy walking path. There are picnic tables, interpretive signs, and a covered observation shelter for eagle spotting on inclement days.

FISHING

With its lakes, rivers, creeks, and easily accessed tidewater, Bellingham and the surrounding area is a haven for both salt- and freshwater angling enthusiasts. Several varieties of salmon, including coho, chinook, sockeye, chum, and pinks, can be found in Puget Sound waters, with rainbow, kokanee and cutthroat trout being the goal of most freshwater fishers. Fishing licenses are required of anyone age 15 or older who wants to fish, and they can be obtained at various Bellingham outlets including H & H Sports and Yeager's or online by going to the Washington Department of Fish and Wildlife Web site at www.wdfw.wa.gov and clicking "Licensing."

Here are some popular local fishing holes.

Cain Lake

This small lake about 9 miles south of Bellingham is popular with those with a jones for rainbow trout, largemouth bass, and yellow perch. The season runs from late April to the end of October, and the boat launch is located at the south end of the lake.

Lake Padden

With its long, easily accessed shoreline, this is one of the more popular spots to cast a line, and it's stocked every April with almost 20,000 legal-size trout. The season generally runs from late April

Winter rain got you down? Head for the San Juan Islands, which receive about half as much rain as Bellingham's 36 inches. If you'd rather grin and bear it, try Nooksack Falls. Heavy precipitation ensures the falls will be especially spectacular, and the thick forest canopy actually blocks most of the falling rain. Arroyo and Whatcom Falls parks are good choices.

through the end of October, and only boats without motors are allowed.

Lake Samish

This large lake about 6 miles south of Bellingham offers some great year-round fishing, especially for kokanee, largemouth bass, and cutthroat trout. There's a boat launch on the east side and a county park dock on the north end, and both are well-marked.

Lake Whatcom

Bellingham's largest lake (and water supply), and it's a hotspot for kokanee, large- and smallmouth bass, and yellow perch. The season runs from late April to the end of October, and boat launches are located at the north and south ends of the lake.

Nooksack River

This river, which flows from the glaciers of Mount Shuksan, provides plenty of fishing opportunities and is easily accessed right off the Mount Baker Highway. Coho, chinook, chum, and pink salmon are fished as well as steelhead and cutthroat. Before fishing, you should check current regulations with the Washington Department of Fish and Wildlife.

Silver Lake

About 30 miles east of Bellingham, this lake nestled in the Cascade foothills is a hotspot for rainbow and cutthroat trout. Along with a boat launch, Silver Lake Park, where the lake is located, has boat rentals, a campground, and cabin rentals.

Closer to Mount Baker

Near Artist Point at the end of the Mount Baker Highway, you can find alpine-lake fishing opportunities in sublime settings. Lake Ann, which is accessed via a 4-mile hike and has its trailhead about a mile before Artist Point itself, is stocked with cutthroats. Four of the Chain Lakes, accessed via 3-mile hikes from either

Austin Pass or Artist Point, are stocked with rainbows and brook trout.

Based on San Juan Island, this Friday Harbor boat takes anglers fishing for five species of salmon as well as bottom fish.

Saltwater Fishing

Several companies offer fishing charters to some great fishing areas hidden in the various coves and inlets along Whatcom County's shoreline as well as to spots in the San Juan Islands and Alaska's Inside Passage.

Eagle Point Charters
Gate 7—Slip 33
Squalicum Harbor
(360) 966-3334, (360) 961-8598
www.eaglepointcharters.com
This year-round salmon, ling cod, and halibut fishing charter focuses mainly on the San Juan Islands and fishes for everything from king salmon to rock and red snapper to ling cod.

Jim's Salmon Charter
4434 Boblett Road, Blaine
(360) 332-6724
This north county service has been offering fishing excursions since the late 1960s. Its fully equipped 24-foot boat takes up to four people on salmon excursions.

Pacific Northwest Sportfishing
Squalicum Harbor
(360) 676-1321
www.pacific-northwest-sportfishing.com
This company offers fishing excursions to various western Washington rivers for salmon and steelhead, as well as extended multiday trips out of the southeast Alaska port town of Craig. Everything is bigger in Alaska, with 40- to 60-pound halibut the norm, and even the occasional 200-pounder is brought on board.

Trophy Charters
Dock 2, Spring Street Landing
Friday Harbor
(360) 378-2110, (360) 317-8210
www.fishthesanjuans.com

Fishing-Related Businesses

H & H Anglers & Outfitters
814 Dupont Street
(360) 733-2050
www.hhanglers.com

LFS Marine and Outdoor
851 Coho Way
(360) 734-3336, (800) 426-8860
www.lfsinc.com

Yeager's Sporting Goods
3101 Northwest Avenue
(360) 733-1080

GOLF

Yes, it tends to rain here a bit. But most of the time, it's a gentle, dare I say, refreshing spritz of a rain. Showers, people usually call it, not rain. Rain is what pelts you, what falls so hard you're soaked on a quick traverse from your front door to your car. Most of the time it doesn't do that in Bellingham. And since temps are fairly mild in town and the immediate environs—rarely below 40 and not often above 70 degrees—Bellingham and Whatcom are prime spots for three-season golf. (Some diehards try to go four seasons, but January and February are pretty wet.) In fact, just a few years ago, *Golf Digest* magazine named Bellingham the seventh "best little golf town in America."

Bellingham and Whatcom County have 16 golf courses, the most courses per capita in the state. They range from city-owned Lake Padden Golf Course, one of the best municipal courses you'll find anywhere, to privately owned Bellingham Country Club, which, like Padden, is also right in town, to the Arnold Palmer–

designed Semiahmoo Golf Course near the Canadian border.

Most courses are open to the public, with the exception of the members-only Bellingham Country Club. Semiahmoo Golf and Country Club is semiprivate. Its two courses are open to the public on alternating days on an odd-even basis.

Municipal Golf Course

Lake Padden Golf Course
4882 Samish Way
(360) 738-7400
www.lakepadden.com
Hilly, wooded, and beautiful not only describes Bellingham but also this Bellingham Parks and Recreation gem, named one of the top public courses in the West by *Golf Digest* magazine. The more than reasonable green fees for the 18-hole, 6,675-yard course range between $16 and $28. The full-service club has a clubhouse with snack bar and practice facilities, and it offers lessons.

Private (Members-Only) Golf Course

Bellingham Golf and Country Club
3729 Meridian Street
(360) 733-3450
www.bellinghamgcc.com
This wide-open yet-tree-lined traditional championship course (pretty much everything in the Northwest is tree-lined) is one of the best-conditioned courses in the state, and, as such, it's usually playable 12 months a year. Par is 70; yardage is 6,523. The newly renovated pro shop has three pros and offers the full range of golf merchandise, gear rental and repair, and, of course, lessons. The club also features a full banquet room and restaurant (also refurbished) and a swimming pool.

Semiprivate Golf Courses

Loomis Trail Golf Club
Loomis Trail Road, Blaine

Semiahmoo Golf and Country Club
Semiahmoo Parkway, Blaine
(360) 371-7015, (800) 231-4425
www.semiahmoo.com/golf.asp
About 25 miles northwest of Bellingham are two of the most lauded golf courses in the Northwest. Loomis Trail Golf Course was voted the top public golf course in the state by *Golf Digest* magazine while nearby Semiahmoo Golf Course, which was designed by the incomparable Arnold Palmer, was voted number three. Both are part of the Semiahmoo Resort and open to the public on alternating days—Loomis Trail on even days of the month, Semiahmoo on odd days. Loomis Trail features an extensive network of lakes and canals (there are water features on all 18 holes) that contribute to the course having the second-highest slope rating (difficulty) level of any in Washington state. Semiahmoo features some 70 bunkers with water figuring in on five holes. The courses, which are about 3 miles from each other, each have full clubhouses that offer the full range of services: pro shop, snack bar, and banquet facilities. Semiahmoo also has a restaurant, a lounge, an outdoor pavilion used for events, and a fitness center with sauna. Green fees at the two courses range from $30 to $69.

Public Golf Courses

Dakota Creek Golf and Country Club
3258 Haynie Road, Custer
about 20 miles north of Bellingham
(360) 366-3131
www.dakotacreekgolf.com
Here you get a great golf bang for your golf buck. Greens fees range from $15 to $18 ($10 to $12 for nine holes) on this beautiful par 71, 5,185-yard course that

features rolling hills, water features, and stunning mountain and county views.

Homestead Farms Golf Resort
115 East Homestead Boulevard, Lynden
(800) 354-1196
www.homesteadfarmsgolf.com
This stunning resort course just outside Lynden has a hole that golf aficionados simply lust after. Until they try to play it, that is. The 18th hole is the only par 5 in the Northwest that plays to an island green. Ending your round in the drink is a real possibility on Homestead's 6,927-yard, par 72 course. The course features many water features as well as a terrific open view to Mount Baker. This is a respected course: In both 2004 and 2006 Homestead Farms hosted the Great Links Northwest Open, the Northwest's oldest tournament. Along with a restaurant and banquet facilities, the resort features a hotel, a fitness center, and indoor-outdoor hot tubs.

North Bellingham Golf Course
205 West Smith Road
Three miles north of Bellingham
(360) 398-8300
www.northbellinghamgolf.com
The North Bellingham course is a rarity in western Washington: It's a Scottish links–type course with almost no trees. But what it lack in timber this 6,179-yard, par 72 course more than makes up in bunkers galore and lots of water features, making for a surprisingly tough 18 holes. Green fees are $25 to $40.

Shuksan Golf Club
1500 East Axton Road
About 6 miles north of Bellingham
(800) 801-8897
www.shuksangolf.com
Though Semiahmoo and Loomis Trail are among the most highly rated courses in the state, there are those faithful Shuksan Golf Club devotees who will put their course up against any other. That's because the immaculately maintained course has some of the best views of

Mount Baker and myriad Cascade cousins and challenging holes, with more than 1,000 feet in elevation change among the numerous rolling hills and steep ridges, to be found on any Whatcom County course. Seventeen holes across the par 72, 6,737-yard course have water features. There's also a stunning clubhouse, with full pro shop, restaurant, and banquet facilities. Green fees are $26 to $52.

Sudden Valley Golf Club
4 Clubhouse Circle
About 8 miles east of Bellingham on the south shore of Lake Whatcom
(360) 734-6435
www.svgolf.org
This course shows two completely different faces. The front nine is set against Lake Whatcom and is wide open and mostly flat. The back nine, however, climbs a wooded ridge: the holes are narrow and heavily treed, and the greens are a tad smaller. Oh yeah, and there're 47 bunkers spread across the course's 18 holes and 6,143 yards. (The course is a par 72.) Green fees are $25 to $45.

KAYAKING

With its 143 miles of tidewater shoreline, innumerable coves, inlets, and bays, not to mention the San Juan Islands just a passage crossing or two away, Bellingham is a true destination spot for sea kayakers of all skill levels. Along Chuckanut Bay the incredible swooshes and swirls of the sandstone formations are simply jaw-dropping and are a favorite of passing paddlers. Popular put-in spots include Larrabee State Park (the signed boat launch is just north of the main park entrance), Marine Park, and Semiahmoo Park, about 25 miles northwest of Bellingham.

Elakah Expeditions
Bellingham
(360) 734-7270, (800) 434-7270
www.elakah.com

Kayaking on Baker Lake. MIKE MCQUAIDE

Fairhaven Boatworks
501 Harris Avenue
(360) 714-8891
Located at water's edge on the Fairhaven waterfront, Fairhaven Boatworks rents kayaks and rowboats for those who already know what they're doing when it comes to paddling. You can also store your boat here.

Moondance Sea Kayak Adventures
(360) 738-7664
www.moondancekayak.com

Northern Lights Expeditions
(360) 734-6334, (800) 754-7402
www.seakayaking.com

W.A.K.E.
(360) 383-9139
www.wakekayak.org
W.A.K.E., the Whatcom Association of Kayak Enthusiasts, is a fun group who meet for excursions and extended outings and safety training. They are always willing to help those with little or no experience or those who want to learn where to go.

Whatcom County Parks and Recreation
Sea Kayaking Program
(360) 733-2900
www.co.whatcom.wa.us/parks/outdoor/
classes/kayaking.jsp
The county parks department's outdoor

program offers introductory kayaking classes and outings as well as multiday trips. It's just about the perfect place for first-timers to get some kayaking experience.

In addition, several kayak outfitters offer guided trips to the San Juan Islands, which include whale-watching excursions, the Gulf Islands of British Columbia, and the Inside Passage, among other places.

MOUNTAIN BIKING

Lake Padden

The wide 2.6-mile trail encircling Bellingham's favorite swimming hole is an excellent not-too-challenging but not-too-easy place to ride. About 1.6 miles of it are pancake flat, with the wooded mile on the south end home to a few rollers. Since this is also a very popular route for walkers and runners, it goes without saying to be respectful of other trail users. Luckily this is a wide trail, and unpleasant incidents

between foot- and bike-traffic are rare.

For a little more of a challenge, seek out what are generally called the "horse trails" on the south and east side of the lake. Though unmarked, they're easy to find—any trail leading off the main lake trail in the woods is a horse trail. They're steep, snaky, often muddy, and quite technical. For more information, call the Bellingham Parks and Recreation Department at (360) 676-6985, or call one of the local bike shops listed below.

Interurban Trail

This 6.6-mile abandoned rail bed links Bellingham's Fairhaven district with Larrabee State Park, and it is terrific for easy to moderate, not-too-technical bike riding. Views along the way are spectacular, from a dense, rain forest–like gorge to open, sweeping vistas of the San Juan Islands and Olympic Mountains. Being a rail trail, the Interurban is wide and, except for a couple spots, such as Arroyo Park and a creek crossing near Larrabee State

Mountain biking in Bellingham. BELLINGHAM WHATCOM COUNTY TOURISM

Biking Galbraith Mountain

To many of a certain ilk—that being the human-powered fat-tire set—Bellingham is known for one thing: mountain biking. (Maybe two things: mountain biking and heading to Boundary Bay afterward for a hearty pint of Inside Passage Ale.) Bellingham's calling card in this regard is 2,000-foot-high Galbraith Mountain, a place where on quiet mornings (and afternoons and evenings), shouts of sheer joy, exuberance, and bliss, as well as whoops, yelps, and hollers, can be heard from the multitude of mountain bikers careening down the literally untold (50? 75? 100?—it's impossible to know) miles of singletrack trail that snake up and down its hillside. Though largely privately owned, bikers, trail runners, and hikers have the run of the mountain, so long as they do so responsibly. (That is, they don't hunt or build fires, stunt structures, or meth labs.) Mostly because of Galbraith, *Mountain Bike* magazine named Bellingham one of the top 10 places in the country for mountain biking.

Though long-beloved by off-road users of every stripe—motorcyclists, ATV riders, equestrians, hikers, runners, and mountain bikers—it wasn't until the early 2000s that public access to Galbraith's private lands was officially granted. That's when Trillium Corp., a local developer, became the major landowner on Galbraith and laid down the law. It banned motorized vehicles from the mountain but gave mountain bikers the green light to ride. Mountain bikers did, however, have to dismantle the extreme-riding, gravity-defying structures, such as teeter-totters, ladders, and high bridges that had sprung up over the years.

Trillium even named the Whatcom Independent Mountain Pedalers (WHIMPs), a local mountain-biking club, the official stewards of Galbraith Mountain. The developer now works with the club to determine where trails can and can't be built, and it notifies club mem-

Park, almost perfectly flat. For more information, call the Bellingham Parks and Recreation Department at (360) 676–6985, or call one of the local bike shops listed below.

The following shops offer trail information as well as bike sales and service.

Fairhaven Bike and Mountain Sport
1108 11th Street
(360) 733–4433
www.fairhavenbike.com
This outfit also rents bikes.

Fanatik Bike Company
2025 James Street
(360) 756–0504
www.fanatikbike.com

Jack's Bicycle Center
1907 Iowa Street
(360) 733–1955

Kulshan Cycles
100 East Chestnut Street
(360) 733–6440
www.kulshancycles.com

bers about upcoming logging projects so the WHIMPs can build alternate and detour trails.

Galbraith Mountain has two main access points: a north entrance at the end of Bellingham's Birch Street close to Whatcom Falls Park and a south entrance from Galbraith Lane about a mile east of Lake Padden.

From the Birch Street entrance, follow the road to the end, pick up the obvious trail, and follow it into the woods as it switchbacks and climbs to the Ridge Trail, the northern gateway to many miles of mountain-bike fun on Galbraith. While Galbraith does have trails for riders of various skill levels, much of it is technical and often quite muddy. Because it starts with a significant climb up a winding singletrack, this is probably the more difficult of the two entrances.

For a little easier introduction, access Galbraith from the south entrance, just up the hill from Lake Padden Park's east entrance. Park at the large unmarked parking lot across from Galbraith Lane. Pedal down Galbraith Lane for about 0.3 mile and take a right. Just ahead, bear left at a fork, rounding a gate as you do, and you're there.

Galbraith truly has trails or dirt roads for riders of all abilities. For those who don't necessarily want a technical ride but still want to enjoy some off-road pedaling, the dirt roads are the best option. They reach into the mountain's every corner, offer some great views, and will keep a rider busy for days.

Among the many trails considered hot spots are Bob's Trail, El Pollo Elastico, Cedar Dust, and Purple Heart, but trails are unmarked and known by different names to different people. To get the most out of the mountain, ride with someone who's ridden Galbraith before. You can go to www.galbraithmt.com, which has numerous photos, trail descriptions, and more, including some detailed maps on where to ride that you can download for about $12. Galbraith Mountain Local Knowledge Trail Maps are also available at local bike and outdoor stores. For information on the Whatcom Independent Mountain Pedalers (WHIMPs), including organized rides, check out www.whimpsmtb.com.

R.E.I.
400 36th Street
(360) 647–8955
www.rei.com

MOUNTAIN CLIMBING

Each year about 5,000 people climb, or attempt to climb, to the summit of Mount Baker. Most make the approach from either the Coleman-Deming Glacier route on the north side or the Easton Glacier route from the south. While the routes are not technical, the ascent involves climbing 5,000 vertical feet on glacier, which implies potential dangers—crevasses, avalanches, exposure, bad weather, etc. A couple thousand people also attempt the more challenging rock and glacier climb to the summit of Mount Shuksan each year. Because Mount Shuksan requires rock climbing to scale the final 600-foot rock pyramid, it's a more technical climb than Mount Baker. Therefore, for safety reasons it's best to hook up with a guide

Mount Baker Ski Area

Though world renowned for its gobs and gobs of snowfall and as being one of the birthplaces of snowboarding, the Mount Baker Ski Area is actually a fairly small ski area. Just eight lifts are across 1,000 acres with 1,500 feet vertical. It has no high-speed quads; no trendy shops, boutiques or après ski nightlife at which to spot celebrities; and no beds on which to spend the night. The closest accommodations are 17 miles down the hill in the small, sleepy berg of Glacier.

Still, the Mount Baker Ski Area is one of the most well-known winter playgrounds anywhere. It might rank fourth in Washington State in number of skier visits (as of 2004), but it's ninth in the *world* when it comes to ski areas written about or photographed for ski and snowboard publications.

Why the fuss? First, its terrain—it's steep and deep with naturally occurring half-pipes that look like waves frozen in snow. Second, its epic amounts of snowfall—647 inches per year, the most of any ski area in North America, including a world record 1,140 inches during the 1998-1999 season. And perhaps most important was general manager Duncan Howat's decision way back in the early 1980s to allow a couple kids with what looked like mini-surfboards attached to their boots—the first snowboarders, they were—to ride the mountain. Mount Baker was the first place where snowboarders were not just allowed but welcomed with open arms.

The Legendary Banked Slalom, a snowboarding race down one of the ski area's natural half-pipes, has put the ski area on the map as well. In its 20-plus years, the race has drawn every big name in the sport, including Terje Haakonsen, Karleen Jeffery, Craig Kelly, Tom Sims, Victoria Jealouse, Barrett Christy, and Ross Rebagliati, snowboarding's first Olympic gold-medal winner.

But the Mount Baker Ski Area isn't just for the single-plank set. Skiers love the area and still make up more than half of all rider visits.

Mount Baker's no-frills approach has become, in a way, one of its major appeals.

The lack of distractions—no advertising on ski towers, no video games, no televisions, no neon signs, and, if it weren't for the power they're forced to generate themselves, no electricity—focuses more attention on the ski area's sublime setting at the foot of Mount Shuksan. That's not to say that you're out of luck if you're dying for a steaming bowl of chili or piping mug of hot chocolate after a day on the slopes. Both the White Salmon Day Lodge and the Heather Meadows Day Lodge offer food service with extensive menus and retail shops that carry all the gear you could possibly need. The ski area's rental and instruction programs cater to all snow enthusiasts, from telemark skiers to snowshoers to cross-country skiers to, of course, alpine skiers and snowboarders.

Facts and Figures:

Vertical rise: 1,500 feet

White Salmon Day Lodge Elevation: 3,500 feet

Heather Meadows Day Lodge Elevation: 4,300 feet

Mount Baker Ski Area. MIKE MCQUAIDE

Top elevation: Top of Hemispheres Chair—5,089 feet

Skiable acres: 1,000

Lifts: Four quads, two doubles, two rope tows

Terrain: 31 percent expert, 45 percent intermediate, 24 percent beginner

Lift tickets: $37 for adults

Information: www.mtbaker.us or call (360) 734-6771

Season: Generally opens in mid- to late November and stays open through the end of April.

Getting to the Mount Baker Ski Area: Go east on the Mount Baker Highway for 52 miles to the White Salmon Day Lodge. The Heather Meadows Day Lodge and parking areas are about 3 miles farther up the highway.

service that will teach basic glacier travel and self-arrest techniques as well as (hopefully) get you to the summit. The following guide services offer mountain- and rock-climbing instruction and/or guiding to Mount Baker and Mount Shuksan, among other places.

American Alpine Institute
1515 12th Street, Fairhaven
(360) 671–1505
www.mtnguide.com

Base Camp, Inc., Bellingham
(360) 319–8372
www.basecampwa.com

RIVER RAFTING

From June to August, a 9-mile stretch of the North Fork Nooksack River between Glacier and Maple Falls offers a heck of a roller-coaster ride for adventurous river rafters. The rapids are mostly class III and IV with the scariest section—or most exciting, depending on how you look at it—being the first mile after the put-in at the Horseshoe Bend Trailhead. Farther downstream, the river eventually mellows to the point where the last 6 miles can be a tame river float.

While white-water rafting is great fun, in the glacier-fed, boulder- and snag-riddled Nooksack, it can be quite danger-ous, especially the first 3 miles. Every few years it seems the local newspaper runs a series of stories about safe river rafting, inevitably after someone has drowned in a rafting incident.

For that reason it's best to go with one of the several rafting companies that are permitted by the Forest Service to run guided trips. They provide rafts, trans-portation to the river, and safety equip-ment. The following guide services offer white-water rafting trips on a 9-mile stretch of the Nooksack River between Glacier and Maple Falls.

Alpine Adventures
Seattle
(800) 723–8386
www.alpineadventures.com

River Recreation
Bothell
(800) 464–5899
www.riverrecreation.com

River Riders
Leavenworth
(800) 448–7238
www.riverrider.com

ROAD BIKING

Western Whatcom County's mostly flat terrain makes it a popular place for road cyclists. The Mount Baker Bicycle Club (www.mtbakerbikeclub.org) hosts a num-ber of rides throughout the week, and several rides also just kind of occur on their own. Saturday morning's 7:00 A.M. Donut Ride has been a just-show-up-and-ride institution since the early 1980s, and summer's Tuesday evening rides are way popular, too. Saturday's 10:00 A.M. Jelly Donut Social Ride is a little more low-key. Kulshan Cycles (100 East Chestnut Street, 360–733–6440, www.kulshancycles.com) where many of these rides start, is great place to meet other riders and find info about the local bike scene. For cyclists who believe there's no gain without some pain, mid-September's Mount Baker Hill Climb bike race (www.meyermemorial.org) climbs 4,300 feet over 24.5 miles from the town of Glacier to Artist Point.

RUNNING/JOGGING

With its myriad trails and parks, Belling-ham is certainly a great place to run. Just about all the trails listed in the Parks and Trails chapter are havens for runners. Lake Padden, the Interurban Trail, Whatcom Falls Park, and the South Bay Trail/Boule-vard Trail, which connects downtown to

Fairhaven, are among the most popular places to run.

Bellingham is blessed with an active and very welcome running community, too. Semi-organized runs for people of all abilities meet several times a week, with most folks meeting at Fairhaven Runners (1209 11th Street, 360-676-4955, www.fairhaven runners.com) in Fairhaven. Another great resource is the 600-member-strong Greater Bellingham Running Club (www .gbrc.net), which, along with being a great place to hook up with fellow runners, puts on about a dozen races each year from 5K to 50K long.

SNOW PLAY

Heather Meadows and the Mount Baker Ski Area is the number one winter destination not just for those who want to ride the lifts but also for families who want some free snow fun—tobogganing, snow tubing, and just playing around. That's because the paved Mount Baker Highway is plowed free of snow to the ski area, and in winter and spring it's the easiest and safest access to the snowy alpine country.

Just below the ski area, the Picture and Highwood Lake bowls fill with snow, and folks slide down the white stuff on toboggans, sleds, discs, tractor-trailer tire tubes, plastic garbage bags, river kayaks, and just about anything people can come up with to slide downhill in the snow. It's not a snow-tubing park, so it's free, and of course you get your money's worth—that is, you have to carry your tube, kayak, disc, toboggan, whatever, back up the hill yourself. When your fingers and toes need thawing, head up the hill to the Heather

During the winter of 1998-1999 the Mount Baker Ski Area set the world record for snowfall. In the 28 days of February 1999, the ski area was buried by 304 inches of snow—an average of 11 inches of new snow each day.

Meadows Day Lodge for some hot cocoa or chili.

To get to the action, go east on the Mount Baker Highway to just past milepost 54 and Picture Lake. Start looking for parking here on the shoulder of the road that circles the lake, or park just up the road in the day lodge parking lot.

SNOWSHOEING AND BACKCOUNTRY SKIING

The Heather Meadows Day Lodge upper parking lot is also a popular jumping-off point for snowshoers and backcountry skiers, particularly those heading to Artist Point. It's about 4 miles round-trip, depending on the route taken. Skiers and snowshoers need to be avalanche aware, stay off slopes that are likely to slide, and not go beyond their abilities.

Because so much heavy snow falls in this area, and the potential for avalanche is sometimes so high, it's vital to check current conditions before heading out. For current conditions and route description, contact the Mount Baker Ranger at (360) 856-5700. For more detailed avalanche conditions, check the Northwest Weather and Avalanche Web site www.nwac.noaa .gov or call (206) 526-6677.

NIGHTLIFE ⓨ

Bellingham loves its live music. Bands such as the Posies, Deathcab for Cutie, and the Mono Men all got their start here. (So did Loretta Lynn, as long as we're on the subject.) Numerous other biggies have made it a point to stop by on their way to somewhere else, such as Nirvana and Pearl Jam. So there are shows to check out almost every night of the week at one venue or another. And cover charges are always reasonable.

At the same time, as a college town come the weekends many Bellinghamsters just wanna move. (And be seen moving.) They want loud music, but they don't much care to watch others play it. (It takes away from watching each other.) So Bellingham has a number of dance clubs that specialize in DJ-spun tunes.

And of course, there are more understated places to rendezvous at, clandestinely or otherwise; places where the conversation is muted, and the light is by candles. So Bellingham has a little bit of everything—from places to help you wind down after a day on the water or in the mountains to places to rev you up and keep you going half the night.

BARS

Green Frog Acoustic Tavern
902 North State Street
(360) 756-1213
Several places in B'ham offer Open Mic nights where budding musicians (and

---

ℹ️ *Bars in Bellingham close at 2:00 A.M., and last call is generally around 1:30. Some bars are on bar time, which is 15 minutes ahead of real time.*

---

sometimes those perhaps not so likely to bud) can get onstage and bang out a few tunes. But only the Green Frog Acoustic Tavern provides musical instruments for patrons to play—guitars, banjos, mandolins, basses, a piano, etc. (Given the establishment's name it shouldn't come as a surprise that the instruments need no plugging in.) Inside, the place is a throwback—peanut shells on the floor, picnic bench seating around tables that are little more than long wooden boards, and more than likely, one or two (or maybe five) dogs lying about. Favored by college students as well as anyone who likes good music (it's not just open mics; featured acts grace the stage as well), the Green Frog boasts more than 10 beers on tap as well as about 75 others in bottles or cans. It's Bellingham at its most casual.

Le Chat Noir
1200 Harris Avenue
Third floor of Sycamore Square
Fairhaven
(360) 733-6136
On summer evenings when the sun sets late and the golden light slowly fades over this fine seaside city, there're few more romantic settings from which to bask in such atmospheric finery than the third floor of Fairhaven's Sycamore Square building. It's got the whole French bistro thing going on, too, with exposed brick, soaring archways, and hanging vines. The lighting is low, the mood is sophisticated, and the wine list is extensive. This is the place to go when you want to be reminded that there's more to Bellingham than just kayaking, snowboarding, mountain biking, and a bunch of crazy college kids. The Black Cat, as it's often called, is also a fine restaurant with an extensive French and Mediterranean menu.

Nimbus
119 North Commercial Street, 14th Floor
(360) 676-1307
www.nimbus.to

Let's see: you want a room with a view, some cool sophistication, and maybe later on, something to eat. Head up 14 floors to the top of the Bellingham Towers building, where terrific 360-degree views of Bellingham and the surrounding mountains and sea await. Thankfully, the restaurant's menu and ambience live up to those views. This is another of Bellingham's most romantic nightspots, with an extensive wine and cocktail selection to match not only the views and ambience but also Nimbus's terrific menu, which ranges from prawns with pumpkin-maple butter appetizers to filet mignon.

World Famous Up & Up Tavern
1234 North State Street
(360) 733-4020

The Up & Up is a rite of passage for some Western students. Loud, dark, crowded, and serving cheap beer—especially on Thursday nights when you can get $1.00 mini-pitchers and cheeseburgers for even less—it's probably responsible for more missed 8 o'clock classes than any venue in town. And it's been that way for a long, long time. In fact, the original Up & Up was one of the first bars to open after the repeal of Prohibition in 1933 (though at a different location). As of press time, the owners were in the midst of dividing the Up & Up with hopes to conquer, so to speak. The Up & Up will remain on the left side of the club's 6,000-square-foot downtown space while a new establishment, the Andover—more of a lounge proffering spirits and lounge food—will open on the right. Thus it'll be the Up & Up Andover. (Ahem.)

BREWPUBS/ALEHOUSES

Archer Ale House
1212 10th Street
(360) 647-7002

Located in a unique (and cool) spot in Bellingham—below street level just across from the Fairhaven Village Green—Archer Ale House is one of those Fairhaven standbys that certain out-of-towners make pilgrimages to. Why? Well, along with being a double for a pub in the U.K.— small tables populate the cozy spot as well as a huge, dark wood bar that spans nearly the entire space—Archer is famous for its rotating selection of the finest craft ales, not only from the Northwest but also from Europe. Archer's serves food, too. Among the offerings from its especially tasty pub grub menu are fish and chips (of course), chicken wings, bratwurst, focaccia dip sandwiches, and a selection of soups and salads.

Boundary Bay Brewery and Bistro
1107 Railroad Avenue
(360) 671-5897
www.bbaybrewery.com

Boundary Bay is one of those popular places that does everything well. Along with being a restaurant and award-winning brewery—it regularly takes home a truckload of hardware from the North American Beer Awards—the unpretentious former warehouse is a terrific nightspot with a couple different stages for live jazz, blues, jambands, and rock 'n' roll. When the weather is fine, head to the outdoor beer garden with its deck and moveable tents, all overlooking the downtown waterfront and sunsets through the San

Juan Islands. The nearly 200-foot-wide stage hosts a variety of bands, performers, and acts. When the weather turns ill, Boundary Bay's Tap Room hosts live music, as well as innumerable good times shared over in-house stouts, ales, and dunkels (dark, German lager).

Honey Moon Mead
1053 North State Street
(360) 734-0728
www.honeymoonmead.net
In late 2005 two local couples opened Honey Moon Mead, Bellingham's first meadery and only the fourth in all of Washington State. Located in the alley behind State Street, about half a block from the farmers' market, Honey Moon serves several varieties of the fermented honey and wine beverage that might call up memories of reading Beowulf in high school. The atmosphere is charming with exposed brick and local art on the walls, just about perfect for this little flowering of Bellingham mead subculture. Honey Moon's mead varieties include raspberry, blueberry, orange, and tangerine. They also serve hard cider and wines made with grapes from Yakima. Honey Moon is open evenings Wednesday through Sunday and opens at 3:00 P.M. on weekends.

North Fork Brewery, Pizzeria, Beer Shrine and Wedding Chapel
6186 Mount Baker Highway, Deming
(360) 599-2337
www.northforkbrewery.com
Masquerading as a mere roadside tavern complete with wood beams, old-school

For up-to-date info on the current happenings and shakings, pick up a copy of the Cascadia Weekly, a free alternative paper that comes out on Thursday, or Thursday's Cascadia Herald, for its Take 5 arts and entertainment guide, or visit www.barstop.com.

beer signs, and a couple blaring TVs, this multitasking marvel about 20 miles east of Bellingham makes for fun destination dining and drinking. Super casual, the North Fork brews its own beers and barleywines and boasts one of the smallest breweries in the West. Try the Son of Frog, an English-style ale brewed with caramel and chocolate malts—it's a meal (and dessert) in itself. Crusts for the excellent East Coast–style pizza are made daily on the premises, and the pizza selection includes the usual suspects—your pepperonis, your sausages, your mushroom and olive, and pretty much anything you can come up with. Other entrees include lasagna, and such appetizers as artichoke jalapeno dip and wild smoked salmon salad will knock your socks off. The beer shrine is what it sounds like, a shrine to beer—good beer, bad beer, old beer, it's all here. Just off the main dining room, more than 90 years' worth of beer bottles are displayed under glass. Finally, an ordained minister on the premises actually performs weddings in the summer at the North Fork's "beer backyard," which features a bubbling fountain. This is truly a one-of-a-kind place.

The Temple Bar
306 West Champion Street
(360) 676-8660
www.templewinebar.com
Except for the emphasis on wine as opposed to stout, this narrow, street-level space below the Mount Baker Apartments recalls a boisterous Irish pub. Which is fitting, since owner Liz Dean named this local fave after the Temple Bar section of Dublin. With green walls and mismatched tables and chairs, the quirky interior is like something put together by a garage-sale enthusiast with a fat wallet and some artistic flair. It serves as the perfect backdrop to a laid-back, ultra-casual Bellingham sipping/dining experience. Wine and cheese selection are vast, and the knowledgeable staff is more than willing to help you choose between a Tiefenbrunner Pinot Grigio or Seven Peaks Shiraz or the

Chaource as well as help you pronounce them correctly. The Temple Bar also serves panini sandwiches, soups, salads, espresso drinks, and desserts from next door's mega-luscious Mount Bakery. It's open from 4:00 P.M. to midnight Tuesday through Saturday.

COMEDY

Up Front Theatre
1200 Bay Street
(360) 733–8855
www.theupfront.com
Opened in 2004 by comic Ryan Stiles, known for his appearances on *Whose Line is it Anyway* and The *Drew Carey Show,* the Upfront is the place to go when you're in the mood for some sidesplitting laughter. The small 85-seat venue hosts Friday and Saturday evening improv performed by top regional as well as local groups, who take the form of improv games, one-act improvised plays, and musicals. There are even competitive improv sessions, and Stiles himself often performs at the theater. Tickets are ridiculously cheap—like $10.

DANCE CLUBS

The Royal
208 East Holly Street
(360) 738–3701
www.theroyal.biz
This restaurant, bar, and dance club has the biggest dance floor in town, and it's way popular with the 25 and younger set. Thursday through Saturday are dance nights, with lots of booming bass, lots of gyrating males and females, lots of sweat and smoke—in other words, it's the place to be. Upstairs is a more sedate game room with pool tables, pinball machines, air hockey, etc. The Royal also features bands whose heyday might best be described as having been in the past; Blue Oyster Cult, Sir Mix-A-Lot, and a Flock of Seagulls have graced its stage in recent years.

Rumors Cabaret
1119 Railroad Avenuw
(360) 671–1849
www.rumorscabaret.com
Rumors used to be known more as a strictly gay dance club, but in recent years it's trended more toward being a dance club that celebrates the alternative for everyone. What's alternative? Oh, y'know, foam parties, drag nights, Dolly Parton CD-release parties, and the like. Halloween, Mardi Gras, Cinco de Mayo and any celebration that offers the chance to dress up are big here. Dark, with lots of thumping, bumping bass, Rumors boasts a revolving lining of DJs spinning everything from reggae to hip-hop to retro-80s to . . . did I mention events such as Dolly Parton CD-release parties? Live music too, on occasion.

LIVE MUSIC

Chiribin's
113 Magnolia Street
(360) 734–0817
As of press time, this new (late 2005) downtown eatery had just begun its career as a live music venue for everything from jazz to folk to rock. But given the fact that live music has been a staple at 113 Magnolia for years and years (previous tenants the Beech House Pub and the Calumet both hosted music as far back as the 1970s) chances are good that Chiribin's will host music for the foreseeable future. Also a tasty restaurant, Chiribin's is notable for its colorful wall-size mural of a rooster playing the piano, and it's named for the rooster portrayed.

Fairhaven Pub and Martini Bar
1114 Harris Avenue
(360) 671–6745
www.fairhavenpub.com

A couple things distinguish the Fairhaven from any other place in town: the cover bands and the martini menu. This nightspot, whose owner also owns The Royal, features live music most nights of the week, which quite often is not only a cover band but also a tribute band. Zepperalla and Hell's Belles, all-girl bands playing nothing but Led Zeppelin and AC/DC songs, respectively, are just two of the bands who've graced the club's stage. Then there are the martinis—more than 20 different varieties, including Creamsicle and Funky Munky, as well as more traditional fare such as the Fairhaven Classic. For those who'd like to make a whole evening of it, the Fairhaven Pub and Martini Bar also serves dinner, specializing in steaks, burgers, and sandwiches.

Horseshoe Cafe
113 East Holly Street
(360) 734-0380

The Horseshoe Café is perhaps an acquired taste. In the days before smoking was banned from public establishments, the Horseshoe's Ranch Room (the café's lounge) had a reputation as a dark, smoky, hard-liquor bar that was open all night, and a place where career drinkers practiced their art, as it were. Though public smoking is kaput, the rest still stands. Located smack in the heart of downtown, on weekend nights the college crowd also descends on the Horseshoe drawn not only for specials such as Jaeger-Red Bull and Bourbon nights, but also for the 24-hour menu that offers breakfast all the time, hearty burgers and steaks, and even some vegetarian dishes. Interesting factoid: The Horseshoe opened in 1886 and back then, sold a little bit of everything · including fishing gear and supplies for hunting varmints.

The Nightlight Lounge
211 East Chestnut Street
(360) 527–1531
www.nightlightlounge.com

A recent entry into the Bellingham scene, the Nightlight has made a name for itself as one of Bellingham's best venues for live music. With its killer sound system and huge stage—not to mention a capacity of 500 patrons, huge for B'ham—this Chestnut Street club across from the Bellingham Herald building has attracted some big names in the underground-indie-altish world. Reverend Horton Heat, Son Volt, and Henry Rollins have all played here. As more than one fan in this music-crazed town has stated: "The Nightlight is what Bellingham has always needed."

Wild Buffalo House of Music
208 West Holly Street
(360) 752–0848
www.wildbuffalo.net

In the late 1990s when the Wild Buffalo opened, it targeted a market that nobody had really thought about before: the 30- to 50-year-old set who love live blues, jazz, soul, and rock 'n' roll, but who don't want their clothes to reek of cigarettes when they get home. Smoke-free since the day it opened, it's been one of Bellingham's most popular nightspots ever since, offering live music six nights a week. The best local bands grace the Buffalo's stage, as do top regional ones (slide guitar impresario Roy Rogers, blues harp man Curtis Salgado) once or twice a month. A cool Southwest motif with Indian blankets, stuffed buffaloes, and cacti greets visitors (as does the seemingly ubiquitous Bellingham exposed brick walls), and the good-size dance floor ensures that you have plenty of room to get jiggy wid it. A nice touch is the free water that's available right next to the dance floor, just where you need it. Along with serving a wide selection of microbrews, wines, and non-boozy beverages, Wild Buffalo offers tasty sandwiches, dinners (including pizza), and appetizers. And it isn't just nondescript, no-taste bar food. Entrees include wild

Alaskan coho salmon and hickory-smoked chicken breast, and pizzas are gourmet, with Thai chicken and roasted garlic veggie among the offerings. The place opens at 4:00 P.M. Tuesday through Sunday, and is closed on Monday. The cover charge for weekend shows is usually less than $10; more for regional acts.

MOVIE THEATERS

Sometimes, even if you deck yourself out in Gore-Tex socks, Gore-Tex pants, Gore-Tex jacket, and a Gore-Tex hat, the rain is just going to win. And you're not going to want to play outside. So, see a movie. Bellingham has three cinemas in town, and all are members of the Regal Entertainment Group. Most showings cost $8.25 for adults ($5.50 before 6:00 P.M.), $5.50 for children, $5.25 for seniors, and $7.00 for students. Here are the locations. The number in the name indicates how many theaters each venue has.

Regal Bellis Fair 6 Cinema
5 Bellis Fair Parkway
(360) 676–2280

Regal Sehome 3 Cinemas
3300 Fielding Avenue
(360) 676-7595
Regal Sunset Square Cinema 6
1135 East Sunset Drive
(360) 647-4755

In addition, Bellingham has an independently owned movie house.

The Pickford Cinema
1416 Cornwall Avenue
(360) 738-0735
www.whatcomfilm.org/pickford
Started in 1998, the beloved 88-seat Pickford Cinema, named in honor of silent-screen star Mary Pickford, is owned by the Whatcom Film Association and shows artsy and independent and foreign films that B'hamsters used to have to travel to Seattle or Vancouver to see. The present downtown location has only one screen, but there are plans to move the theater in fall 2006 into an expanded space on Bay Street (next to the American Museum of Radio) that would afford the space to have two screens.

SHOPPING

When it comes to shopping, Bellingham looks out for its own. The push to buy local is strong, and it's helped largely by Sustainable Connections (www.sustainableconnections.org), the network of local independently owned businesses and farms that encourage shoppers to buy from local stores rather than the national big box chains. Started in 2001, Sustainable Connections now counts more than 400 businesses, farms, and nonprofit organizations among its members throughout Whatcom, Skagit, and San Juan Counties. Participating members usually display the organization's distinct Think Local—Buy Local—Be Local logo.

Sustainable Connections fits nicely with Bellingham's Downtown Renaissance Network. This is a group of downtown Bellingham business owners who in recent years have banded together to ensure that downtown Bellingham continues to evolve as a vibrant district with diverse and exciting shops, galleries, restaurants, and other businesses and attractions. In the late 1980s when Bellis Fair Mall first appeared, downtown Bellingham was somewhat in dire straits. Many stores, including Bon Marche, JCPenney, and Sears left downtown for the mall, and in the early 1990s, downtown Bellingham had more than its share of empty storefronts and little to entice shoppers.

Thankfully, things have improved and downtown Bellingham, as well as Fairhaven, along with new shopping districts such as Barkley Village, now offer an enticing area of diverse and interesting shops, cafes, and restaurants.

ART AND ANTIQUES

Aladdin's/Old Town Antique Mall
427 West Holly Street
(360) 671-3301
This is kinda the heart of Bellingham's antique row, aptly located in Old Town, within a stone's throw of where Henry Roeder and Russell Peabody first rowed ashore in 1852 and put the wheels in motion to found the city of Bellingham. A little bit of everything can be found here, not just antiques but also collectibles including thousands of LPs (remember them?), 45s (remember them?) and 78s (I don't remember them).

Artwood
1000 Harris Avenue
(360) 647-1628, Fairhaven
www.artwoodgallery.com
Bellingham is surrounded by forests, so a visit to Artwood is enlightening because you get to experience firsthand some of the truly amazing things that humans can do with wood. (It's the other end of the spectrum from say, slash-and-burn forest practice.) You'll discover highly artistic furniture pieces—tables, settees, rocking chairs—as well as sculptures and just cool things to touch, such as Jim Hume's Easter Eggs. Hume is one of a roster of wood artists who sell their wares on consignment at Artwood, which is a cooperative gallery of Northwest wood artists.

Barbo Furniture
1321 Cornwall Avenue
(360) 734-1997
www.barbofurniture.com
This downtown store sells some truly incredible pieces for the home, office, and patio. Among them are one-of-a-kind wood furniture pieces handcrafted by owner Chris Barbo as well as high-quality manufactured goods by Kingsley-Bate,

Sherrill Furniture, and others. In addition, Barbo sells art, furniture, and woven goods by local artists, such as photographer Tore Ofteness and potter Jeff Mildner.

Chuckanut Bay Gallery and Sculpture Garden
700 Chuckanut Drive
(360) 734-4885, (877) 734-4885
www.chuckanutbaygallery.com
This popular gallery, located just south of the South Side on Chuckanut Drive, is a true melding of art and nature. On-site are works by more than 300 Northwest Artists that are perfect for the home, patio, and garden—birdhouses and feeders, wind sculptures, and hand-carved granite sculptures and the like. Indoor pieces include decorative and functional pottery, handcrafted wood boxes, and artist prints. If you're not looking to buy, just take a pleasant stroll in the sculpture garden and bask in the gurgle-gurgle of sundry water features. You'll be transported to another world, one of serenity and peace.

Eartha Kitties
405 West Holly Street
(360) 714-1832
Just up the street from Aladdin's, this establishment has the best name of any shop in town, according to this author. And inside it's as unpretentious as the name is clever. "A veritable flea market of trash and treasure" is Eartha's motto, and well, yeah, it's pretty much right on.

Gallery West
1300 12th Street, Fairhaven
(360) 734-8414
www.artgallerywest.com
Located at the corner of 12th Street and Harris Avenue—in other words, as can't-miss-it-smack-in-the-heart-of-Fairhaven as it's possible to be—Gallery West offers two floors of fine arts and crafts, and unique furniture as well as picture-framing services. A Fairhaven mainstay since 1971, the elegantly appointed emporium deals in fine jewelry, woodwork, handblown glass, pottery, and lots more, including authentic Northwest Native American carvings.

Lucia Douglas Gallery
1415 13th Street, Fairhaven
(360) 733-5361
www.luciadouglas.com
A true Fairhaven and Bellingham treasure, Lucia Douglas hosts exhibits of some of the Northwest's finest painters, printers, and sculptors. Jazz concerts and poetry readings are held monthly. The gallery is usually closed for most of January.

Looking for interesting, one-of-a-kind gifts for the holiday season? Regional artists and craftspeople sell their wares at the Holiday Festival of the Arts (360-676-8548, www.alliedarts.com/hf.htm) and the Roeder Home Holiday Arts and Crafts Sale (360-733-6897). The Holiday Festival of the Arts generally runs from just before Thanksgiving to Christmas Eve; the Roeder Home event generally runs the last week of November.

Mud in Your Eye Pottery
911 Harris Avenue, Fairhaven
(360) 650-9007
www.mudinyoureyepottery.com
In the 1970s and 1980s, Mud in Your Eye was located in Los Gatos, California, and it was known as a beloved little place that sold the handcrafted pottery of more than 100 different artists. In the mid 1990s owners Frank and Cate Howell moved to Bellingham's South Side, where they opened a beloved little place that sells the handcrafted pottery—lamps, vases, cookware, quicheware, bowls, bread trays, stoneware water crocks, and more—of more than 100 different artists. Frank makes many of the pieces himself.

BOOKSTORES

Barnes and Noble
4099 Meridian Street
(360) 647-7018
www.barnesandnoble.com
Bellingham and Whatcom County are
served by a single Barnes and Noble store
that's located just north of Bellis Fair Mall.
The selection is huge, and there are nice
comfy chairs in which to lose oneself in
the pages of the latest Harry Potter or the
earliest Patrick O'Brian (or whomever).
There's also a Starbucks Café, and live
readings and children's events are held at
the store, too.

The Newstand
111 East Magnolia Street
(360) 676-7772
Want to read the latest headlines from
Sydney, Australia? Or London? Or pick up
a copy of Sunday's *Los Angeles Times,* or
New York Post? Or is there some obscure
tattoo magazine you need to pick up? Or
a knitting pattern from *Knitting Digest*
magazine that you're dying to get your
hands on? Chances are, The Newstand,
whose well-stocked racks are stuffed with
magazines and newspapers from around
the world, has you covered. The store also
carries popular and obscure paperbacks
and well as silly gifts such as Albert Ein-
stein action figures.

Village Books
1200 11th Street, Fairhaven
(360) 671-2626
www.villagebooks.com
Since 1980, Village Books, one of the
Northwest's largest independent bookstores, has been as much a part of the
Fairhaven landscape as are the town's historic brick buildings and tales of the
exploits of Dirty Dan Harris. Newly settled
in a three-story brick building at the corner of 11th Street and Mill Avenue that
thankfully maintains its late 19th-century
flair, Village Books offers a huge selection
of new and used books, live events including readings and slide shows, and a fine
cafe and restaurant—Book Fair—on its top
floor. Terrific views to the west include
San Juan sunsets, and below and to the
back of the store is the Fairhaven Village
Green, a public square and park that hosts
a farmers' market and outdoor cinema
among many other events.

Used Books

Bellingham is also known for its several
fine used bookstores. The three stores
below usually stock more than 100,000
books each. In the case of Henderson and
Michael's, which are across a downtown
street from each other, it's not uncommon
to see shoppers going from one to the
other in search of some title the other
didn't have. Each store is always in the
buying mode as well.

Eclipse Bookstore
1104 11th Street, Fairhaven
(360) 647-8165

Henderson Books
116 Grand Avenue
(360) 734-6855
www.michaelsbooks.com

Michael's Books
109 Grand Avenue
(360) 733-6272

BOUTIQUES/GIFT SHOPS

Cresswell Boggs
1300 Railroad Avenue
(360) 752-0522
www.cresswellboggs.com
Along with a terrific selection of greeting
cards, stationery, and related accessories,
this newish (2004) downtown emporium
specializes in fine silver jewelry for both
men and women.

Old Fairhaven Winery
1106 Harris Avenue, Suite 104, Fairhaven
(360) 738-WINE
This charming Fairhaven boutique offers nine varietals as well as a wide selection of wine-related gifts and accessories. What's wine-related? How about wine-cask furniture? The wines, which come from Eastern Washington, are each named for a historic Fairhaven building, which makes a nice touch for gift giving. Old Fairhaven also sells gourmet food, chocolate, coffees, and salad dressings. Private wine tastings are offered as well.

Paper Dreams
1206 11th Street, Fairhaven
(360) 676-8676
Another Fairhaven mainstay, Paper Dreams is located right next to Village Books. In fact (and not surprisingly since they share the same owners), they open in to one another on the ground floor so you can walk from one to the other without stepping outside. In Paper Dreams, you'll find every kind of high-quality and unusual tchotchke you could care to find, from upscale glassware pieces to Northwest Art to silly toys to a wide selection of greeting cards, calendars, and stationery. There's candy too, Mount Baker Fudge, and coffee from Fairhaven Finest Coffee.

CHILDREN'S CLOTHING

Kids Northwest
1319 Cornwall Avenue
(360) 676-6051
Locally owned, Kids Northwest specializes in apparel and shoes that are both functional and fun, proving that clothes are meant not only to be worn but to be worn out. The store also sells interesting and stimulating toys.

FARMERS' MARKETS

Bellingham Farmers' Market
(three locations)
(360) 647-2060
www.bellinghamfarmers.org

Barkley Village
Tuesday, 3:00 to 7:00 P.M., July to September

Downtown—Railroad Avenue and Chestnut Street
Saturday, 10:00 A.M. to 3:00 P.M., April to October

Fairhaven—Village Green
Wednesday, 3:00 to 7:00 P.M., June to September

The downtown farmers' market runs Saturdays from April through October and is the place to go for fresh fruits, veggies, seafood, plants and flowers, arts and crafts, and lots more. Starting in 2006 the market will be housed in Depot Market Square, a 7,000-square-foot open-air pavilion that will host other community events as well. Be there on opening day the first Saturday in April to see the mayor kick off the market season with his annual cabbage toss to a long-standing market vendor. The Barkley and Fairhaven farmers' markets, though scaled-down versions of the downtown market, are vibrant and unique affairs in their own rights.

HOME AND GARDEN

Bakerview Nursery
945 East Bakerview Road
(360) 676-0400
www.bakerviewnursery.com
Bellingham residents love to garden. (Just check their fingernails; chances are they're darkened with topsoil or compost.) And for the past 30-plus years, local garden and yard putterers have been able to find everything they could possibly want to grow and help it grow in the healthiest

way possible at Bakerview. But it ain't just green stuff. Bakerview sells pond fish, outdoor furniture, gloves, tools, and seemingly every garden accessory known to man and woman. It also delivers dirt, bark, rock, sand, etc., so you needn't get dirty while making your garden beautiful.

Greenhouse
1235 Cornwall Avenue
(360) 676–1161
This downtown store boasts three floors of everything imaginable to make your home worthy of a feature in *Sunset* magazine. (Or to just find some fun little knick-knack for your bathroom windowsill. Whatever.) Mahogany tables, pots and pans, ultra-cush sofas, candles and candlesticks, pillows and blankets—all high-quality stuff that you're not going to find at Fred Meyer.

MEN'S AND WOMEN'S CLOTHING

Garys' Men's & Women's Wear
128 West Holly Street
(360) 733–2180
For more than 25 years, Garys' has been catering to the City of Subdued Excitement's fashionistas. (Such as they are.) The store specializes in upscale clothing, mostly from smaller manufacturers who sell only to independent retailers so the selection offered is, along with being high-quality, unique. Garys' also boasts some of the best window displays in town.

Hilton's
113 West Magnolia Street
(360) 734–3090
Providing solely to Bellinghamsters since the mid-1920s, Hilton's has your feet covered. Offering everything from Birkenstocks to the dressiest of dress-ups to hiking boots to gardening clogs, Hilton's fits all Northwesterner's passions, whether they be indoor or outdoor shoe passions.

Sojourn
1317 Railroad Avenue
(360) 671–5704
Playful, sassy, coquettish, and reasonably priced—those are attributes of this downtown establishment that specializes in funky (good funky), colorful textures and fabrics. Along with apparel, Sojourn sells shoes, accessories, and quirky gifts.

MUSIC STORES

Avalon Discs
1330 Railroad Avenue
(360) 676–9573
With its oversize rock star posters, intricate pipes for smoking, uh, tobacco, and tie-dyed shirts, Avalon gives one the impression that they've stepped back in time. Like say to the 1970s. Except Avalon's a lot cleaner, and its big windows are brighter than most of those shops of yore. The space specializes in new and used CDs and records, as well as the aforementioned rock–pop culture merchandise, and cool postcards are available, too.

Everyday Music
115 East Magnolia Street
(360) 676–1404
www.everydaymusic.com
Now occupying the corner site where Cellophane Square held court for so long, Everyday Music is a company based in Portland, Oregon, that buys and sells new and used CDs, DVDs, cassettes, and records. Sporting oversize wall posters like its predecessor and music flyers in the windows, you'd pretty much swear it was still Cellophane. Everyday Music opens early (9:00 A.M.) and closes late (midnight).

OUTDOOR GEAR

Fairhaven Bike and Mountain Sport
1108 11th Street, Fairhaven
(360) 733–4433
www.fairhavenbike.com

Along with carrying several lines of popular mountain, road, comfort, and kids bikes (and offering gear and repairs, too), this Fairhaven institution also sells gear for sliding down the snow. Snowboards, snowshoes, skis (cross-country and tele-mark) are offered, as well as the appropriate apparel and accessories for staying warm and dry. (Read: Gore-Tex.) The store also rents bikes, skis, and snowboards.

Fairhaven Runners and Walkers Too
1209 11th Street, Fairhaven
(360) 676-4955
www.fairhavenrunners.com
This is a full-service store for running and walking enthusiasts. Along with stocking all manner of bipedal-related footwear, apparel, and accessories, Fairhaven Runners helps foster the burgeoning running and walking community with organized runs, walks, clinics, and other events, most of them free.

H & H Anglers & Outfitters
814 Dupont Street
(360) 733-2050
www.hhanglers.com
Outdoorsmen and women of the angling and hunting stripes head to H & H, which provides just about everything they could possibly need—not only equipment and apparel but guide services, too. And H & H has been doing it for more than 50 years.

Kulshan Cycles
100 East Chestnut Street
(360) 733-6440
www.kulshancycles.com
Downtown's biggest and oldest bike shop, Kulshan Cycles sells and repairs mountain, road, and kids' bikes and pretty much all manner of two-wheeled conveyances. Also, its Chestnut Street location is where many loosely organized cyclists meet up to head out, in particular for the Donut Ride, a Saturday morning habit since the 1980s for many riders.

Prostock Athletic Supply
110 North Samish Way
(360) 647-0410
www.prostockathletic.com
This is the place to go for your team sports needs—soccer, baseball, softball, football, basketball, etc. Gear, apparel, balls, pucks—it's all here, which is why this is the first choice of local high school and college teams. Prostock recently relocated here from Cornwall Avenue downtown.

REI
400 36th Street
(360) 647-8955
www.rei.com
Since Base Camp and Great Adventure closed a few years ago, this Sehome Shopping Center satellite of the popular outdoor retailer has become *the* place to go for all your human-powered outdoor fun needs. There's gear for camping to climbing and snowshoeing to bicycling, not to mention extensive, book, map, and travel departments. And a whole lot more. REI rents camping gear and snowshoes and also sells cool camping tchotchkes such as boomerangs, hacky-sacks, Frisbee-type items, and the like.

Sportsman Chalet
114 West Holly Street
(360) 671-1044
Upstairs, it's mostly tennis, soccer, and swimming—as well as just a lot of great casual outdoor apparel—downstairs, it's Bellingham's biggest ski and snowboard shop. Along with all the single- and double-plank gear and clothing you could ever care to choose from, Sportsman offers repairs, tune-ups, and rentals, too. You can also find information galore on all ski areas in the region.

SPECIALTY FOOD STORES

Community Food Co-Op
1220 North Forest Street
(360) 734-8158
www.communityfoodcoop.com
Since 1970 the co-op has, in its various forms and locations, been offering Belling- hamsters and other locals the best in organic produce, meat, seafood, and grocery items. In 1970, it was a 900-square-foot space that sold about 10 different items. Now it boasts 10,000-plus members, a beloved vegetarian deli-restaurant-cafe and, come 2007, a second store that is expected to open in the fall of that year.

ATTRACTIONS

Whether you're an inny or outty—someone whose passions are indoor pursuits or outside ones—Bellingham truly has something for everyone. The Mount Baker Ski Area is perhaps the Whatcom County attraction that's garnered the most press over the years, but it's certainly not the only one. It's not even the only one in the mountains. In summer and fall, when the mountains' heavy snow melts away, dozens of hiking and sightseeing trails emerge and draw outdoor lovers by the thousands. That, and the myriad trails and parks in and around Bellingham itself, are true havens for the outty set.

But innies have their havens too. Whatcom Museum, housed in the historic circa-1892 City Hall building, showcases rotating art exhibits as well a comprehensive photo collection that traces Bellingham's history from its earliest days. It's one of several museums around town. History buffs will be charmed also by turn-of-the-20th-century Fairhaven, the South Side commercial district and neighborhood that's maintained much of its 1890s flair.

Downtown's historic Mount Baker Theatre hosts fine music, theater, and dance performances, and the charmingly tiny Pickford Cinema screens independent and avant-garde films. On weekends the Upfront Theatre hosts some riotously ridiculous improv and stand-up comedy. And three casinos in the area offer the chance to strike it rich (or not), and/or see a show.

The waters that lap the shores of Bellingham are certainly an attraction too, not only for waterfront boat tours but also for the several whale-watching excursions offered by local companies. They head toward the San Juan Islands, where in summer about 90 orca whales cruise the surrounding waters of Puget Sound.

So you see, Bellingham and Mount Baker have you covered. Inside, outside, day or night—you're sure to be able to find an attraction that suits your passion.

PRICE CODE

The following price key is for adult prices in the summer. In many instances discounts are available for students, seniors, and children.

$	Less than $5.00
$$	$5.00 to $10.00
$$$	$11.00 to $20.00
$$$$	More than $20.00

Artist Point and Heather Meadows $
End of the Mount Baker Highway

Yes, Bellingham is a seaside town, but no visit to this city by the bay that's renowned for its natural splendors is complete without an up-close-and-personal audience with the mountains. And there's no better place than at the end of the curving swerving Mount Baker Highway about 54 to 57 miles east of Bellingham. (The mileage varies because of the snow level; the last 3 miles are cleared of snow for only about three months each year.)

The last 5 miles of the highway are referred to as Heather Meadows, and the Mount Baker Ski Area is located along this stretch. In summer and fall, it's here that you'll find some of the best—and certainly the most easily accessed—alpine hiking around. There's everything here from barrier-free paved paths, perfect for the casual sightseer and those with small children, to more rugged trails leading deep into the wilderness and right up to the toes of the big peaks, Mount Baker and Mount Shuksan. Artist Point is at the very end of the road, at 5,100 feet, and the views here are the best around and the most easily earned.

In winter, Heather Meadows is a winter playground, not just because of the Mount Baker Ski Area but also because the terrain is perfect for sledding, tobogganing, and snow tubing. Families head here by the hundreds for free snow fun. Call the Glacier Public Service Center (360–599–2714) for the latest conditions and to find out how far the Mount Baker Highway is open. Parking at Heather Meadows requires a Northwest Forest Day ($5.00) or Season Pass ($30.00). They're available at the Glacier Public Service Center, on the east end of the small town of Glacier, near milepost 33 on the Mount Baker Highway.

CASINOS

Nooksack River Casino   **$$$$**
5048 Mount Baker Highway, Deming
(360) 592–5472, (877) 935–9300
www.nooksackcasino.com
Along with 400-plus slot machines, the Nooksack River Casino, which is run by the Nooksack Indian Tribe, offers the most popular Las Vegas-style table games— blackjack, craps, mini baccarat, roulette, three- and four-card poker, etc. There are a couple of restaurants, and, like the Lummis' Silver Reef Casino, the casino will be undergoing an expansion. A 200-room hotel with restaurants and an RV park are planned to open in the coming years. The casino is located on the Mount Baker Highway about 15 miles east of Bellingham.

Silver Reef Casino   **$$$$**
4876 Haxton Way, Ferndale
(360) 383–0777, (866) 383–0777
www.silverreefcasino.com
Located just north of Bellingham, Silver Reef Casino is a 50,000-square-foot gaming emporium owned and operated by the Lummi Nation. Along with video slot machines and table games such as blackjack, craps, and Spanish 21, the casino boasts five bars and restaurants, a 400-seat performance space, and, starting in 2006, a whole lot more. A 20,000-square-foot expansion will include a 100-plus-

room hotel, a couple more restaurants and bars, and about 200 more slot machines and other games of chance. To get there, head north on Interstate 5 to exit 260, and then go west on Slater Road for about 4 miles.

Skagit Valley Casino Resort   **$$–$$$**
5984 North Darrk Lane, Bow
(360) 724–7777, (877) 275–2448
www.theskagit.com
The biggest casino in the area, the Skagit is about 15 miles south of Bellingham and offers a slice of the Vegas experience. (For better or worse.) The casino has more than 650 slot machines, all the table games you could want, 3 restaurants, and a 103-room hotel. In addition, the 460-seat Pacific Showroom hosts semi-big-name (or one-time big-name) comedians, musicians, and revues. Head south on I-5 to exit 236 and go east on Bow Hill Road to Darrk Lane. (The signs and lights of the casino are visible from the freeway.)

MOVIES

Fairhaven Outdoor Cinema   **$–$$**
(360) 733–2682
www.epiceap.com

The Pickford Cinema   **$$**
1416 Cornwall Avenue
(360) 738–0735
www.whatcomfilm.org/pickford
Bellingham has one independently owned movie house, the beloved 88-seat Pickford Cinema. Started in 1998, the Pickford, named in honor of silent-screen-star Mary Pickford, is owned by the Whatcom Film Association and shows artsy and independent and foreign films that B'hamsters used to have to travel to Seattle or Vancouver to see. The present downtown location has only one screen, but there are plans to move the theater in fall 2006 into an expanded space on Bay Street (next to the American Museum of Radio) that would afford the space to have two screens. The Whatcom Film Association

Haunted Haven

To experience a little turn-of-the-20th-century Fairhaven, take one of the Friday Fairhaven Haunts and History Tours. You'll follow a period-costumed Dan Harris and "lady of the night" and learn about the South Side district's origins, its colorful characters, and the time Mark Twain spent a night at the old Fairhaven Hotel, among other things. The one-hour walking tour costs $4.00; $2.00 for children and seniors. Tours leave at 11:00 A.M. and 2:00 P.M. from Fairhaven Village Inn. Call (360) 650–9691.

also sponsors NW Projections, an annual film festival that runs in November.

Traveling Pickford Show $-$$
(206) 571-1816
www.whatcomfilm.org/tps
On Saturday nights from late June to early September, on grassy park lawns throughout Bellingham, families, friends, and individuals can be found lounging about on blankets, often bundled up and enjoying popcorn and hot cocoa while taking in the onscreen exploits of Bogey and Bacall, Indiana Jones, Pee Wee Herman, Spider-Man, and others. They're taking in the picture show. Drive-ins may be a thing of the past, but outdoor cinema is thriving in Bellingham. Movies are screened every other Saturday night at Fairhaven Village Green, and weekly on a rotating basis at the Bellingham Public Library, Bellwether on the Bay near the Hotel Bellwether, and just across the waterway at Zuanich Point Park. Movies are shown on the sides of buildings or on portable billboard-size screens, and there's live music or entertainment before each screening. Cost is $4.00 per person or $10.00 per family.

MUSEUMS AND HISTORIC SITES

The American Museum of Radio $
1312 Bay Street
(360) 738-3886
www.americanradiomuseum.org
Jonathan Winter, an admitted radio geek since he was 15 years old, opened his personal collection of more than 800 radios to the public when he started the Bellingham Antique Radio Museum in 1985. Among the fellow radio enthusiasts who visited the old cramped, cavelike museum was John Jenkins, an avid collector who owned more than 1,500 early radio and electrical instruments. Jenkins and Winter combined their collections in 1995 and opened a museum. Five years later they moved to this expansive 25,000-square-foot space. A fascinating place, the museum is stuffed with hundreds of pre- and post-war antique radios, including familiar hardwood arch-fronts from radio's heyday and bizarre, unwieldy types with consoles the size of sofas. There are also vintage electrical devices that date back hundreds of years and chronicle man's early attempts to bottle lightning. Upstairs there's a radio station, KMRE 102.3 FM, which rebroadcasts classic radio shows.

Museum Pharmacy

Head downstairs at the Fairhaven Pharmacy and you take a step back in time. Pharmacist Gordy Tweit keeps a mini-museum down there—shelves are stocked with ancient homeopathic cures in stopper bottles, there are cans of salmon from the old canneries days, and vintage photographs line the walls. Tweit will answer pretty much any question you could ever have about what it used to be like in Fairhaven, and he knows of what he speaks. In 1941 he started as a delivery boy at Fairhaven Pharmacy and eventually worked his way up to pharmacist, and eventually he owned the store. Remarkably, Tweit is one of four such folks to go the delivery boy–pharmacist–owner route since the store opened in 1889. The museum is open from about 1:00 to 5:00 P.M. on Friday, and it's located at 1115 Harris Avenue, at the corner of 12th Street and Harris Avenue.

Chuckanut Drive
Fairhaven

Like a mini version of Highway 1 along the Northern California coast, historic Chuckanut Drive weaves and winds along the water, offering stunning vistas of the San Juan Islands and Northern Puget Sound. Completed in 1896, it has been a day trip favorite for Northwesterners for more than 100 years. In fact, between 1913 and 1931 it was part of the Pacific Highway that reached from San Diego to Vancouver, B.C. From Bellingham's Fairhaven district, Chuckanut Drive heads south along the base of Chuckanut Mountain for 15 miles.

Fairhaven
Harris Avenue and 12th Street and the surrounding area
www.fairhaven.com

Head to Bellingham's South Side for a tour of Bellingham's artsy-historic district. In Bellingham's early days (late 1800s), Fairhaven was one of four towns on the bay, and the one known for its rough 'n' tumble ways—bars and sporting houses (brothels) by the dozens, nearly as many economic booms and busts, and even a spot along Harris Avenue where unidentified dead folks were lain in the hopes that someone would come ID them and take them away. But you know how things like that work—100-some-odd years later it's a charming little spot with unique cafes, shops, restaurants, and parks that hearkens fondly back to those days. In its architecture, style, and flair, that is. Many buildings—and all new buildings including the condos and shops that have been mushrooming in recent years—retain the original brick and sandstone look that makes a stroll down one of Fairhaven's streets feel like a saunter back in time.

Mindport $
210 West Holly Street
(360) 647-5614
www.mindport.org

One part of this hands-on sciencey place is stuffed full of cool optical illusions, contraptions with marbles that roll across ramps then drop through chutes onto spinning wheels, weird sound systems where the human voice forms patterns in grains of sand, a telephone which plays your voice backward, and a whole lot more. The other part is an art gallery featuring photographs that are sometimes suitable for adults only. Ask when you enter. Mindport was started by Kevin Jones and is a melding of science

The interior of Mount Baker Theatre. MOUNT BAKER THEATRE

and art; it's patterned after San Francisco's Exploratorium. (Mindport, however, is much smaller.) Most Mindport exhibits are appropriate for kids age 6 and older; it's pretty much the perfect place to keep the young ones occupied for a few hours on a rainy morning. Exhibits change on a fairly regular basis.

Mount Baker Theatre
104 North Commercial Street
(360) 734-6080
www.mountbakertheatre.com

With its imposing 110-foot Moorish towers, the Mount Baker Theatre—like the red-brick cupolas of the nearby Whatcom Museum—is one of Bellingham's most recognizable man-made icons. Built in 1927 by West Coast Theaters to be one of the true movie palaces, the venue's 80-foot stage and elaborate interior feature ornate plasterwork, gold leaf, and a 600-pound chandelier that hangs from the domed ceiling. (The same architect also designed Seattle's 5th Avenue Theater.) Built for both vaudeville and silent movies (which would soon be overtaken by the advent of talkies), the 1,500-seat theater also boasted a $25,000 (a lot of money in those days) Wurlitzer organ with pipes 16 inches wide. These days the theater is city-owned and hosts productions by road companies from throughout the United States as well as popular acts in rock, jazz, and classical music. Local arts groups such as Whatcom Symphony Orchestra and Whatcom Chorale also present concerts here. In recent years, a smaller 150-

seat studio theater has been added for more intimate performances. In 1978 the Mount Baker Theatre was named to the National Historic Landmark Register.

Outdoor Sculpture Collection   Free
Western Washington University
(360) 650-3000
www.outdoorsculpture.wwu.edu

Anyone who's explored Western Washington University's beautiful hilltop campus has surely taken note of its renowned (and free) Outdoor Sculpture Collection. Anyone who's been there with kids has no doubt spent an afternoon or two chasing them about as they go from one of the collection's very climbable pieces of land art to the next. *Log Ramps,* as its name suggests, are logs placed at about a 9-foot-high incline, an angle that makes young ones (and students) like to climb and descend and climb and descend, repeatedly. *Stone Enclosure: Rock Rings* is a 40-foot circular wall of rock cut with holes that correspond to the North Star and the four points of the compass. One of the most recent, and most popular, additions to the collection is *Feats of Strength,* seven foot-high bronze figures placed amid sandstone boulders that are either reposing jauntily or straining under the weight of heavy rocks they lift over their heads. There are about 25 pieces in the outdoor collection spaced throughout the 215-acre campus.

Whatcom Children's Museum $
227 Prospect Street
(360) 733-8769
www.whatcommuseum.org

One of Bellingham's most popular spots for kidding around. Located just down the block from the Whatcom Museum of History and Art, the Children's Museum is just about the best place for toddlers through second graders on those too-numerous-to-count Bellingham gray days. Loads of educational hands-on exhibits and activities keep kids occupied (and a-learnin') for hours. There are costumes to try on, games to play, crafts to make, books to read, and loads more to do. Exhibits

change every year or so. Past exhibits have been reptile-, time machine-, and animal home-themed. The museum is open Tuesday, Wednesday, and Sunday from noon to 5:00 P.M.; Thursday, Friday, and Saturday from 10:00 A.M. to 5:00 P.M.; it's closed on Monday. Admission is $3.50 per person.

Whatcom Museum of History and Art $
121 Prospect Street
(360) 676-6981
www.whatcommuseum.org

Bellingham's perhaps most recognizable icon is also one of its most popular attractions. Located on a bluff just above where Bellingham's earliest white settlers first made land, the distinctive redbrick cupolas and clock tower of the former City Hall, now Whatcom Museum, beckons visitors from throughout the region. Along with a collection of more than 200,000 artifacts, including a spectacular photograph archive, the museum campus is composed of four buildings, all of which feature rotating exhibits. Victorian Homes of Bellingham, Northwest Motorcycle History, and Women Painters of Washington are just a few recent exhibits. The museum also hosts a number of events, including history talks, musical performances, puppet shows, local documentary films, family Halloween parties, and lots more. Extremely popular are the museum-sponsored summer Bellingham Bay History cruises, which run on Thursday evenings from June to August. On a 2½-hour boat tour across Bellingham Bay, a museum curator details the area's colorful past and some of its enigmatic characters.

WHALE WATCHING

Each summer three pods of orca whales, about 90 individual whales in all, cruise the waters surrounding the San Juan Islands to the wonder and amazement of all. To watch these great black-and-white sea pandas frolicking in the sea, by leap-

The Whatcom Museum of History and Art. DAVID SCHERRER

ing completely out of the water and then crashing with a spectacular watery splash is truly one of the quintessential Northwest experiences. Several companies run whale-watching boats from Bellingham, offering both half-day and daylong trips. Here are a few.

Island Mariner Cruises   **$$$$**
5 Harbor Loop
Squalicum Harbor
(360) 734-8866, (877) 734-8866
www.orcawatch.com

Sea Orca Adventures   **$$$$**
Bellingham Cruise Terminal
355 Harris Avenue
(360) 734-3431, (800) 480-4390
www.orcawhales.com

Victoria San Juan Cruises   **$$$$**
Bellingham Cruise Terminal
355 Harris Avenue
(360) 738-8099, (877) 443-4552

OTHER ATTRACTIONS

Bellingham Bells   **$-$$**
Joe Martin Field
(360) 527-1035
www.bellinghambells.com
Since the 1920s, they've been playing pro- or semi-pro baseball in Bellingham. Whether it's been for the Bellingham Baby Ms, a Seattle Mariners' farm team whose roster featured future stars Edgar Martinez and Ken Griffey Jr., or the original Bellingham Bells, who played in the 1940s,

Bellingham fans have a history of turning out by the thousands to watch the boys of summer. The current Bells squad is a member of the six-team West Coast Collegiate Baseball League and features mostly 18- to 22-year-olds hopefully on their ways to the big leagues. Tickets are cheap—like $5.00 to $8.00—and there are all sorts of fun family promotions, including birthday parties and baseball camps.

**Bellingham Farmer's Market
(three locations)
(360) 647-2060
www.bellinghamfarmers.org**

**Downtown—Railroad Avenue and
Chestnut Street   Free admission**
Saturday, 10:00 A.M. to 3:00 P.M., April to October

**Barkley Village   Free admission
Tuesday, 3:00 to 7:00 P.M., July to
September**

**Fairhaven—Village
Green   Free admission**
Wednesday, 3:00 to 7:00 P.M., June to September

Starting in 2006, the downtown Bellingham Farmer's Market will be housed at Depot Market Square, a 7,000-square-foot open-air building, which will host other community events as well. As always, the downtown farmer's market runs Saturdays from April through October and is the place to go for fresh fruits, veggies, seafood, plants and flowers, arts and crafts, and lots more. The Barkley and Fairhaven farmers' markets, though scaled-down versions of the downtown market, are vibrant and unique affairs in their own rights. The downtown market kicks off the season in April when the mayor of Bellingham does the annual cabbage toss to a long-standing market vendor.

**Birch Bay Waterslides $$–$$$
4874 Birch Bay–Lynden Road
(360) 371-7500
www.birchbaywaterslides.net**
When temperatures soar, Birch Bay Waterslides, located about 20 minutes northeast of Bellingham, offers one of the best options for cooling off in Whatcom County. Multiple slides, including the 60-foot Hydrocliff drop slide, offer a sampling of what happens when gravity, humans, and slippery surfaces meet—they fall at great speeds accompanied by a high-fun, high-thrills content. A mega-size elongated hot tub lets you warm up when you need to. (That's the only slight downside—located so close to Birch Bay, even on the hottest days there almost always seems to be a cool offshore breeze.) Sand-pit volleyball courts, a kids' play area, and a restaurant and snack bar round out the offerings.

**Larrabee State Park $
245 Chuckanut Drive
(360) 676-2093
www.parks.wa.gov**
The oldest of Washington's state parks, Larrabee is kind of a microcosm of all the natural splendors that the Bellingham and Mount Baker area have to offer. There's the sea (Chuckanut Bay), there's a mountain (1,900-foot Chuckanut Mountain, which rises practically straight up out of the bay), and there's forest everywhere (some 2,700 acres' worth). There are trails that go up (to Fragrance Lake on Chuckanut Mountain's shoulder) and trails that don't (the Interurban Trail leads 6 mostly flat miles to Fairhaven on Bellingham's south side). The park also has picnic, barbecue, play structure, and other day-use facilities.

**Mount Baker Ski Area $$$$
Mount Baker Highway Milepost 52
(360) 734-6771
www.mtbaker.us**
Accolades galore and a world-record have

Snowboarding below Mount Shuksan. MIKE MCQUAIDE

gone to this relatively small ski area near the end of the Mount Baker Highway. Recently named by *Skiing* magazine as the best ski area in the state and one of the 20 best areas in North America, Baker is also the single-season record holder for snowfall. It *averages* about 650 inches of snow per year, the most of any ski area in North America, and during the 1998-1999 season, it was dumped on by a world-record 1,140 inches of snow. That's 95 feet! Beloved by both skiers and snowboarders, Baker has no lodgings or glitzy après-ski scene, just it's own unique vibe that's made it loved by skiers and snowboarders the world over.

Up Front Theatre $$
1200 Bay Street
(360) 733-8855
www.theupfront.com
Opened in 2004 by comic Ryan Stiles, known for his appearances on W*hose Line is it Anyway* and *The Drew Carey Show,* the Upfront is the place to go when you want to go somewhere you'll be guaranteed to laugh. The intimate 85-seat venue hosts Friday and Saturday evening improv performed by top regional as well as local groups, who take the form of improv games, one-act improvised plays, and musicals. There are even competitive improv sessions, and Stiles himself often performs at the theater.

Waterfront Boat Tour $-$$
Victoria San Juan Cruises
Bellingham Cruise Terminal
355 Harris Avenue
(360) 738-8099, (877) 443-4552
Victoria San Juan Cruises, which also runs whale-watching tours and walk-on ferry service to the San Juan Islands and Victoria, B.C., offers waterfront boat tours in Bellingham Bay. Get a spy-hopping orca's view of Fairhaven, Boulevard Park, and the emerging downtown waterfront while also being treated to a bit of Bellingham's natural and cultural history. Tours run from late May to early September and start at either the Bellingham Cruise Terminal in Fairhaven or Squalicum Harbor at the north end of the bay. You can enjoy the tour as either a two-hour round-trip excursion that drops you off where you board or a one-hour point-to-point cruise, e.g., board in Fairhaven and depart at Squalicum Harbor.

KIDSTUFF

In many ways this area is just one giant playground for kids. For along with having many terrific community parks (Cornwall Park, Whatcom Falls Park, etc.), Bellingham is blessed with a plethora of smaller neighborhood parks (Elizabeth Park, Forest and Cedar Park, etc.), most of which have cool play structures, picnic areas, ball fields, or just open areas to explore and play chase. One in seven acres in Bellingham is park or trail and for kids, meaning that just about everywhere you look, there's a place to play.

But of course in the Northwest it has a tendency to rain. And during winter it turns dark rather early. No matter. Grab the kids and head inside to some of Bellingham's numerous indoor attractions. Choose from museums, rock walls, libraries, swimming pools, an ice arena, and more.

Both Bellingham's and Whatcom County's parks and recreation departments have terrific programs that offer year-round classes, outings, and trips that are great fun and super experiences regardless of the weather. Whatcom Family YMCA also has terrific programs. Summer is a great time not only because the weather is just about perfect without fail, but also because of the many fun events, festivals, and fairs held—Ski to Sea, Northwest Washington Fair, Summer Concerts in the Park, Summer Outdoor Cinema, and much more. There are summer camps too—from sports camps to music camps to art camps to dance camps and everything in between.

ART/MUSIC/DANCE CLASSES AND WORKSHOPS

Clan Heather Dancers
2919 Birchwood Avenue
(360) 715-8682, (877) HOPTOIT
www.nas.com/clanheather
For more than 30 years, Heather Richendrfer has been teaching kids how to get in touch with their Celtic heritage, even if they don't have any. Classes focus on Scottish Highland, Irish step dance, tap, as well as choreography. Students have the option of taking part in performances at area fair and festivals, as well as competing at regional Highland Games competitions.

Monart School of Art
1701 Ellis Street, Studio 203
(360) 738-8379
www.bellinghamart.com
Here kids (and adults) learn to draw using the Monart method, based on a drawing system devised by Mona Brookes, a renowned California art educator. The Bellingham school is one of 49 Monart schools worldwide. Classes are held for students four years old and older, all the way to adult classes. The school also offers summer art camps for kids focusing on cartooning, Chinese dragons, mermaids, pirates, and more.

Nancy Whyte School of Ballet
1412 Cornwall Avenue
(360) 734-9141
www.nancywhyteballet.com
This is the place for kids to go to learn about battement tendue, porte de bras, and every other balletic movement and position there is. The school offers everything from an Early Childhood Dance Pro-

gram for kids ages 3 to 6 to opportunities to dance with the Mount Baker Ballet in the annual production of *The Nutcracker* at the Mount Baker Theatre to private lessons for kids and adults. It also puts on weeklong summer dance camps in July.

North Sound Youth Symphony
Bellingham
(360) 733-6632
www.nsysymphony.com
Young people can make some beautiful music, as this symphony of more than 100 musicians age 9 to 22 proves several times each year in performances at Western Washington University. The organization has levels of ensemble that are dependent on the musician's skill level—symphonia, Philharmonia, and symphony. Entry is by audition.

Wendy Setter's Dance Studio
1820 Cornwall Avenue
(360) 734-1595
www.thedancestudio.net
For those who want to learn how to get a bit more jiggy widdit, the Dance Studio teaches not only ballet but also jazz, tap, and hip-hop. Dance students perform at local events such as the Holiday Port Festival and a summer event called Tour de Dance, held at the Mount Baker Theatre.

BOOKSTORES

Along with having extensive children's sections, each of the following stores has weekly story times or reading groups for toddlers to 12 year olds. Call the individual store for more information.

Barnes and Noble
4099 Meridian Street
(360) 647-7018
www.barnesandnoble.com

Village Books
1200 11th Street, Fairhaven
(360) 671-2626
www.villagebooks.com

In addition, several of Bellingham's fine used bookstores have voluminous kids' sections. These are great places to load up on already-been-loved books at great prices.
Eclipse Bookstore
1104 11th Street
(360) 647-8165

Henderson Books
116 Grand Avenue
(360) 734-6855

Michael's Books
109 Grand Avenue
(360) 733-6272

CAMPS

Art in the Garden Summer Camps
(360) 201-9038
web www.nas.com/meloyco
These popular weeklong camps are geared toward kids age 6 to 15 and focus on watercolors, oil painting, pen and ink drawing, and other media. Noted regional artist Rebecca Meloy, assisted by her corgi, Finn, leads the camps in her award-winning garden.

Bellingham Bells Youth Baseball Camp
Joe Martin Stadium
(360) 527-1035
www.bellinghambells.com
This weeklong summer camp gives kids the chance to learn how to pitch, hit, and field from the pros. Kids are taught by players, coaches, and scouts for the Bellingham Bells baseball team, a minor league club in the West Coast Collegiate Baseball League. All instruction takes place on Joe Martin Field, where Ken Griffey Jr. and Edgar Martinez played many years ago on their way to the bigs.

Bellingham Junior Sailing Program
Bellingham Yacht Club
2625 Harbor Loop
(360) 733-7390
www.byc.org/juniors
The Bellingham Yacht Club holds both

basic and intermediate sailing programs for kids age 8 to 18. The two-week sessions offer six hours of daily instruction and the opportunity to partake in dinghy and keelboat races, which teach kids about the teamwork that's necessary in sailing larger boats.

Bellingham Parks & Recreation
3424 Meridian Street
(360) 676-6985
www.cob.org/parks
The city's terrific parks department offers numerous day- and half-day camps and overnight trips throughout the summer for preschoolers to teenagers. Camps and trips focus on everything from Irish step dancing to computers, skateboarding to rock climbing, entomology to ecology, and more. There are also training programs in areas such as service, babysitting, and leadership.

Southside Summer Camp
Bellingham Boys and Girls Club
1715 Kentucky Street
(360) 527-9777
www.whatcomclubs.org
The Boys and Girls Club offers weeklong camp sessions throughout the summer at two different locations. Geared for kids of all ages, the camps have a different theme each week, from computers to outdoor games to art and more.

Summer Enrichment Program
St. Paul's Episcopal School
3000 Northwest Avenue
(360) 733-1750
Want your child to have an interesting and enlightening summer? Enroll them here. Among the eclectic mix of one- to three-week day-camp offerings: Music Composition and Technology; Fun with French; Digital Photography and Computers; and one called If The Queen Comes To Lunch, where kids learn table manners and etiquette appropriate for royals.

Four times each year (usually early September, December, March, and June), the Bellingham Herald *publishes a pull-out Leisure Guide that's stuffed with information on recreation and educational events, programs, and camps. Though the information contains activities for people of all ages, a majority of the activities are for kids and teens. The guide is also available for free at the Arnie Hanna Aquatic Center and the YMCA.*

Western Kids Camp
Western Washington University
(360) 650-4094
www.wwu.edu/campusrec/kidscamp
Held at Western Washington University's brand-spanking-new Wade King Campus Recreation Center, this camp's weeklong sessions have both an academic and recreational component. Kids learn about science, bugs, and plants in the morning, and then swim, play tennis, go on scavenger hunts, and the like in the afternoon. Each week features a different theme, from Vikings to the Olympics.

Whatcom County Parks and Recreation Summer Art Program for Children and Teens
2600 Sunset Drive
(360) 733-6897
This very popular cultural art program offers day camps and classes in unique (for kids) areas such as carpentry, woolworking, pottery, cooking, as well as standbys like science, magnetism, drawing, and painting. Offerings are for kids and teens age 3 to 17, and all camps and classes take place at the historic Roeder Home.

Whatcom Family YMCA
Summer Programs
1256 North State Street
(360) 733-8630
www.whatcomymca.org

Bellingham's Y pretty much has it covered when it comes to keeping your child or children occupied in the summer. (Year-round, actually.) Weeklong Summer Explorer and Adventure Camps for kids in kindergarten through sixth grade feature on-site rock climbing and swimming as well as three field trips per week. Teen Xtreme and Teen Caravan for middle- and high-schoolers boast extended trips to places such as the San Juan Islands. Among the Y's many other offerings are Sport Camps for kids age 3 to 12 in golf, soccer, gymnastics, T-ball, flag football, basketball, and more.

Sports Camps

Bellingham Parks & Recreation
(360) 676-6985
The ubiquitous Parks and Rec department runs summer sports camps for boys and girls in a number of team sports. Choose from basketball, soccer, baseball, softball, volleyball, golf, tennis, gymnastics, and more. Most camps are a week long and are held at various high schools and middle schools throughout the area.

Summer Tennis Camps
Bellingham Tennis and Fitness Club
800 McKenzie Avenue
(360) 733-5050
www.bellinghamtennis.com
Little ones as young as five years old can learn how to get in the swing of things, serve and volley, and eventually leap over the net in victory in these weeklong camps held at this Fairhaven club. Camps are for players from 5 to 18 years old.

FREE RAINY-DAY FUN

Alaska Ferry Terminal
355 Harris Avenue, Fairhaven
(360) 676-8445
Sometimes all the little ones need is a change of pace and a change of place. The big, open, high-ceilinged ferry termi-nal provides such a space. Check out the big relief maps of Alaska on the walls while your little ones pretend they're giants striding through the mountains. Also check out the waterfront comings and goings through the many windows. Climb the stairs, where, except for the twice weekly sailing, it's devoid of people. This is a great place where kids can climb on benches, explore little nooks and crannies, and the like. Need a treat—head downstairs for some hot cocoa or a big cookie.

Great Harvest Bread
305 East Magnolia Street
(360) 671-0873
www.bellinghambread.com
It seems like every kid in Bellingham has been on the Great Harvest Bread Tour. It's a true Bellingham rite of passage. Kids learn what goes into making bread, including not only the ingredients and all the cutting and kneading but also the big barrels of flour and yeast and especially honey—sweet stuff. Not to mention the huge oven. And, what could be cooler than this: Each kid gets to take home a miniloaf of bread.

Toddler Time
Bloedel Donovan Multipurpose Room
2214 Electric Avenue
(360) 676-6888
Many props to Bellingham Parks and Recreation for opening up the gym at Bloedel Donovan a couple mornings a week during the school year and letting the little ones, some barely able to walk, have the run of the place. Many a tod-dler's first friendship has been formed here (perhaps also their first mortal enemy/adversary but that's not worth getting into) while kicking a ball, sharing turns on a tricycle (as much as they can share), or chasing an errant hula hoop. During those rainy winter months when cabin fever is raging and the concept of getting outside to play seems as remote a possibility as learning to fly, Toddler Time

is a godsend and sanity maker to parents. It's for itty-bitty kids to those age 3, and it's usually open 10:00 to 11:30 A.M. on Tuesday and Thursday.

KID-FRIENDLY FAIRS AND EVENTS

May

Procession of the Species
Bellingham Parks and Recreation
(360) 676-6985
www.ncascades.org/procession
This downtown festival combines two things Bellinghamsters love—dressing up in imaginative animal-, bug-, plant- and fish-type costumes and celebrating the wilderness, which the procession and after-procession events do. Starting in January, Parks and Rec offers workshops for children and adults in puppet, mask, costume, and banner making especially for the procession. There are workshops featuring percussion instruments, too.

Junior Ski to Sea
Lake Padden Park
(360) 734-1330
www.bellingham.com/skitosea
A week before the adults have their Ski to Sea race, the kids get their own relay race at Lake Padden Park. Teams of six partake in the five-event race that includes running, three-legged racing, biking, soccer-dribbling, and an obstacle course. Talk about a "gas-gas-gas, jack," this is it. A Ski to Sea Junior parade takes place the night before for *all* kids (not just those doing the race) age 14 and younger. Ski to Sea events are sponsored by the Bellingham/Whatcom Chamber of Commerce.

June to September

Concerts in the Parks
Various parks throughout Bellingham
Bellingham Parks and Recreation
(360) 676-6985
www.cob.org
What kid doesn't like picnics in the park, chasing their friends, and dancing with Mom and Dad? Ice cream and cotton candy too? Throughout the summer, Parks and Rec puts on free concerts at various parks throughout the city, and kid-popular performers such as Dana Lyons and Buck and Elizabeth are often on the schedule. Two of the highlights are the weekly Thursday evening concerts at Elizabeth Park and the Friday noontime children's concerts behind the Bellingham Public Library.

August

Bellingham Kids' Festival
Civic Field
Bellingham Parks and Recreation
(360) 676-6985
The first Saturday in August is almost always sunny, and the Bellingham Kids Festival is the best place to take the little ones for some summertime face painting, inflatable maze maneuvering, rock climbing, juggler watching, arts, crafts, food, and more. Usually held on the infield at Civic Field or the outfield at Joe Martin Stadium, the shindig draws some 4,000 folks and is a true 4-F event: Fabulous Family Fun that's Free.

Northwest Washington Fair
Northwest Washington Fairgrounds
1775 Front Street, Lynden
(360) 354-4111
www.nwwafair.com
Amusement-park rides and farm animals. Farm animals and amusement-park rides. If your kid likes these (in other words, if he or she is breathing), they'll love this north Whatcom County institution, held for six

The Ferris wheel at the Northwest Washington Fair. MIKE MCQUAIDE

days in mid-August in Lynden. It's not just animals and rides of course; it's stuff to eat like cotton candy and ice cream and live music and Elvis impersonators and ferris wheels too. This farm-themed fair that draws 200,000 people annually is a slice of Americana from another time, it seems. Great family fun.

Chalk Art Festival
Streets of downtown Bellingham
Allied Arts of Whatcom County
(360) 676-8548
www.alliedarts.com

Every August, the kids (and adults) of Whatcom County get down on their hands and knees and create beautiful art-work on the sidewalks of Bellingham. Using pastel chalks, they sketch scenes from Harry Potter, orca whales spy-hop-ping in Puget Sound, butterflies, dragons, froggies, bunnies—pretty much anything they can come up with. And the sidewalks remain beautiful until the next hard rain, which can be a couple months away.

October

Stoney Ridge Farm Pumpkin Patch
2092 Van Dyk Road, Everson
(360) 966-3919

Nothing says fall quite like a wagon ride on a pumpkin farm with the kids, or a stroll through a hay maze, or a steaming cup of hot apple cider, made fresh from apples right there on the farm. For these and other potential family-photo-album fillers—farm animals, exotic (i.e., weird) chickens, train rides, and local crafts too—head out in the county to Stoney Ridge Farm near Everson. To get there, take the Mount Baker Highway for about 6 miles to Everson-Goshen Road and turn left. Fol-low Everson-Goshen Road for about 8 miles to Van Dyk Road and turn left. Stony Ridge Farm is just ahead on the right, and parking is on the left. The farm is open Thursday through Saturday in October.

Stoney Ridge Farm Pumpkin Patch. MIKE MCQUAIDE

Barkley Pumpkin Patch
Corner of Woburn Street and Barkley
Boulevard
(360) 676–0109
Along with those big unwieldy orange things (pumpkins), this popular in-town pumpkin patch features train rides and an organized trail run, usually held the third Saturday in October. The Pumpkin Patch, which is a fund-raiser for the Whatcom Hospice Foundation (it raised $112,000 over its first four years), usually opens about the second week of October and is open seven days a week.

Trick-or-Treating
Downtown, Fairhaven
Every Halloween, downtown and Fairhaven merchants open up their doors and hand out candy to all manner of ghouls, goblins, ghosts, Ninja Turtles, Darth Vaders, and whoever else shows up. Trick-or-treating starts in the afternoon and is mostly for the very little ones, those who won't be doing much tricking or treating in the dark. Participating merchants are easy to find in the main downtown area (Holly Street, Railroad and Commercial avenues, etc.) and Fairhaven's main drags, too—Harris Avenue and 10th, 11th, and 12th Streets. The YMCA on State Street usually has some free Halloween events, so downtown trick or treaters should stop by there, too.

December

Holiday Port Festival
Port of Bellingham
(360) 676–2500
www.portofbellingham.com
Held at the Alaska Ferry Terminal, this event celebrates the season to be jolly with live music (much caroling), dance performances, free horse and wagon rides, and lots and lots of holiday lights. Among the most impressive lights are those of the Bellingham Yacht Club's

lighted boat parade. Also a huge draw is the annual Gingerbread House Decorating Contest, where groups and families build and decorate some of the most amazing gingerbread houses you'll ever see. The houses are then auctioned off with the proceeds going to such groups as the Red Cross. Expect Santa Claus to drop by. The event takes place the first Friday through Sunday in December, and is free.

KID-FRIENDLY TRAILS, PARKS, AND BEACHES

Bellingham is blessed with numerous beautiful trails, parks, and beaches, and just about all of them are kid friendly. Therefore, the following list is not meant to imply that these are the only trails and beaches that are appropriate for children; they're just some of the highlights. (For more comprehensive coverage of parks and trails, see that chapter.)

Connelly Creek Trail
Donovan Avenue and 30th Street
(360) 676–6985
This trail is a gentle forested meander along Connelly Creek, past wetland meadows croaking with froggies and chirping with red-winged blackbirds. Interpretive signs point out that the trail passes through the Connelly Creek Nature Area, which boasts some of the largest Sitka spruce in town.

Cornwall Park
3424 Meridian Street
(360) 676–6985
This is kind of a smaller version of Whatcom Falls but no less fun. Along with a tree-covered disc golf course (you can pretty much play in the rain), Cornwall boasts a newish kids spray park and play structure. Three miles of trail wend and wind in and out of forest and along Squalicum Creek, creating an exploratory jungle of fun. There are tennis courts, horseshoes courts, barbecues, and picnic tables, too.

Elizabeth Park
Madison and Elizabeth Streets
(360) 676-6985
With its massive deciduous trees, this smallish neighborhood park is beloved for its way-popular playground and for being the venue of the Thursday night summer concerts. Families spread out here by the hundreds, enchanted by the trees, the old-time fountain, and each other.

Heather Meadows and Artist Point
End of Mount Baker Highway
In the mountains, Picture Lake Path, Bagley Lakes-Lower Wild Goose Trail, Artist Ridge, and a couple other trails are certainly short enough and easy enough for small children. The Austin Pass Picnic Area, just outside the Heather Meadows Visitor Center, makes for a perfect picnic spot as well as the starting point for various hikes.

Larrabee State Park
245 Chuckanut Drive
(360) 676-2093
Twenty-six hundred acres of spectacular wilderness, about 15 miles of trails, swirly sandstone bluffs just asking to be scrambled upon by young homo sapien-types, and a couple of great beaches make Larrabee a close-to-perfect spot for a family outing. The park also has an 80-site campground, picnic facilities, and a new play structure. At Larrabee's south end, Clayton Beach is a tucked-away oasis, a sandy beach where the water's a little warmer, the sun seems a little hotter, and the fun is perhaps a little funner. The park has picnic, barbecue, play structure, and other day-use facilities.

Little Squalicum Beach Park
Marine Drive and Lindberg Avenue
(360) 676-6985
Here's a terrific beach to just let the kids run loose to explore and imagine to their heart's content. There's no playground equipment, just driftwood by the ton, a billion shells and cobbles to skip across the water, and a stream emptying onto the beach. Perfect for damming up. Then diverting. Then damming up. Then diverting. In summers, when the tide is out, the water is warm enough for wading, which is more than you can say for most Puget Sound beaches.

Mud Bay Beach Walk
End of Fairhaven Street, Fairhaven
What kid doesn't love the mud? (Parents, of course, don't always share that love.) When the tide is out, the bay empties of water and, it seems, fills with the slimy, grimy dark stuff, complete with millions of crabs, sand dollars, and squirting razor clams. So pull on some boots and head out exploring. The sandstone cliffs here are Larrabee-esque, and you just might see more purple and orange sea stars here than you thought existed on earth.

Whatcom Falls Park
1401 Electric Avenue
(360) 676-6985
Along with crashing waterfalls, a swimming hole right out of Tom 'n' Huck, and 5 miles of wooded trails that are excellent for exploring both nature and one's imagination, this park features a newish play structure that helps build strong bodies in more than 12 ways. It also has basketball and tennis courts, barbecues, a really cool trout hatchery with interpretive displays, and a children's fishing pond.

LIBRARIES

Bellingham Public Library
210 Central Avenue
(360) 676-6864
The children's library is located in the lower floor of the main library building downtown. Along with offering a great selection of books, magazines, videos, and DVDs to borrow, the library holds several free story times each week for kids up to eight years old. In addition, once a month the library presents Thursday Night Spotlight, when they host kids' entertainers such as jugglers, storytellers, puppeteers,

and more. In summer the lawn on the library's north side becomes the venue for the Friday noontime children's concerts. All events are free.

**Whatcom County Library System
Locations in Blaine, Deming, Everson,
Ferndale, Lummi Island, Lynden, Maple
Falls, Point Roberts, and Sumas
(360) 354-4883
www.wcls.org**
There is a network of nine libraries throughout the county, from Sudden Valley just east of Bellingham to Point Roberts, which is a nubbin of land that you can't get to without traveling through Canada for 20-some miles. All of them have children's sections and programs involving stories, songs, and other amusements for toddlers and preschoolers as well as school-age kids.

MUSEUMS

**Mindport
210 West Holly Street
(360) 647-5614
www.mindport.org**
One part of this hands-on sciencey place is stuffed with cool optical illusions, contraptions with marbles that roll across ramps then drop through chutes onto spinning wheels, weird sound systems where the human voice forms patterns in grains of sand, a telephone which plays your voice backward, and a whole lot more. The other part is an art gallery featuring photographs which are sometimes suitable for adults only. Ask when you enter. Mindport was started by Kevin Jones and is a melding of science and art; it's patterned after San Francisco's Exploratorium. (Mindport, however, is much smaller.) Most Mindport exhibits are appropriate for kids age 6 and older; it's pretty much the perfect place to keep the young ones occupied for a few hours on a rainy morning. Exhibits change on a fairly regular basis.

**Whatcom Children's Museum
227 Prospect Street
(360) 733-8769
www.whatcommuseum.org**
This is one of Bellingham's most popular spots for kidding around. Located just down the block from the Whatcom Museum of History and Art, the Children's Museum is a terrific place to take toddlers through second graders on those too-numerous-to-count Bellingham gray days. Loads of educational hands-on exhibits and activities keep kids occupied (and a-learnin' for hours). There are costumes to try on, games to play, crafts to make, books to read, and loads more to experience. Exhibits change every year or so. Past exhibits have been reptile-, time machine-, and animal home-themed. The museum is open Tuesday, Wednesday, and Sunday from noon to 5:00 P.M.; Thursday, Friday, and Saturday from 10:00 A.M. to 5:00 P.M., and closed on Monday. Admission is $3.50 per person.

OTHER INDOOR ATTRACTIONS

**Marine Life Center
1801 Roeder Avenue
(360) 671-2431**
I know kids aren't the types who like to reach down into touch pools and stroke the backs of orange and purple sea stars, to stick their fingers in sea anemones and giggle in delight as their frilly mouths close around their fingers, or to look a giant Pacific octopus in the eye, but if they were, the Marine Life Center would be the place for them. I jest, of course. Kids love this Squalicum Harbor mini-aquarium. The small, semi-outdoor structure boasts three huge tanks and two floor-mounted pools, one which kids (and adults) can poke their fingers in. The other, much larger tank is for observation only, but oh, the observing one can do. Giant Dungeness crabs, spike-red sea cucumbers, sunflower sea stars, giant green anemonea—there are more than 175

species of sea critter in all, including the thorny head rockfish who'll swim slowly to the surface to check you out. The price of admission for all this great fun? A $1.00 donation for adults and 50 cents for kids. This is a great place for marine education-slash-entertainment.

Tube Time
1522 Cornwall Avenue
(360) 715-9167
A plethora of oversize tubes for the young ones to crawl over under on and through, ball pits to dive in and hide from little siblings in, and numerous slides to slide down—what more could a kid want? (Or parent, to tire their kids out.) Tube Time also has a toddler area with plastic toys for climbing and soft blocks for building (the tube network can be daunting for the real little ones) and a game room. The site of countless birthday parties, Tube Time has party rooms and serves pizza and other party-appropriate food and drink.

Rock Walls

Leading Edge North Academy
1710 Express Drive
(360) 733-6969
www.leadingedgenorth.com
This 12,000-square-foot facility is not only a fully equipped gymnastics facility that offers instruction, camps, and competition but it's also a popular indoor-climbing destination. The 100-foot-long wall is 25 feet high and offers everything from easy-breezy beginner routes to hang-on-for-dear-life advanced ones. The wall is available for lessons and private parties.

Whatcom Family YMCA
1256 North State Street
(360) 733-8630
www.whatcomymca.org
Along with boasting the highest indoor rock wall in the state, the Bellingham Y also has a kinder, gentler, not-so-high wall

that's great fun for kids and the not so hard-core. The Y offers classes, open times when families can get together to scale the walls, and climbing parties, too. Two- and four-week classes often include an outdoor component, such as a climbing excursion to Larrabee State Park. The Y wall is open to nonmembers as well as members.

SPORTS AND RECREATION

All-Comer's Track and Field Meets
Civic Field
(360) 676-6985
Every Monday evening from mid-June to late August, hundreds of people of all ages gather at Bellingham's Civic Field to see how fast they can run, how far they can throw, and how high they can jump. It's a low-key affair that's crazy fun. How could it not be? The sight of giggling three-year-olds running as fast as they can while hopping over 6-inch-high hurdles is adorable beyond belief. And all kids get ribbons, too.

Bellingham Boys and Girls Club
1715 Kentucky Street
(360) 527-9777
www.whatcomclubs.org
For youth baseball, softball, football (tackle and flag), and basketball, the local boys and girls club is the fountainhead. Leagues run year-round with opportunities for kids starting as young as kindergarten age.

Bellingham Parks & Recreation
3424 Meridian Street
(360) 676-6985
www.cob.org/parks
Along with offering myriad summer and school vacation camps (see above), the parks department also offers a bevy of day and overnight trips throughout the year to places such as Mount Baker, Seattle's Woodland Park Zoo, Seattle Mariner's baseball games, and more.

Sportsplex
1225 Civic Field Way
(360) 676-1919
www.bellinghamsportsplex.com
This is one of the coolest places to play—literally. Along with indoor soccer leagues, camps, and drop-in play sessions, the Sportsplex has an indoor ice-skating rink, which means the temperature inside is always just a little chilly. Along with ice hockey leagues, the Sportsplex offers instructional camps and sessions for kids who've never played or who want to improve their skills. Complete skating programs are also offered, including speed and figure skating. The Sportsplex also has a batting cage.

Whatcom County Parks and Recreation
Young Naturalists and Family programs
Tennant Lake, Ferndale
(360) 384-3064
www.whatcomcounty.us/parks/tennant lake
Just outside Ferndale, Tennant Lake is a magical place that's perpetually a-croak with frogs, a-buzz with dragonflies, and a-hoot with owls. Thus it's perfect for Whatcom County's Young Naturalists and where 5- to 9-year-olds explore the park's wetlands searching for critters, insects, bladderworts and other insectivorous, and lots more. The six-week program is held one day a week in the late afternoon. Family Program offerings take place both at night (search for owls and study the night skies for faraway stars, planets, and constellations) and afternoon (learn to identify bald eagles and other avian visitors to the Bellingham area).

Sports Camps

Bellingham Parks & Recreation
(360) 676-6985
The ubiquitous Parks and Rec department runs summer sports camps for boys and girls in a number of team sports. Choose from basketball, soccer, baseball, softball, volleyball, golf, tennis, gymnastics, and more. Most camps are week long and are held at various high schools and middle schools throughout the area.

Whatcom County Youth Soccer Association
Northwest Soccer Park
(360) 384-6323
www.whatcomsoccer.com/youth.htm
It's safe to say that Bellingham and Whatcom County grown-ups are fairly soccer-crazed, and here is where that mania is passed on to the next generations. Leagues start for kids as young as age 4 and continue, not just through elementary, middle and high school, but into adulthood as well. Youth games are played on weekends at the Northwest Soccer Park just a few miles north of Bellingham, but teams practice throughout the week at various school fields in town.

TOY STORES

Fountain Drug & Galleria
2416 Meridian Street
(360) 733-6202
Need to get a gift for someone still in their single digits but you're not into the latest movie tie-in hunk of plastic? Head downstairs to this north-of-downtown (it's in the Fountain district, actually) pharmacy for a selection of challenging, interesting, skill-building, and most important, *fun,* toys that you're not likely to find in the chain stores. Here is everything from stuffed animals to challenging puzzles and games to musical instruments to lots and lots of Thomas the Tank Engine toys, this last laid out in a little village that'll keep your little ones enthralled for hours. The pharmacy often features special monthly game nights for kids with tea time for the adults; call for a schedule.

Wild Blueberries
1106 Harris Avenue, Fairhaven
(360) 756-5100
Specializing in toys for the age 10 and

younger set, this Fairhaven shop hand-picks its merchandise from various trade shows and cottage industries around the country, which accounts for its unusual and exciting selection. Nothing here is electrical or battery-operated, there are just a lot of imagination- and interaction-inspiring toys, books, science kits, games, and the like.

Yeager's
3101 Northwest Avenue
(360) 733-1080

This old-school, blast-from-the-past sporting goods store, which sells hunting, fishing, and camping gear as well as all you'll need for baseball, soccer, skiing, and snowboarding, has a surprisingly good toy selection that, chances are, you might not find on your own. It's downstairs with nary a sign pointing it out. Just ask someone who works there; you'll be pleasantly surprised.

WATER FUN

Arnie Hanna Aquatic Center
1114 Potter Street
(360) 647-7665
www.cob.org/parks/aqua

Sure, there's lap swimming and water aerobics for the adults, but this is definitely a kids place. Besides the 135-foot winding, swirling tube slide, the center boasts a kids' pool and a mini-tot play area to amuse the little ones when their older sibs are taking lessons in one of the many year-round programs. Lessons are offered for those as young as six months old. Local swim teams, not all associated with a school, also use the pool and are always looking for new members. The aquatic center can be rented out for birthday parties, and it also has something called H2O Child Care, where the center provides in-water child care while you go swim laps, take a water aerobics class, or just hang out in the hot tub if you're so inclined.

Birch Bay Waterslides
4874 Birch Bay-Lynden Road
(360) 371-7500
www.birchbaywaterslides.net

When temperatures soar, Birch Bay Waterslides, located about 20 minutes northeast of Bellingham, offers one of the best options for cooling off in Whatcom County. Multiple slides, including the 60-foot Hydrocliff drop slide, offer a sampling of what happens when gravity, humans, and slippery surfaces meet—they fall at great speeds accompanied by a high-fun, high-thrills content. A mega-size elongated hot tub helps you warm up when you need to. (That's the only slight downside—located so close to Birch Bay, even on the hottest days there almost always seems to be a cool offshore breeze.) Sand-pit volleyball courts, a kids' play area, and a restaurant and snack bar round out the offerings.

Spray Parks

Cornwall Park
3424 Meridian Street
(360) 676-6985

Fairhaven Park
Chuckanut Drive
(360) 676-6985

Kids need to beat the heat? Or just get wet for the heck of it? In summer, Fairhaven Park in the South Side of Bellingham and Cornwall Park at the north end turn on the water jets at their free spray parks, much to the squealing delight of the city's kids. All kinds of mini-geysers and sprinklers squirt high and entice kids to run through them on the hard rubber surface. This is quite possibly the best fun a kid can have for free in the summer. Don't forget the towels and sunscreen.

Whatcom Family YMCA
1256 North State Street
(360) 733-8630
www.whatcomymca.org

The Spray park at Cornwall Park. MIKE MCQUAIDE

Along with a shallow kids' pool, the bigger Y pool features a wave machine where it's fun to pretend you're shipwrecked in the middle of the Pacific and there are circling sharks all around only too eager to topple you from their perch atop an inflatable tractor-trailer tube. (This is what I've heard.) Both pools can be rented for parties, and swim lessons are available for those age 6 months to 12 years.

ANNUAL EVENTS

Bellingham and Bellingham-area residents tend to celebrate everything. Beautiful music, lousy weather, the annual gathering of bald eagles, busted-up loggers, fruit harvests, bagpipers, tulips, really long relay races—you name it, chances are there's a festival here in Northwest Washington that celebrates it.

The biggies are Ski to Sea, the 82.5-mile relay race from the Mount Baker Ski Area to Bellingham and its attendant festivals and parades that generally take place the last couple weeks of May; and the Northwest Washington Fair, six days of farm animals, amusement park rides, live music, and more, that takes place in mid-August and draws about 200,000 folks. Though Ski to Sea is spread out over a couple weeks and many venues, the biggest events in terms of crowds and things to do are the downtown parade on the Saturday of Memorial Day weekend and the next day's It All Ends In Fairhaven finish-line festival.

Conversely, the Northwest Washington Fair takes place at one site, the Northwest Washington Fairgrounds in Lynden. The fair runs Monday through Saturday. (Like just about everything else in Lynden, it's closed on Sunday.)

Independence Day is another biggie for Bellingham, with formal and informal celebrations throughout the city. The city-wide fireworks display takes place over Bellingham Bay. On the night of the fourth, it's an odd sensation when about 9:30 P.M. the city suddenly springs to life again with traffic and thousands of people walking the streets trying to squeeze into the remaining open waterfront spots to watch the fireworks.

Other big events include Ferndale's Pioneer Days, the Skagit Valley Tulip Festival (about 25 miles south but included here because of its popularity), the Belling-

ham Farmer's Market, and the Mount Baker Blues Festival. Find details on these and others in the following pages.

FEBRUARY

Pacific Northwest Rain Festival
Fairhaven Village Green
(360) 738-1574
www.fairhaven.com

A low-key celebration of all things wet and rainy held the first Saturday after Groundhog Day, this one-day event features rain-themed poetry readings, rain dances, rain songs, and a fashion show featuring—what else—the latest in Gore-Tex and other raingear. Usually there's an appearance by the Fairhaven Ladies of the Evening Society, too, a group of local women who dress up in 1890s tart attire in tribute to Fairhaven's first working women. The festival is free.

Mount Baker Legendary Banked Slalom
Mount Baker Ski Area
(360) 734-6771
www.mtbaker.us

What started out in the mid-1980s as a little competition among friends has since blossomed into one of the biggest events in snowboarding. It's been featured in *Sports Illustrated* and *Outside* magazines and draws everyone who's anyone in snowboarding circles—among them, superstar Terje Haakonsen and Ross Rebagliati, snowboarding's first Olympic gold-medal winner. The three-day bash features rock and hip-hop concerts, a salmon barbecue, and a bonfire so big they say it's visible from outer space. Industry bigwigs come from all over to schmooze and showcase their latest and greatest gear. Race spectators must purchase lift tickets (you can ride or ski between heats), which cost about $40 for

adults and $30 for those age 7 to 15; they're free for those age 6 and younger.

MARCH

**Whatcom County Home
and Garden Show
Northwest Washington Fairgrounds
Lynden
(360) 671–4247
www.whatcomhomeshow.com**
Held the first Friday through Sunday in March, this event is the largest home show north of Seattle and one of the largest events in Whatcom County. Sponsored by the Building Industry Association of Whatcom County, the expo annually boasts several hundred vendors showing off wares, plants, and supplies all in time for spring cleaning, building, planting, and renovating. There's often an appearance by a home and gardening luminary such as Ciscoe, the Seattle one-named gardening guru. Admission is about $6.00 and free for those age 16 and younger.

APRIL

**Dirty Dan Days
Fairhaven Village Green
(360) 676–8990
www.fairhaven.com**
Come celebrate the dirty one, Dan Harris, oft-credited with founding the town of Fairhaven and certainly one of the area's pioneers. This two-day celebration of all things dirty includes a rowing race (Dan was a notorious smuggler), an uphill piano race (before Dan shook the dust of Bellingham off his feet when he left town, he pushed his piano down the street and into the bay that now bears his name), a chowder cook-off, live music, a vintage car show, yacht tours, and more. DDD takes place the last weekend in April at the Fairhaven Village Green, and it's free.

**Bellingham Farmers' Market
(three locations)
Downtown—Railroad Avenue
and Chestnut Street**
Saturday, 10:00 A.M. to 3:00 P.M., April to October

Barkley Village
Tuesday, 3:00 P.M. to 7:00 P.M.,
July to September

Fairhaven—Village Green
Wednesday, 3:00 P.M. to 7:00 P.M.,
June to September

**(360) 647–2060
www.bellinghamfarmers.org**
This Bellingham institution runs every Saturday from April through October. Be there on opening day the first Saturday in April and you'll see the mayor kick off the market season with his annual cabbage toss to a long-standing market vendor. Along with local food, flowers, and arts and crafts, the market is also a great place to catch street performers—costumed stick-figure folks on giant stilts, musicians playing everything from banjos to hand-saws to dobros, jugglers of all sorts—most of whom entertain and will gladly receive your pocket change if you'd like to get rid of it. Saunter, meet friends, and munch; that's the farmers' market in a nutshell. Admission is free.

**Skagit Valley Tulip Festival
Many locations throughout western
Skagit County and Mount Vernon
(360) 428–5959
www.tulipfestival.org**
Each year about half a million folks from points all over flock to this mega-flower fest that takes place over two-and-a-half weeks about 25 miles south of Bellingham. Set against the Cascade Mountains, with Mount Baker appearing to hold court, the endless rainbow fields in the Skagit Flats of daffodils, tulips, irises, and lilies are truly stunning, enough so that visitors pump some $14 million into the local economy in checking out the petals and

Summer snowshoeing at Heather Meadow. MIKE MCQUAIDE

their associated events. Those events include arts and craft shows, bike rides through the flower fields, a street fair and tulip parade, and something that's billed as the world's biggest garage sale. There are various charges for different events.

MAY

Holland Days
Lynden Chamber of Commerce, Lynden
(360) 354-5995
www.lynden.org
Held the first Friday and Saturday in May, this Dutch-themed festival is a celebration of the Netherland Liberation of 1945. Most events take place within a 4-block downtown stretch and include an open-air market with kids events, such as a family bike ride, a parade, a fun run, and, this being

Lynden, klompen dancing and street sweeping. That's right, street sweeping, with brooms and everything; it's a Dutch thing. Remember, the event is held on Friday and Saturday; Lynden is pretty much closed on Sunday.

Ski to Sea
Various locations throughout
Bellingham and Whatcom County
Bellingham/Whatcom Chamber of
Commerce
(360) 734-1330
www.bellingham.com
Bellingham's biggest event is a two-week-long celebration of its outdoor riches and recreation opportunities. At the center of this mostly Memorial Day weekend celebration is the race itself, in which more than 400 teams compete in a seven-leg relay race from the Mount Baker Ski Area

to Fairhaven's Marine Park in Bellingham Bay. Teams of eight cross-country ski, downhill ski, run, road bike, canoe (two persons), mountain bike, and kayak the 82.5 miles, all in the hopes of being the first to ring the finish-line bell. (Or to at least ring it before the time cut-off.)

It's estimated that almost 100,000 spectators line the course somewhere to watch, which is remarkable given that the county's population is about 166,000. Though the race itself is just one morning and part of an afternoon, Ski to Sea events take place throughout the last two weeks of May. There's a Sea to Ski Grand Parade, Junior Ski to Sea Race, Junior Ski to Sea Parade, Sea to Ski Junior Sail Regatta, Ski to Sea Carnival, Ski to Sea Book Sale. (You get the idea.) The accompanying It All Ends in Fairhaven festival, with live music, arts and crafts, food booths, pony rides, and the like, and other events pump more than $5 million into the local economy.

JUNE

Bellingham Scottish Highland Games
Hovander Homestead Park
(360) 647-8500
www.bhga.org
Lotsa bagpipes, lotsa Scottish dancing, lotsa sheepdog trials, and, of course, what are highland games without lotsa tossin' of the haggis? Despite its name, this two-day, first-weekend-in-June event, which also features arts, crafts, and food vendors, is actually held at Hovander Homestead Park in the fields outside Ferndale. But wherever it is you can't miss it; just follow the sounds of the bagpipes. Admission is $8.00 for adults, $6.00 for seniors and those ages 6 to 12, and free for children younger than age 6.

Deming Logging Show
Deming Logging Show Grounds
3295 Cedarville Road, Deming
(360) 592-3051
www.demingloggingshow.com

Since 1962, this has been the place to go if you want to see some serious (and sometimes seriously fast) log rolling, speed climbing, ax throwing, choker setting, hand bucking, and the like. And there are clowns, too. The whole wood-chip flyin' atmosphere is like a rodeo, but with loggers instead of cowboys. The two-day event takes place the second full weekend in June and is a fund-raiser to help injured loggers and their families. Admission is $6.00 for adults and $3.00 for seniors and those age 6 to 12. Children younger than age 6 get in for free.

Concerts in the Parks
Various parks throughout Bellingham
Bellingham Parks and Recreation
(360) 676-6985
www.cob.org
On various nights throughout the summer, Bellingham Parks and Rec sponsors free concerts at a number of parks throughout the city. These family-friendly events usually feature folk, blues, jazz, and World music as well as children's performers. They're a great time for picnic dinners on the grass; at some venues vendors sell food, ice cream, cotton candy, and even hula hoops. This is a time when squealing children chase and play, tickled pink beyond belief, and hippies, former hippies, and nonhippies join hands to twirl to some live tunes. Weekly Thursday evening concerts take place at Elizabeth Park, and weekly Friday children's concerts take place at noon behind the Bellingham Public Library. Other parks with monthly or twice-monthly concerts include Boulevard Park, Big Rock Garden Park, and Fairhaven Village Green. In 2005 Wednesday-night alley concerts were held in a downtown alley (as the name implies) between Wild Buffalo and Mindport. Admission is free; contact Parks and Rec for a schedule.

A free concert at Elizabeth Park. MIKE MCQUAIDE

OUTDOOR MOVIES

Fairhaven Outdoor Cinema
(360) 733-2682
www.epiceap.com

Traveling Pickford Show
(206) 571-1816
www.whatcomfilm.org/tps

On Saturday nights from late June to early September, on grassy lawns in parks throughout Bellingham, families, friends, and individuals can be found lounging about on blankets, often bundled up and enjoying popcorn and hot cocoa, while taking in the onscreen exploits of Bogey and Bacall, Indiana Jones, Pee Wee Her-

man, Spider-Man, and others. They're taking in the picture show. Drive-ins may be a thing of the past, but outdoor cinema is thriving in Bellingham. Movies are screened every other Saturday night at Fairhaven Village Green, and weekly on a rotating basis at the Bellingham Public Library, Bellwether on the Bay near the Hotel Bellwether, and just across the waterway at Zuanich Point Park. Movies are shown on the sides of buildings or on portable billboard-size screens, and there's live music or entertainment before each screening. The cost is $4.00 per person or $10.00 per family.

JULY

Haggen Fourth of July Celebration
Bellingham Bay

Bellingham's big fireworks blastoff features a spectacular 30-minute display of sound and fury over Bellingham Bay. Be aware, however, that since this is the far Northwest corner of the far Northwest and daylight tends to linger a while in early July, the show doesn't start until at least 10:30 P.M. The best places to watch are anywhere along the water, such as Boulevard, Marine, or Zuanich Park, anywhere along Squalicum Harbor or Little Squalicum Beach, or anyplace up high. Outside the Performing Arts Center at Western Washington University is also a good place.

Bellgrass Music and Food Festival
Bellwether on the Bay
(outside the Hotel Bellwether)
(360) 738-6701
www.hospicehelp.org/bellgrass.htm

This Independence Day festival features live music, local food, wine, and arts and crafts booths in a splendid outdoor setting at harbor's edge by the Bellwether Hotel. The event is a fund-raiser for the Whatcom Hospice Foundation, which helps terminally ill people in Whatcom County. The festival often features popular Bellingham bands, such as The Walrus, who specialize in Beatles' covers, and the Chryslers, who've been wowing Bellingham audiences for more than 20 years. Admission is free.

Whatcom County Old Settlers Picnic
Pioneer Park, Ferndale
(360) 384-3693
www.whatcomoldsettlers.com

If there was ever a slice of Whatcom County Americana this is it. Held annually since 1896 (that's right), this four-day Thursday-to-Sunday festival at the end of July features horse-drawn wagon rides through Ferndale, a grand parade, a softball tournament, and a kids' talent show as well as tours of authentic cabins from the days of Whatcom County's earliest European settlers. There are arts and crafts, hot dogs and hamburgers, patriotic music, and a petting zoo, too. All that's missing are lawnmower races. No, wait, the picnic has that, too. All this fun is free.

Mount Baker Blues Festival
River's Edge Christmas Tree Farm, Deming
(360) 671-6817
www.bakerblues.com

Started little more than a decade ago, this fest held the last weekend in July has quickly earned both a name for itself and a huge following. Named "Best Blues Event" several times already by the Washington Blues Society, the festival takes place 12 miles east of Bellingham River's Edge ChristmasTree Farm in Deming and features the West's top bluesmen and women. Past performers have included David Lindley, Eric Sardinas, Robbie Laws, the blues group Incognito, and Blues Cousins, which is generally regarded as Russia's top blues band. (Funny, I thought it was . . .) Lots of folks who are attending both days of the festival camp out at the Deming Speedway right next door. Tickets are generally about $30 per day and $55 for the weekend. Campsites are available for another $35.

AUGUST

Bellingham Kids' Festival
Civic Field
Bellingham Parks and Recreation
(360) 676-6985

The first Saturday in August is almost always sunny, and the Bellingham Kids Festival is the best place to take the little ones for some summertime face painting, inflatable maze maneuvering, rock climbing, juggler watching, arts, crafts, food, and more. Usually held on the infield at Civic Field or the outfield at Joe Martin Stadium, the shindig draws some 4,000 folks and is a true 4-F event: Fabulous Family Fun that's Free.

The Northwest Washington Fair. MIKE MCQUAIDE

Northwest Washington Fair
**Northwest Washington Fairgrounds
1775 Front Street, Lynden
(360) 354–4111
www.nwwafair.com**

This fair is a true Whatcom County tradition. Since the early 1920s thousands have flocked to Lynden during the second full week of August for this six-day celebration of all things farm related—cows, horses, pigs, cows, hogs, exotic (and just weird-looking) chickens, and lotsa cows. There's also lots of food—waffle fries, elephant ears, hot dogs, and hamburgers—and entertainment. Everyone from Loretta Lynn to Johnny Cash to Garth Brooks has played here and shared the stage with tractor pulls and demolition derbies. The fair also has a terrific carnival with ferris wheels, Tilt-a-Whirl rides, and games of chance. Parking lots in and around the fairgrounds aren't quite sufficient to handle the parking load, so you may end up parking at a nearby Lynden shopping center or civic group lot, but shuttle buses provide transportation from many of the lots. Admission is $8.00 for adults, $3.00 for those age 6 to 11, and free for kids age

When heading to Lynden for the Northwest Washington Fair or other events, for that matter, consider taking Hannegan Road instead of the Guide Meridian. Hannegan bypasses all the Guide Mall sprawl, and for the most part it's a jaunt through farmland. When you reach Lynden, just head west on Front Street for about a mile to reach the fairgrounds.

5 and younger. Carnival rides cost extra—$2.50 per ride or $15.00 to ride all day.

Bellingham Festival of Music
Various locations throughout
Bellingham and Whatcom County
(360) 676-5997
www.bellinghamfestival.org
For two weeks each August, this celebration of classical music and jazz takes over the city and has become one of the premier music fests in the West. The American Sinfonietta, the 40-piece symphony in residence, forms the festival's centerpiece by performing at most concerts, which usually also feature a number of world-class soloists and ensembles. Past performers have included the Miami String Quartet, Pepe Romero, Frederica Von Stade, Garrick Ohlsson, and Heidi Grant Murphy, a world-renowned soprano who actually grew up in Bellingham. Concerts take place at several Bellingham and Whatcom County locations, including Western Washington University, Mount Baker Theatre, Fairhaven Village Green, and the White Salmon Day Lodge at the foot of Mount Shuksan, a simply stunning venue. Tickets for this reasonably priced festival range from $16 to $35.

Chalk Art Festival
Streets of downtown Bellingham
Allied Arts of Whatcom County
(360) 676-8548
www.alliedarts.com
On the second Saturday of each August an amazing transformation takes place in downtown. Hundreds of artists and art wannabes descend upon the sidewalks with pieces of chalk the colors of the rainbow in their hands. On bended knee they

White Salmon Day Lodge. MIKE MCQUAIDE

spend hours scribbling and scratching and sketching away with the concrete sidewalk panels as their canvasses, and when they're through the sidewalks are beautifully transformed forever. Or until the next good rain. Seriously though, the colors and images that some of these artists come up with are truly stunning. Everyone is welcome to participate, even if you're all thumbs when it comes to drawing. And everyone can spend a couple hours sauntering about checking out the ground-level gallery or watching the artists create. Watching inspiration in action is a wonderful thing. If you want to draw, it's $20.00 for adults and $8.00 for those age 12 and younger to participate. Simply appreciating the art is free.

SEPTEMBER

Bellingham Traverse
Downtown to Lake Samish mostly
via various trails and parks
(360) 527-2722
www.bellinghamtraverse.com
This is Bellingham's other relay race. Started only about five years ago, this run–mountain bike–road bike–trail run–kayak trek has become hugely popular. It's kind of a mini Ski to Sea though the Traverse is more of an ecoenviromentally themed event—participants are required to raise funds for their favorite environmental group. The course simulates the journey of local salmon dealing with life in an urban environment and roughly follows their route from downtown to Lakes Padden and Samish and back into town again. Good places to spectate include the Bellingham Farmer's Market, where the start and finish take place and there's all manner of food and beverage to keep one sated, and Lake Padden, where the run–mountain bike–road bike transition area is.

Though much smaller than Ski to Sea and just a one-day event, the Traverse has, like that event, spawned its own peripheral festivities. One such festival is Eco Expo,

where environmental and wilderness advocacy groups and outdoor recreation clubs gather to educate and show what they have to offer. Participants usually include groups such as the Whatcom Land Trust, which seeks to preserve wilderness habitat, and WHIMPs, the Whatcom Independent Mountain Pedalers, a local mountain-biking club.

OCTOBER

Stoney Ridge Farm Pumpkin Patch
2092 Van Dyk Road
(360) 966-3919

Barkley Pumpkin Patch
Corner of Woburn Street
and Barkley Boulevard
(360) 676-0109
www.hospicehelp.org
Come autumn when the temperatures begin to drop and the leaves change color, there's something in our DNA that tells us: It's time for a wagon ride through a pumpkin field. Or if not a wagon ride, at least a muddy saunter through a pumpkin field. Luckily, a couple local places provide just that. Out in the country about 20 minutes from Bellingham, Stoney Ridge Farm has the wagon rides and a lot more, too, including a hay maze, hot apple cider, kids' train rides, local crafts and some pretty bizarre chickens and other fowl. In Bellingham itself, at Barkley Village, the Barkley Pumpkin Patch is a super in-town alternative. Along with pumpkins and kids' train rides, Barkley features a fun run. The Barkley event is a fund-raiser for the Whatcom Hospice Foundation. Stoney Ridge is open Thursday through Saturday in October, and admission is $2.00 per person or $7.00 per family. Barkley opens about the second week of October, and is open seven days a week for free.

Trick-or-Treating
Downtown, Fairhaven
Every Halloween, downtown and Fairhaven merchants open up their doors

and hand out candy to all manner of ghouls, goblins, ghosts, Ninja Turtles, Darth Vaders, and whoever else shows up. Trick-or-treating starts in the afternoon and is mostly for the very little ones, those who won't be doing much tricking or treating in the dark. Participating merchants are easy to find in the main downtown area (Holly Street, Railroad and Commercial Avenue, etc.) and Fairhaven's main drags too—Harris Avenue and 10th, 11th, and 12th Streets. The YMCA on State Street usually has some free Halloween events, so downtown trick or treaters should stop by there too.

NOVEMBER

Northwest Projections Film Festival
Various downtown Bellingham venues
www.whatcomfilm.org/projections/
(360) 752-0933
This four-day fest in early November started in 2000 and has grown almost exponentially each year, both in attendance and number of film submissions. Along with screenings of locally and regionally produced films, the festival boasts unique features such as the Guerilla Film Fest, where high-school students are given 65 hours to write, edit, and produce a film to be screened on the final day of the festival. Panels include guest speakers; past panelists have included R.W. Goodwin, a Bellingham resident and former producer of *The X-Files.* Northwest Projections culminates with an award ceremony where the top films and filmmakers take home the Golden Ham-

Because of many Bellinghamsters' love of fireworks, two times each year the city takes on the sound, if not the sight, of a war zone. Fireworks can be discharged in Bellingham from 9:00 A.M. to midnight on July 4, and from 6:00 P.M. to 1:00 A.M. on New Year's Eve.

ster, short for Bellinghamster. (Get it?) Admission prices vary.

Holiday Festival of the Arts
Pickford Dream Space
1318 Bay Street (next to the American Museum of Radio and Electricity)
(360) 676-8548
www.alliedarts.com/hf.htm
A holiday tradition for more than 25 years, the Holiday Festival is a great way to get into the holiday spirit and pick up some unique and unusual gifts for those on your shopping list. More than 120 Northwest artists and artisans will offer their wares—everything from blown glass to hand-woven scarves and hats to photographs to garden art to jewelry to gourmet food and more. Local musicians provide live holiday songs and other tunes. The festival opens the Saturday before Thanksgiving and runs until Christmas Eve. (Closed Thanksgiving.)

DECEMBER

Sinterklaas and Lighted Christmas Parade
Downtown Lynden
(360) 354-5995
www.lynden.org
The town of Lynden, about 15 miles due north of Bellingham, has deep Dutch roots. So each December they celebrate the arrival of Sinterklaas, the patron saint of the Dutch. Sometime after noon, Sinterklaas rides into town atop a regal white horse, accompanied by Zwarte Piet and the Lynden Klompen Dancers. Kids get to visit with Sinterklaas, no doubt dropping hints as to what they wouldn't mind receiving on Christmas, and at about 6:00 P.M. the lighted Christmas Parade begins. It's a sight to behold as all manner of floats and farm equipment and antique cars are decked out in dazzling, multicolored lights. This terrific holiday tradition is free.

Holiday Port Festival
Port of Bellingham
(360) 676-2500
www.portofbellingham.com
Held at the Alaska Ferry Terminal, this event celebrates the season to be jolly with live music (much caroling), dance performances, free horse and wagon rides, and lots and lots of holiday lights. Among the most impressive luminaries are those of the Bellingham Yacht Club's lighted boat parade. Also a huge draw is the annual Gingerbread House Decorating Contest, where groups and families build and decorate some of the most amazing gingerbread houses you'll ever see. The houses are then auctioned off with proceeds going to groups such as the Red Cross. Expect Santa Claus to drop by. The event takes place the first Friday through Sunday in December, and it's free.

THE ARTS

Bellingham ain't just the outdoors. In fact, in 2005 *USA Today* named Bellingham one of the 10 best small-city arts communities in the United States. The town has a thriving art scene consisting of museums, galleries, and various music, choral, and theater groups. In addition, throughout the year several arts organizations host special events such as downtown and Fairhaven's Summer Solstice gallery walks and the Potpourri of Art and Allied Arts Holiday Festival of the Arts, where dozens of local artists gather to offer their wares at one venue.

Bellingham also plays host to events such as the Bellingham Festival of Music, a two-week celebration of classical music and jazz that's become one of the premier music fests in the West. And along with being home to the longest-running community theater in Washington State, Bellingham is the home of many fine choral and symphonic groups, such as the Whatcom Chorale, the Bellingham Chamber Chorale, and the Whatcom Symphony Orchestra.

CHOIRS

Bellingham Chamber Chorale
(360) 738-8982
www.bellinghamchamberchorale.org
This relatively new entry into the Bellingham music scene has made an immediate impression and gained a devoted following. Founded in 2003 and focusing on everything from Renaissance pieces to 20th-century jazz, as well as creative musical meldings such as poems by Dylan Thomas set to music by American composer John Corigliano, the 40-member Bellingham Chamber Chorale always offers some unexpected musical delight. The group presents three concerts each year, usually at Western Washington University.

Whatcom Chorale
(360) 738-7166
www.whatcomchorale.org
This long-standing community chorus boasts more than 100 members from Whatcom and nearby Skagit County. The group performs popular works in the classic genre as well as folk songs and spirituals, and the choir presents about four concerts per year. The chorale's Christmas performances, which usually include something from Handel's *Messiah* are always popular. The group is always open to new members by audition. In 1998 the chorale toured Europe and performed six concerts in three countries.

MUSIC

Bellingham Festival of Music
Various locations throughout
Bellingham and Whatcom County
(360) 676-5997
www.bellinghamfestival.org
Started in 1993, this two-week celebration of classical music and jazz has become one of the premier music fests in the West. Conductor Michael Palmer leads the American Sinfonietta, a 40-piece symphony that serves as the festival's centerpiece, in numerous concerts that feature world-class soloists and ensembles. Past performers have included the Miami String Quartet, Pepe Romero, Frederica Von Stade, Garrick Ohlsson, and Heidi Grant Murphy, a world-renowned soprano who grew up in Bellingham. Concerts take place at several Bellingham and Whatcom County locations, including Western Washington University, Mount Baker Theatre, Fairhaven Village Green, and the White Salmon Day Lodge at the foot of Mount Shuksan, a simply stunning venue.

Whatcom Symphony Orchestra (WSO)
2915 Newmarket Street, Suite 104
(360) 756-6752
www.whatcomsymphony.com
Delighting classical music fans for more than 30 years, the WSO is a community orchestra that's led by Western Washington University professor of composition Roger Briggs. Concerts, which are performed at the Mount Baker Theatre, feature the orchestra playing in concert with noted guest artists from throughout the region. Performances take place about every two months. For true music aficionados, the WSO often offers such pre-concert events as talks by accomplished musicians, music scholars, and other notables. Always popular is the annual free children's concert that takes place in spring, a great introduction for little ones to both classical music and the wonder that is the Mount Baker Theatre.

THEATER

Bellingham Theatre Guild
1600 H Street
(360) 733-1811
www.bellinghamtheatreguild.com
The oldest community theater in Washington State, the Bellingham Theatre Guild got its humble beginnings in 1929. It moved around a bit in its first 15 years, but in 1944 it moved to its current space, the former Congregational Church at 1600 H Street just a little northwest of downtown. (Thus the distinct Theatre Guild steeple visible throughout much of the neighborhood.) The season, which generally includes five or six well-known musicals, comedies, and dramas, runs from September to July. The Guild benefits from having not only a talented community but also students and faculty up the hill at Western Washington University from which to draw. Speaking of talent, two-time Oscar-winner Hilary Swank performed in several Theatre Guild productions while growing up in Bellingham.

iDiOM Theater
1418 Cornwall Avenue
(360) 201-5464
www.idiomtheater.com
While the Theatre Guild offers a more traditional evening, the iDiOM, which opened in 2001, specializes in fare that's a bit more cutting-edge. Original works including serial plays, comedy duos who border on the vaudevillian, and midnight cabaret that's a tad risqué, are all typical fare for this innovative group run by local alt-theater impresario Glenn Hergenhahn. Locals have been flocking to iDiOM's downtown space since day one and continue to do so.

Western Washington University
Performing Arts Center
(360) 650-6146, (800) 998-2372
www.wwu.edu/depts/theatre
Western puts on many fine productions not just during the school year but also through its highly successful Summer Stock season. Being a university, the production values tend to be a bit higher than more local Whatcom County productions. Also, given that most of the people on and behind the stage are professionals, or hope to be someday, the productions themselves are often quite good. Shows can be anything from recent Broadway hits to edgy comedies and dramas to old standbys such as *Cabaret* or *A Funny Thing Happened on the Way to the Forum*. Most performances during the school year take place at Western's Performing Arts Center Mainstage, while some Summer Stock shows move to interesting venues such as Elizabeth Park and Fairhaven Village Green.

ARTS ORGANIZATIONS

Allied Arts of Whatcom County
1418 Cornwall Avenue
(360) 676-8548
www.alliedarts.com
This organization helps local artists of all stripes increase their visibility to the gen-

eral public via education and its down-town gallery and by sponsoring popular arts events such as the Chalk Art Festival and the Holiday Festival of the Arts. (See the Annual Events chapter for more information.) Exhibits at Allied Arts Gallery change monthly and can feature just about anything from surreal paintings to Native American art to metal sculpture to photography to whatever Allied Arts members can come up with. Allied Arts also helps sponsor the Downtown Gallery Walks, which take place three times each year, usually in July, September, and December.

VENUES

Mount Baker Theatre
104 North Commercial Street
(360) 734-6080
www.mountbakertheatre.com
This beautiful and historic city-owned Bellingham landmark hosts top dance, theater, and music productions from across the country and around the world. Built in 1927 for vaudeville and silent movies, the 1,500-seat theater offers a spectacular venue for experiencing anything from the Harlem Gospel Choir to the Seattle Opera to the Moscow Chamber Orchestra and more. In addition, road companies of Broadway productions such as *Tap Dogs, The Full Monty,* and productions of beloved shows such as *Oklahoma* often pull into town and put on a show. The theater also hosts concerts by national and regional rock, pop, and jazz acts. Local arts groups such as the Whatcom Symphony Orchestra and the Whatcom Chorale also present concerts here. In recent years a smaller 150-seat Studio Theatre has been added for more intimate performances.

SCULPTURE

Outdoor Sculpture Collection
Western Washington University
(360) 650-3000
www.outdoorsculpture.wwu.edu
Anyone who's explored Western Washington University's beautiful hilltop campus has surely taken note of its renowned (and free) Outdoor Sculpture Collection. Anyone who's been there with kids has no doubt spent an afternoon or two chasing them about as they go from one of the collection's very climbable pieces of land art to the next. *Log Ramps,* as its name suggests, are logs placed at a 9-foot incline, an angle that young ones (and students) like to climb and descend and climb and descend, repeatedly. *Stone Enclosure: Rock Rings* is a 40-foot circular wall of rock cut with holes that correspond to the North Star and the four points of the compass. One of the most recent, and most popular, additions to the collection is *Feats of Strength,* seven-foot-high bronze figures placed amid sandstone boulders that are either reposing jauntily or straining under the weight of heavy rocks they lift over their heads. There are about 25 pieces in the outdoor collection spaced throughout the 215-acre campus.

MUSEUMS

Whatcom Museum of History and Art
121 Prospect Street
(360) 676-6981
www.whatcommuseum.org
This four-building downtown campus boasts a collection of more than 200,000 artifacts and works of art, including a spectacular photograph archive. While most people think of the museum as only the former city hall building, the striking redbrick building on the bluff above Whatcom Creek that was built in 1892 boasts three floors of gallery space, and the museum also includes the Syre Education Center, the Arco Exhibits Building,

and the popular Whatcom Children's Museum. The Syre center is housed next door to the main museum building in a former fire hall, and it offers classroom space and permanent historical exhibits on local Native American history and early pioneer days. The Arch building, right across from the former city hall, hosts revolving exhibits by local, regional, and national artists in just about every medium. *Victorian Homes of Bellingham, Northwest Motorcycle History,* and *Women Painters of Washington* are just a few of the museum's recent exhibits. The museum also hosts a number of events, including history talks, musical performances, puppet shows, local documentary films, family Halloween parties, and lots more.

EVENTS

Lummi Island Artists Tour
Lummi Island
(360) 758-7121, (360) 758-7499
www.lummi-island.com
Three times each year about a dozen artists on Lummi Island open their studios to the public on this getaway tour that's not really that much of a getaway. (The island is just a six-minute ferry ride from Gooseberry Point, itself only about 20 minutes from Bellingham.) The tour is self-guided: You can pick up a map at the Beach Store Café, near the ferry landing, or you can print one from the Web site. Lummi Island is spread out a bit, so bicycling or driving are probably the best ways to get from studio to studio. Among the artists are sculptors who work in stone and metal, photographers, musicians, potters, glassworkers, handcrafted knitters, and more, and several of the artists offer demonstrations. The weekend tours generally take place on Memorial Day and Labor Day weekends and on the first weekend of December.

Fairhaven Holiday Tour d'Art Gallery Walk
Fairhaven
(360) 647-1628
www.fairhaven.com
The official (kinda) kickoff of the holiday season in Fairhaven takes place the weekend after Thanksgiving. That's when 30 or so galleries, shops, and cafes stay open late, have their establishments decorated for the holidays, and offer seasonal drinks and treats. Along with an official-esque Fairhaven Christmas tree lighting, the historic district decks itself out with some 30,000 tiny white lights. It's quite a spectacle and a terrific holiday tradition. Fairhaven is also the site of a Solstice Gallery Walk in June.

Northwest Projections Film Festival
Various downtown Bellingham venues
www.whatcomfilm.org/projections/
(360) 752-0933
This four-day fest in early November started in 2000 and has grown almost exponentially each year, both in attendance and number of film submissions. Along with screenings of locally and regionally produced films—narrative, shorts, experimental, pretty much everything—the festival boasts unique features such as the Guerilla Film Fest, where high-school students are given 65 hours to write, edit, and produce a film to be screened on the final day of the festival. Panels include guest speakers; past panelists have included R.W. Goodwin, Bellingham resident and former producer of *The X-Files.* Northwest Projections culminates with an award ceremony where the top films and filmmakers take home the Golden Hamster, short for Bellinghamster. (Get it?) Admission prices vary.

DAY TRIPS 🚗

Washington State is unique in many ways, and perhaps none more so than in its diversity of terrain. The Evergreen State has everything from temperate rain forests where the average precip is an inch a day, to arid desert environments where triple-digit temperatures are not uncommon in summer. And of course there are the mountains of the Cascades, which include five glacier-draped volcanoes, four of which are more than 10,000 feet high. The one that's below 10,000 feet is perhaps Washington's most well-known: Mount St. Helens, which erupted in a cataclysmic explosion in 1980.

Then there's the water: Washington kinda drifts into the Pacific Ocean on its west flank and the mighty Columbia River separates much of the state from Oregon to the south. Puget Sound, a deep 135-mile-long inlet, is the second busiest container port in North America and home of about three-quarters of the state's 6.2 million-plus population.

Then there's the city side of things. Washington is certainly home to natural wonders, but its largest city, Seattle, is not too shabby either. Along with being one of the most beautiful cities in the United States, it's also a leader when it comes to industry, particularly the high-tech variety. In the early to mid-1970s, a couple guys named Bill Gates and Paul Allen started Microsoft, which would go on to become the world's largest software company. Today the company's headquarters are in Redmond, about 15 miles northeast of downtown Seattle.

SEATTLE

The Emerald City, as it's called, is 90 miles due south of Bellingham on Interstate 5, and, like Portland and San Francisco, it's one of the West Coast's truly great cities. Left-leaning, alternative, and funky in a good way, Seattle is known for among other things its coffee culture (Starbuck's got its start here), its music (it's the home of grunge music as well as Jimi Hendrix), Microsoft (though that's actually headquartered in Redmond, just northeast of the city), and for just being simply a stunning jewel of a city set on the hills above glistening Puget Sound. Seattle's population is about 600,000 with about 4 million people living in the greater metropolitan area.

The city was founded in the early 1850s, just about the same time Bellingham was getting its start, and is named for Chief Sealth, head of the Duwamish and Suquamish Indian tribes and referred to by many as Chief Seattle. A true frontier town, Seattle experienced numerous booms and busts, most of which were lumber-, shipping-, fishing- or gold rush–related. The Great Seattle Fire of 1889 destroyed much of downtown, but the city's desirable location on a deepwater bay ensured that it would be rebuilt and prosper. Shipbuilding carried the economy through much of the early 20th century and after World War II, the aviation industry, with Boeing at the forefront, began to drive the Puget Sound economy. In the late 1960s and early 1970s, tough times in the industry (at one point, Boeing cut its workforce from 80,000-plus to less than 40,000) drove one Seattle businessman to post a billboard reading: "Will the last person leaving Seattle turn out the lights." In 2001 Boeing eventually moved its headquarters to Chicago, though the company retains its Everett production plant.

Luckily, though it took a few years, the burgeoning technology industry, led by Bill Gates and Paul Allen, was there to pick Seattle back up again. Throughout the 1980s and 1990s, Seattle's proximity to such natural beauty as Mount Rainier (just 60 miles away), the San Juan Islands, and the Olympic Peninsula, as well as the fact that it wasn't prohibitively expensive, made Seattle one of the most desirable places to visit and live. Its reputation as being the epicenter for hipness didn't hurt, either. In the early 1990s, rock radio was dominated by Seattle bands such as Nirvana, Pearl Jam, Soundgarden, Alice in Chains, Queensryche, Presidents of the United States of America, and others. A film scene and popular film festival emerged also. These days Seattle is also home to industry giants such as Amazon.com, REI, Costco, Nordstrom, Safeco, and many other companies.

In early 2001, an earthquake measuring 6.8 on the Richter scale rocked the Puget Sound area. Its epicenter was about 50 miles south of Seattle, and it caused about $1.5 billion in damage but no deaths.

So, what to do on a visit to this vibrant, exciting city? Pike Place Market (1531 Western Avenue, 206–682–7453, www.pike-placemarket.org) is a good place to start. This bustling Seattle institution on the downtown waterfront is not only a great place to pick up fresh fruit and veggies but also the place to duck flying fish. At Pike Place Fish, fishmongers don't hand fish to one another. They throw it through the air—accompanied by the requisite street performer-type patter—and give you a salmon's-eye view of what it's like to be stream salmon at spawning time. Set on the side of a hill leading down to the water, the market, which opened in 1907, has several floors that are crammed with unique shops, restaurants, and cafes. In fact, the first Starbuck's opened here in 1971.

Then there's the 605-foot-high Space Needle (206–905–2100, www.spaceneedle .com). With its observation deck at 520

Seattle skyline. WWW.PHOTOS.COM

feet, this is perhaps the city's most recognizable landmark, and it's at the heart of Seattle Center, a 74-acre park complex built for the 1962 World's Fair. (Actual conversation I once had with an elevator operator: ME: This job must have a lot of ups and downs, huh? SHE: Yeah, but it's the jerks along the way that keep it interesting.) Seattle Center is also the home of the Pacific Science Center (200 Second Avenue North, 206-443-2001, www.pacsci.org), a super-fun complex of five buildings with IMAX theaters, the Butterfly House, planetarium and laser shows, and tons of stuff to keep the kids (and adults) in jaw-dropping wonder. Also great for kids is the Children's Museum Seattle (305 Harrison Street, 206-441-1768, www.thechildrensmuseum.org), which boasts interactive multicultural- and environmentally themed exhibits such as Global Village and Mountain Forest. Also fun are the Imagination Station, where kids can make art via a variety of mediums, and the Mindscape Technology Studio.

Nearby is the center's whirly-swirly, multicolored, Frank Gehry–designed Experience Music Project (325 Fifth Avenue North at the base of the Space Needle, 877-EMPLIVE, www.emplive.org), Paul Allen's monument to all things rock 'n' roll. Among the 80,000-plus rock artifacts are Jimi Hendrix's Woodstock guitar and a ton of Beatles' paraphernalia, such as Fab Four wallpaper. Visitors can make their own noise, er, music in the many interactive studios.

Literally next door is the Science Fiction Museum (325 Fifth Avenue North, 877-367-5483, www.sfhomeworld.org), a virtual nirvana for fanatics of the *Star Wars/Star Trek/Matrix*-type movies and novels of authors such as Ray Bradbury. Along with a lot of high-tech whiz-bang, the museum's collection includes movie props and costumes such as Darth Vader's helmet, and the B9 robot used in the TV series *Lost in Space*.

And of course there's the Space Needle, which offers at a somewhat hefty price ($13 per person) the most incredible bird's-eye view of the city possible. Feeling peckish? Grab lunch or dinner at SkyCity (206-905-2100, www.spaceneedle.com/restaurant), the rotating restaurant at the top.

Seattle Center is also the home of the Seattle Opera (1020 John Street, 800-426-1619, www.seattleopera.org) and the Seattle Children's Theatre (201 Thomas Street, 206-441-3322, www.sct.org), as well as the Key Arena (305 Harrison Street, 206-684-7200, www.seattlecenter.com), where the SuperSonics, and Springsteen, if he's in town, play.

The center is also the site of some of Seattle's biggest festivals, including Folklife (Memorial Day weekend), Bite of Seattle (mid-summer), and Bumbershoot (Labor Day weekend), which features four days of national and regional music acts, arts and crafts, literature, film, comedy, theater, and much more.

Another of Seattle's biggest bangs is SeaFair (www.seafair.com), a monthlong regionwide celebration of all things waterlike. With boat parades, land parades, and the Blue Angels, not to mention the hydro races (a Seattle tradition that often leaves out-of-towners scratching their heads) it's all part of an annual summer festival that's been going on for almost 60 years.

Zoo-philes will find a bit of nirvana in Seattle at the award-winning Woodland Park Zoo (750 North 50th Street, 206-684-4800, www.zoo.org) in the Wallingford District. With its naturalistic setting, Woodland is one of the oldest zoos on the West Coast, and it delights all generations. You'll experience jaguars in the tropical rain forest, forests of elephants, hungry hippos, grizzlies, gorillas, giant reptiles, snakes, amphibians, and more—more than 300 different species are represented by 1,100-plus individual specimens. But it ain't just animals; the zoo's botanical collection boasts more than 1,000 different plant species.

Just north of Woodland Park Zoo is Green Lake, where Seattlelites go to walk, roller blade, jog, swim, paddle, and do just about anything else they can think of for fun. An expansive lake and green space smack in the middle of an urban neighborhood, Green Lake is encircled by a 2.8-mile trail and surrounded by numerous ball fields, basketball courts, an amphitheater, a pitch and putt golf course, and lots more. Green Lake is a true oasis in one of the country's most beautiful cities.

Sports fans have much to chose from in the way of spectator sports—the NFL's Seattle Seahawks (www.seahawks.com), the NBA's Seattle Supersonics (www.nba .com/sonics), and Major League Baseball's Seattle Mariners (www.mariners.org). Both the Mariners (Safeco Field) and Seahawks (Qwest Field) play in new state-of-the-art, yet coolly retro stadiums that are worth a visit even for those who aren't sports fans.

If art is more your speed, downtown's Seattle Art Museum (SAM) (100 University Street, 206-654-3100, www.seattleart museum.org) is the place to go. You can't miss it—just look for the giant Hammering Man out front. SAM is the Emerald City's biggest museum and the permanent home of an incredible artistically and culturally diverse collection of some 25,000 pieces. Among the museum's specialties are Northwest Native American, Asian, and African art; works by world-renowned artists such as Andy Warhol and Jackson Pollock; and contemporary works by Northwest artists such as Dale Chihuly. Recent temporary exhibits have included photographs from Annie Liebowitz and Spain in the Age of Exploration from 1492 to 1819.

One of the best places to watch the sea comings and goings of day-to-day Seattle is the Hiram M. Chittenden Locks (206-783-7059, www.nws.usace.army.mil/ lwsc.cfm), which controls the entry and exit to the waterway connecting Puget Sound to Lake Union. Each year more than 100,000 vessels—from million-plus-dollar yachts to individual kayaks—make the passage, and watching as engineers control the flow of water is fascinating. The locks tell a fish tale, also. A fish-ladder viewing room allows up-close-and-personal look-sees at salmon making their way back to freshwater (Lakes Union and Washington) or out to sea (Puget Sound). June is the best month for salmon views as the two groups' paths often cross.

Seattle is also the home of the University of Washington (www.washington.edu), not only the biggest university in the Northwest but also one of the oldest on the West Coast. With a beautiful 643-acre campus on the shores of Portage Bay and Lake Washington, the school is perfect for casual strolls, as is the surrounding University District, with its plethora of interesting shops, cafes, and restaurants.

VANCOUVER, BRITISH COLUMBIA

One of the most beautiful cities in all the world, Vancouver is just more than an hour north of Bellingham. Set at the edge of Burrard Inlet and the Strait of Georgia, at the foot of the North Shore Mountains, this ethnically diverse, very cosmopolitan city boasts world-class museums, shops and galleries, and the second-largest seaport in North America. (Only New York's is larger.) It has the second-largest Chinatown in North America, and, to continue its eclectic run of runner-upisms, the second-biggest film production center, second only to Hollywood's. And of course there's Stanley Park—1,000 acres of manicured gardens and tidewater beaches, not to mention an aquarium, an amphitheater, and one of the largest stands of old-growth forest in mainland British Columbia.

Stanley Park (www.city.vancouver.bc .ca/parks/parks/stanley) is, in fact, a terrific

---

To get to Vancouver, head north on Interstate 5 and after crossing the U.S.-Canada border, head north into Vancouver via Highway 99 for about 25 miles.

Vancouver Aquarium. WWW.PHOTOS.COM

place to start exploring. Not only is it a natural wonder, but since it's located on a spit poking into the Burrard Inlet, this 1,000-acre park affords a stunning city vista and is a good way to orient yourself to the city and its surroundings. To get the most of those city and mountain views, consider walking, roller blading, or bicycling the 5.5-mile Seawall Promenade. Along the way, check out the incredible authentic totem poles from the Kwagiulths, a coastal British Columbia First Nations tribe. As for the park itself, along with being crisscrossed by numerous wilderness trails and being the home of a way-cool children's spray park and miniature railway, it's the home of the Vancouver Aquarium (604-659-3474, www.vanaqua .org), Canada's largest and the third-largest aquarium in North America. Along

with beluga whales and Pacific white-sided dolphins, you can check out more than 600 different species, including crocodiles and—every kid's favorite—piranhas.

For the downtown cosmo experience, head to Robson Street, where you'll find unique shops, galleries, and restaurants as well as the center of cultural offerings. The Vancouver Art Gallery (750 Hornby Street; 604-662-4719, www.vanartgallery.bc.ca), which is the largest in Western Canada and presents more than 8,000 pieces from both Canadian and international artists, is not to be missed. Just down the way, get above it all by taking the elevator to the top of the 581-foot Harbour Centre Tower (555 West Hastings Street, 604-689-0421, www.vancouverlookout.com), where the city, harbor, and mountain views are out of this world. Like Seattle's Space Needle, there's a restaurant at the top, the aptly named Top of Vancouver Revolving Restaurant (604-669-2220). You might not build up that much of an appetite on the 50-second elevator ride to the top, but it's a great place to eat, nonetheless.

For fun, science-type stuff, a trip to Science World (1455 Quebec Street, 604-443-7443, www.scienceworld.bc.ca) is a must. (It's the big, metal, golf ball–looking building at water's edge that you no doubt noticed on your way into the city, and it was built for Expo '86.) Along with having a cool OmniMax theater, where the domed screen seems to surround you on all sides, Science World is a very hands-on kind of place where kids can build things and partake in "experiments" that involve magnets, bubbles, water, ball doohickey things, and the like.

Among other things, Vancouver is renowned for its scenic beauty and two of the best places to experience it just north of the city. Grouse Mountain (6400 Nancy Greene Way, North Vancouver, 604-980-9311; www.grousemountain.com) offers a gondola ride to mountain ridge 4,000 feet above the city. From here, all of Vancouver and the surrounding area—including everything from Mount Baker to Bellingham to the San Juan and Gulf Islands—is spread out in front of you, seemingly in miniature, in a simply breathtaking panorama. In summers it's a mecca for sightseers, hikers, and eco-tourists who let the gondola do all the uphill work and then have miles of ridgeline trails to enjoy. And if they get hungry or thirsty, there are several restaurants and cafes along the way, all with stunning views. In winter Grouse Mountain becomes a snowboarder's and snowshoer's playland with a ski area. (It's actually one of three ski areas on this North Shore ridge, each less than 30 minutes from downtown.)

Also on the north side, pretty much on the way to Grouse Mountain, the Capilano Suspension Bridge (3755 Capilano Road, North Vancouver, 604-985-7474; www.cap bridge.com) offers the spectacular experience of dangling 230 feet over the Capilano River. On a wood plank, two-person-wide bridge, that is. One of the city's most popular attractions with almost a million visitors annually, the compound also has restaurants, guided tours, and awesome totem poles that date from the 1930s.

BICYCLING ON LUMMI ISLAND

The closest of all the San Juan Islands, tranquil Lummi Island (www.lummi-island.com) is accessible by a six-minute ferry from Gooseberry Point, which is about 15 minutes northwest of Bellingham. Though ferry served—the 18-car *Whatcom Chief* makes the short crossing 38 times each weekday, 18 times daily on weekends—the island has no public trails, campgrounds, or parks (except boat-in ones) that might draw Orcas Island-esque crowds. So it's peaceful with secluded beaches and about 20 miles of paved, mostly deserted roads that make for an excellent easy-paced biking day trip. There are also some neat places to stop such as the Willows Inn (www.willows-inn.com) and the Beach Store Café near the ferry landing.

The Lummi Indians were the island's first inhabitants, though most fled sometime in the 19th century to avoid raiding tribes from the north. (Lummi Island is not a part of Lummi Reservation.) About 800 people live on Lummi Island year-round, many of them artisans who annually host an Artists' Studio Tour on Memorial Day weekend, Labor Day weekend, and the first weekend in December.

You can either pedal from Bellingham to the ferry landing at Gooseberry Point (about a 15-mile ride one-way) or drive there, park your car, and walk on the ferry with your bike. To drive there, take I-5 to exit 260, and drive west on Slater Road for 3.5 miles to Haxton Way. Head south on Haxton Way for 6.5 miles to the ferry terminal at Gooseberry Point on the Lummi Nation Reservation.

Lummi Island is 9 miles long and about

2 miles wide. From the ferry, it looks like a giant evergreen-covered soupspoon flipped upside-down. The bike riding on Lummi is basically flat, because all the roads are on the handle side—the flatter north side—of the island.

Once across from the Lummi Island ferry landing at Hales Pass, turn right onto Nugent Road. The road heads northwest and follows the shoreline. Through breaks in the trees, there are unfamiliar views of familiar places—the bluffs of Sandy Point and western Whatcom County; Boundary Bay and Point Roberts, that nubbin of U.S. land that hangs south of the U.S.–Canada border like a branch from a neighbor's tree; and beautiful Vancouver, B.C. backed by the North Shore Mountains.

After 2.5 miles, the road veers left abruptly at Point Migley, the island's northernmost tip, and heads almost due south, becoming West Shore Drive. The next 0.5 mile climbs a bit, but the views west into the Strait of Georgia and the Gulf Islands are grand and mostly unobstructed. Orca whales are often seen frolicking in the waters of Rosario Strait from here in the summer.

After cresting the hill, the road drops quickly, and you may feel like one of the bald eagles you're likely to see soaring the skies high above the westside bluffs as you fly down the other side. But slow down because you'll want to stop at the Willows Inn, even if you're not staying overnight. The Willows has been an inn since 1910 and, along with a restaurant featuring organic foods grown next door at the Nettles Farm, it has the Taproot Pub and Espresso, a low-ceilinged, downstairs cafe where everybody feels like a strapping six-footer. It's a great place to stop to quaff or for something to munch.

Once sated, continue south to Village Point and follow as the road heads east along Legoe Bay, the site of the island's first non-Native settlement, which dates from 1871. At the start of the 20th century, there was even a cannery there. After climbing a small hill above the bay, spot the Lummi Island Congregational Church.

Just beyond the gravel parking lot, a small sign points to the short trail to the beach, pretty much the only public beach access on the island.

Park your bike here and head down the couple-hundred-yard trail to a little slice of heaven by the sea. Chances are, it'll just be you, a forest's worth of driftwood strewn across the millions of black-, gray-, and salmon-colored cobbles and shells along the beach. Islands and sea stretch on seemingly to infinity. Orcas Island rises nearly a half-mile straight up out of Rosario Strait, looking like an impenetrable wall of timber. Watching a sunset from here is truly one of the Northwest's great pleasures.

Back on the road, it's only about a mile back to the ferry dock from the church—continue east past the church and take a left at the bottom of the hill onto Nugent Road.

EAGLE-WATCHING IN BRACKENDALE, BRITISH COLUMBIA

This trip is mostly a seasonal one, best visited from November to February, when the weather is at its worst and the need for a nice day trip is at its greatest.

Starting in November, the cottonwoods on the Squamish River about an hour north of Vancouver, B.C., are already decked out for the winter holidays. As they are each winter, the mostly bare trees are trimmed with white bulbs, sometimes two and three dozen in a single tree. Set against the rugged Tantalus Mountain Range, it's awe-inspiring, and it's an annual tradition that's gained this small town called Brackendale (population: 1,500) worldwide recognition.

Truth be told, the white "bulbs" are the heads and tails of bald eagles that flock to this area literally by the thousands. Most years, about 2,000 make the Brackendale Eagle Reserve their winter home, drawn by dying chum salmon making their way from Howe Sound up the Squamish River system, which includes the Squamish, Cheakamus, and Mamquam Rivers. (Compare that to the Skagit River about an hour south of Bellingham, which boasts one of the highest concentration of wintering eagles in the Lower 48, averaging about 400 eagles each year.)

In January 1994 at the annual eagle census, counters tallied 3,766 bald eagles along a 10-mile stretch of the Squamish, breaking the previous single-day record of 3,495 held by the Chilkat Bald Eagle Preserve in Haines, Alaska. Given that an eagle eats on average a pound of fish daily, on the day the record was broken the eagles ate two tons of fish.

Pull over just about anywhere around Brackendale and eagles are seemingly everywhere. On the sandbars and in the shallow braids of the Squamish River and its tributaries, they pick and tear at their salmon with no real urgency. They're on eagle time. Pesky seagulls and crows encircle the eagles, often outnumbering them by about 5 to 1. The gulls and crows are smart enough to stay just out of an eating eagle's way, but once an eagle is finished and flies away, they swoop in like eager busboys clearing plates.

The Brackendale Eagle Reserve is on the Squamish and Cheakamus Rivers, 36 miles north of Vancouver, B.C. (34 miles south of Whistler). From Vancouver, follow Highway 99 (Sea-to-Sky Highway) north. About 4 miles north of Squamish, turn left onto Depot Road and follow it for about 0.5 mile to Government Road. To get to the Eagle Run viewing area, turn left onto Government Road and continue for about 0.5 mile. The viewing area and parking lot are well signed.

An interesting eagle-related stop is the Brackendale Art Gallery (41950 Government Road, 604–898–3333, www.bracken daleartgallery.com) which, along with having a lot of eagle-related art as well as maps and general eagle information, boasts a nice teahouse and a small theater. To get to the gallery, turn right onto Government Road (you would turn left to get to the viewing area). The gallery is about

half a block farther on the right. Look for the giant white unicorn.

MOUNT ERIE NEAR ANACORTES

When many people think of Anacortes, they think only of the Washington State Ferry, but with Mount Erie literally in its backyard, Anacortes makes for a nice day-trip destination on its own. With trails for hiking, a summit you can drive to, and nearby lakes to dive and frolic in, the area is like a theme park for anyone who enjoys the outdoors. Visible for miles because it's more or less the first and highest hill west of the sprawling Skagit Valley, Mount Erie is the centerpiece of the 2,800-acre Anacortes Community Forest Lands.

More than 50 miles of trails snake through dense forests and wildflower meadows, past wetlands and streams, and around several lakes, making Mount Erie and its surroundings a favorite of hikers, mountain bikers, equestrians, paddlers, swimmers, and runners. Combine the fact that the 1,273-foot-high Mount Erie's diorite rock is solid and very grippy with the fact that, by being in the Olympic Rain Shadow, Erie receives a little more than half as much rain as Bellingham and Seattle, and you have all the makings of a rock-climbing hot spot. Which it is.

But Erie is not just for those who like to huff, puff, or sweat. Paved Mount Erie Road leads 1.8 miles to the summit, where scenic viewpoints afford almost 360-degree views of the Cascade and Olympic Mountains and countless tree-covered islands that rise from the Sound like stepping-stones for a giant on his way to the Pacific. It's one of the finest panoramas you'll find anywhere—you'll observe everything from the flatland farms of Skagit County to the rugged beauty of the Olympic Mountains to northern Puget Sound and practically every single one of the 428 to 743 (depending on the tide) San Juan Islands. Since early last century, the city of Anacortes has shown amazing foresight by purchasing and setting aside land (as well as having had the fortune to be gifted key tracts) that today add up to an impressive wilderness within the city limits.

Like downtown Anacortes just 2 miles north, Mount Erie is itself on an island— Fidalgo Island. It's separated from the mainland by narrow Swinomish Channel but easily accessed via Highway 20. To get there, head south on I-5 to exit 230 at Burlington and go west on Highway 20 for 11.5 miles to where Highway 20 divides. Turn left, following Highway 20 toward Whidbey Island. After 1.8 miles, turn right onto Campbell Lake Road. In another 1.6 miles, bear right onto Heart Lake Road. At another 1.3 miles, turn right at the sign for Mount Erie viewpoint. Park there to hike or ride such trails as the Sugarloaf Trail. To drive to the summit of Mount Erie, continue for a few hundred yards to Mount Erie Road on the right. The summit is 1.8 miles ahead.

For a more scenic approach along the water, take Chuckanut Drive south from Bellingham's Fairhaven district for about 15 miles to Edison–Bow Hill Road and turn right. Follow the road as it winds then eventually heads due south and in about 10 miles, intersects with Highway 20. Turn right and follow the above directions from there.

For eats and drinks, the town of Anacortes offers all you could want and more. To get there from Mount Erie, follow Heart Lake Road north for a couple miles to Commercial Street, which is Anacortes' main drag.

Detailed trail maps of Mount Erie and the Anacortes Community Forest Lands are available at the Anacortes Parks and Recreation Department at 904 Sixth Street (360-293-1918) and at the Anacortes Chamber of Commerce visitor information center at 819 Commercial Avenue (360-293-3832). The Friends of Anacortes Community Forest Lands Web site (www.friendsoftheacfl.org) provides valuable information on the park as well.

SCENIC DAY-TRIP DRIVES

A visit to Bellingham and Mount Baker is not complete without taking at least one (if not both) of the following driving tours. One is a not-too-long 15-mile bayside jaunt south along the folds and curves of Chuckanut Mountain to the Skagit Flats; the other is more of a daylong affair that involves driving the Mount Baker Highway for 57 miles to some mile-high alpine splendor.

Chuckanut Drive weaves and winds at water's edge, in and out of forest, and the lower sections offer both peek-a-boo and full-on views of Northern Puget Sound and the San Juan Islands, like countless forested jewels strewn across the water. Many visitors liken it to a mini version of Highway 1 along the Northern California coast.

The Mount Baker Highway, on the other hand, heads due east, straight for the mountains, starting near sea level in town but ending up just a skosh over 5,000 feet at Artist Point. (Most of that climbing takes place over the last 10 miles.) Along the way, visitors experience many shades of Whatcom County—from pastoral farmlands to wild rivers to dense rain forests to sleepy communities nestled in the foothills to the rugged North Cascade Mountains.

What follows are access points, listed by milepost number, to viewpoints, lodgings, restaurants, trailheads, and other points of interest. Many of these are detailed elsewhere in this book.

Chuckanut Drive (State Route 11)

The following description assumes you will be heading south from Bellingham's Fairhaven neighborhood. Once in Fairhaven, drive south on 12th Street. At the intersection with Old Fairhaven Parkway, 12th Street becomes Chuckanut Drive. The following mileposts start with 20 and count downward.

MP 20: Intersection with Cowgill Avenue. Bear left onto Chuckanut Drive.

MP 20: Fairhaven Park, one of Belling-

ham's largest and most popular parks, features a children's spray park, rose garden, ball fields, and ample meeting spaces. It's located on the Interurban Trail, with trail access north to downtown Bellingham and south to Larrabee State Park. (For more information on Fairhaven Park and the Interurban Trail, see the Parks and Trails chapter).

MP 19: Chuckanut Bay Gallery and Sculpture Garden (360–734–4885, www .chuckanutbaygallery.com), a popular gallery that features works from more than 300 Northwest artists. (See The Arts chapter.)

MP 19: Lake Samish Road (on the left). Arroyo Park, a densely wooded gorge, and Interurban Trail parking are just ahead on the right.

MP 19: North Chuckanut Mountain Trailhead. There's also a large parking area for Arroyo Park, Interurban Trail, and Teddy Bear Cove. (See the Parks and Trails chapter.)

MP 16: Hiline Road (also called Cleator Road). Here is yet another parking area and access for the Interurban Trail. This logging road also climbs about 4 miles to the top of Chuckanut Mountain. The road-end parking lot features spectacular views of the San Juan Islands and Puget Sound.

MP 15: Fragrance Lake Trail (on the left) and Larrabee State Park (on the right). The 2-mile trail climbs through dense forest to a gentle minialpine pond, and the park offers campground and salt-water access, not to mention amazing rock sculptures that the waters of Puget Sound have been working on for thousands of millennia. A $5.00 State Park day-use fee is required to park here.

MP 15: Clayton Beach Trailhead Parking Area. A half-mile trail leads to sandy beach, amazing rock formations, and cool tide pools. A parking area on the left requires a $5.00 State Park day-use fee. Look for free, marked parking spaces on the right side of the road. (See the Parks and Trails chapter.)

MP 13: Heritage Marker pullout. The spacious parking area on the right has great views across Samish Bay to Anacortes and San Juan Islands. An inter-

pretive sign tells Chuckanut Drive's history—completed in 1896, a 3-mile section of the road was illegally sold to the Great North Railway in 1901 and was impassable until 1910. From 1913 to 1931, it was part of the Pacific Highway that stretched from San Diego to Vancouver, British Columbia. Today, as then, it's a great place to watch the sunset.

MP 13: Fossils! About 50 yards south of the Heritage Marker parking area is a smaller unmarked pullout area. Park here and, very carefully, cross Chuckanut Drive and walk right (south) for about 10 yards to an obvious rock outcrop tattooed with imprints of ancient palm fronds.

MP 12: Another big pullout parking area with sound and island views. There's also interpretive signage on the area's clamming and fishing history.

MP 11: Hairpin turn to the Taylor Shellfish Farm and Oyster Creek Inn. Taylor Shellfish harvests everything from oysters to clams to mussels to geoducks. Next door's Oyster Creek Inn, a true mecca for seafood lovers, has been perched atop this salmon-rich creek for some 70 years. (See the Restaurants chapter.)

MP 11: Oyster Bar. About 0.5 mile south of the hairpin turn, sits the Oyster Bar Restaurant, another very popular Chuckanut Drive seafood eatery that has terrific sunset views, too. (See the Restaurants chapter.)

MP 10: Bat Caves Trailhead. Pullout parking is on the right just before milepost 10 for this strenuous trail up Blanchard Mountain. Sweeping views of the San Juans, Samish Bay, and the Skagit Flats await those who put tread to trail. (See the Parks and Trails chapter.)

MP 10: Chuckanut Manor Restaurant. This is the third in the trio of Chuckanut Drive's super seafood eateries, and it's also a bed-and-breakfast.

MP 10: Chuckanut Ridge Wine Company, which produces quality local wines. It's open for tastings on Friday, Saturday, and Sunday.

MP 10: Skagit Flats. Once you cross the bridge, you're no longer riding across the flanks of the Chuckanuts. You're in the flat-lands, just a skosh above sea level. Keep your eyes peeled for swans, eagles, snowy owls, and various raptors.

MP 10: Karma Place, Japanese Garden and Nursery, an amazing nursery and Japanese garden that's a true spot of tran-quility.

MP 7: Rhododendron Café, a terrific cafe and restaurant in the Skagit flatlands that features foods from around the world. It also has a gift shop with works from Northwest artists, and it's located at the corner of Chuckanut Drive and Bow Hill Road.

Chuckanut Drive continues another 7 largely pastoral miles south to I-5 exit 231 in Burlington.

Mount Baker Highway (State Route 542)
The following description assumes you will be heading east on Sunset Drive, which becomes the Mount Baker Highway just east of Hannegan Road. For more information on the Mount Baker Highway, including the current conditions, go to www.wsdot.wa.gov/traffic/passes and click on "Mount Baker Highway," or call (800) 695-7623.

MP 10: Nugent's Corner, a small com-munity with a grocery, a bakery, and an espresso stand.

MP 11: Various U-Pick berry and U-cut Christmas tree farms, and the Mount Baker Vineyards.

MP 12: Small town of Deming, where you'll find the Nooksack River Casino, gas stations, cafes, a bakery, a deli, a restaurant and a library. (See the Attractions chapter.)

MP 15: Truck Road. Turn here to reach Deming Homestead Eagle Park, about a half-mile ahead. (See the Other Outdoor Recreation chapter.)

MP 16: Mosquito Lake Road, where you can enjoy bald eagle viewing from Novem-ber to February. Park about three-quarters of a mile ahead on the right. (See the Other Outdoor Recreation chapter.)

MP 20: The North Fork Brewery, Pizze-ria, Beer Shrine and Wedding Chapel, a cool, casual eatery that brews its own

beers and barleywines. It has a roadside tavern feel, top of the line pizza, and beer tastings. (See the Nightlife chapter.)

MP 25: Maple Falls. This small town has restaurants, cafes, a tavern or two, a post office, and the Maple Falls Wash-a-Ton, a combination market, gas station, and laun-dromat. This is the last gas station on the highway, by the way. Silver Lake Park, a popular camping and day-use park, is 3 miles north on Silver Lake Road. (See the Parks and Trails chapter.)

MP 33: The sleepy, 4-square-block town of Glacier which, despite its small size, has much to offer in the food, lodg-ing, and essentials departments. The world-famous Mount Baker Snowboard Shop is here, as is Milano's Restaurant and Deli and Graham's Store and Restaurant, which makes a great end-of-day stop for ice cream. (See the Restaurants chapter.)

MP 33: Glacier Public Service Center (360-599-2714). Stop here for the latest trail conditions, to purchase a Northwest Forest Pass, or to pick up area-related maps, postcards, or books. The center's stone and cedar-shingled building was built in 1939 by the Civilian Conservation Corps and is on the National Register of Historic Places. The center is open daily from Memorial Day to mid-November and on some weekends the rest of the year.

MP 34: Glacier Creek Road (Forest Road 39). This mostly paved road climbs 9 miles to the popular Heliotrope Ridge Trail, and about a mile beyond that to a picnic area and viewpoint with jaw-dropping views of Mount Baker, just 4 air miles away. (That's 2 miles closer to the mountain than Artist Point, at the end of the Mount Baker Area.) This road is not plowed year-round but its upper reaches are usually free of snow from mid-July to late September. Check with the ranger at the Glacier Public Service Center (see above) for the latest conditions.

MP 35: Enter Mount Baker-Snoqualmie National Forest.

MP 35: Douglas Fir Campground. Located just across the Nooksack River bridge on the left, the campground also

Glacier Public Service Center. MIKE MCQUAIDE

has a day-use picnic area. (See the Other Outdoor Recreation chapter.)

MP 40: Nooksack Falls. Turn right onto Wells Creek Road (Forest Road 33) and in a little more than a half-mile, you'll reach a parking lot just before a bridge. The falls are to the right. Listen; you can't miss them. Obey all signs and stay behind the fence while viewing. (See the Parks and Trails chapter.)

MP 43: North Fork Nooksack Research Natural Area. This is an easy forest walk with roadside access through ancient trees, some more than 700 years old.

MP 46: Silver Fir Campground, which also has a day-use picnic area. (See the

Other Outdoor Recreation chapter.)

MP 47: The Mount Baker Highway begins climbing in earnest, gaining 3,000 feet over the next 10 winding, snaking miles. There are steep drops and no guardrails; the scenery is spectacular but keep your eyes on the road!

MP 52: Mount Baker Ski Area White Salmon Day Lodge. (The lower lodge, which is closed in the off-season. (See the Other Outdoor Recreation chapter.)

MP 53: Enter Heather Meadows. A Northwest Forest Pass ($5.00 for day-use, $30.00 for seasonal) is required to park along the remainder of the highway. (See the Parks and Trails chapter.)

Nooksack Falls. MIKE MCQUAIDE

MP 54: Picture and Highwood Lakes, offering stunning views of Mount Shuksan and its reflection. This spot is a photographer's dream. Mountains, meadows, lakes, and wildflowers—it's all here. Paved trail and picnic tables make it perfect for families. Park along the wide shoulder. (See the Parks and Trails chapter.)

MP 54: Mount Baker Ski Area Heather Meadows Day Lodge. (The upper lodge, which is closed in the off-season.) From sometime in October until sometime in July, the Mount Baker Highway closes just beyond the upper parking lot here because of heavy snowpack. (See the Other Outdoor Recreation chapter.)

The following highway mileposts are applicable only during the summer months that the last 3 miles are open.

MP 55: Heather Meadows Visitor Center and Austin Pass Picnic Area. Staffed by Forest Service employees and volunteers, the center offers interpretive displays, guided walks, and a gift shop. It's open from mid-July through late fall. Outside, you'll find interpretive signs and trailheads for the Wild Goose, Bagley Lakes, Fire and Ice, and Chain Lakes Trails. (See the Parks and Trails chapter.)

MP 56: Lake Ann Trailhead. This trail leads to a magical alpine lake and stunning front-row views of Mount Shuksan. (See the Parks and Trails chapter.)

The best views from Glacier Creek Road are actually about a quarter-mile before the road-end viewpoint and picnic area. Trees at the picnic spot have become overgrown and block the best views.

MP 57: Artist Point, the end of the Mount Baker Highway, and pretty much smack in the middle of the mountains. To the south, Mount Baker is just 6 air miles away; to the east, Mount Shuksan is less than half that. At 5,100 feet, Artist Point is one of the highest points accessible by road in the state, but it's accessible only for part of the year. In winters it's piled under by 25-plus feet of snow, and the only way to get here is with snowshoes or backcountry skis. Even in August, there are usually some lingering snow patches, which make for great August snowball-fight photos.

Hiking options here are numerous. There's Artist Ridge for closer views of Mount Shuksan, Ptarmigan Ridge to get close to Baker, Chain Lakes for alpine ponds hidden by the great prow of Table Mountain, and Table Mountain for that top-of-the-world feeling. There's also a short, barrier-free paved path for those needing assistance. (See the Parks and Trails chapter.)

WEEKEND GETAWAYS

In addition to having a great many worthwhile destinations within about two hours of Bellingham, several places just a little farther away make for terrific weekend getaways. Eastern Washington, across Highway 20 or State Route 2, is a land of bright sunshine, ponderosa pines, about a third as much rainfall as the west side (often called the "wet" side), and some charming towns with abundant recreation, shopping, and cultural opportunities.

To the north in beautiful British Columbia sits the world-class, year-round resort town of Whistler. And of course the San Juan Islands, a seeming collection of oversize evergreen jewels out there in Northern Puget Sound, aren't far away.

WHISTLER

More than 40 years ago, a handful of Vancouver, B.C., movers and shakers decided to open a ski resort in the hopes of one day drawing the Winter Olympics. Nice idea, but the site they chose—a remote, glaciated massif called London Mountain 75 miles north of Vancouver—had between not much and absolutely nothing going for it. No road to get in or out, no water, no electricity, no sewers. The last was no big deal though, because no one lived there anyway.

Fast forward to the 2000s, however, and London Mountain, since renamed Whistler in a nod to the whistling marmots who make the mountain's upper reaches their home, perennially tops or is near the top of every ski and snowboard mag's list of North America's best ski resorts (866–218–9690, www.whistlerblackcomb.com). The reasons: two huge mountains boasting 5,000-plus feet of vertical with ski and snowboard runs up to 7 miles long;

more than 100 restaurants, bars, and bistros; and hotels, condos, bed-and-breakfasts, and other accommodations that add up to 5,400-plus rooms. (In 2004, a 273-room Four Seasons Resort Whistler opened, just the second foray into the ski resort world for this posh and prestigious hotel chain.)

And in 2010, the nearly 50-year-old dream of those early visionaries will become reality when Whistler hosts the lion's share of snow events in the Vancouver Winter Olympics. (See the Close-up in this chapter for more details.)

But Whistler is more than just winter. In summers, when the snow finally melts, those ski and snowboard trails on Whistler-Blackcomb, as the ski area is officially called, transform themselves into more than 100 miles of trails for lift-serviced hiking, mountain biking, hiking, and sightseeing, included guided nature walks. And down in Whistler village and the surrounding valley, myriad golfing, river rafting, fishing, kayaking, and canoeing opportunities await, as well as numerous kids' activities.

Whistler is located about 75 miles north of Vancouver, thus about 125 miles north of Bellingham. Something to keep in mind, however, if you're planning a trip to Whistler is the $600 million worth of work being done between now and 2009 to accommodate anticipated Olympics traffic. Much of the road will be widened, straightened where possible, and otherwise improved to cut the travel time by 15 minutes for the 75-mile drive between Vancouver and Whistler. For now, though, it's a different story. Expect delays—up to an hour at certain times of the day and night. Thankfully, the Web site www.seatosky improvements.ca offers up-to-date information on the delays.

Whistler.

Whistler-Blackcomb and the Olympics

WHISTLER-BLACKCOMB STATS:

Elevation: Whistler Mountain, 2,214-7,160 feet; Blackcomb, 2,214-7,494 feet.

Lifts: 37 (both mountains). Blackcomb: one high-speed gondola, six high-speed quads, three triple chairs, seven surface lifts. Whistler: two high-speed gondolas, six high-speed quads, two triples, one double, nine surface lifts.

Lift prices: Whistler and Blackcomb: $72 for an adult; $62 for those age 13 to 18 and older than 65; $38 for those age 7 to 12, and free for children 6 and younger. (All prices in Canadian dollars.)

Opening day: Usually around November 25.

Closing Day: Early June.

Operating hours: Midweek 9:00 A.M. to 3:00 P.M., weekends 8:30 A.M. to 3:00 P.M. Open until 3:30 P.M. or later beginning at the end of January.

Lodging: A wide range available, including hotels, motels, condominiums, rental homes, and bed-and-breakfasts. Call (888) 403-4727 or go to www.whistler blackcomb.com and click on "Accommodation."

Child Care: Offered daily 8:30 A.M. to 4:30 P.M. Reservations are required for infants, and recommended for children 2 years of age and older.

Mountain information: Whistler-Blackcomb: (604) 932-3434; toll-free within **North America:** (866) 218-9690.

Snow phone: (604) 932-4211.

Web site: www.whistlerblackcomb.com.

For information on Sea to Sky Highway delays and work closures, check www.seatoskyimprovements.ca.

The 2010 Winter Olympics will take place from February 12 to February 28. All downhill ski events, bobsled, luge, and skeleton will take place at Whistler-Blackcomb. Nordic events (cross-country skiing, etc.) and ski jumping will be in the Callaghan Valley, south of Whistler at the Whistler Nordic Centre, which will be constructed over the next five years.

Opening and closing ceremonies and ice events—skating, hockey, curling—will be in Vancouver, with snowboarding and freestyle skiing events at Cypress Mountain ski resort in West Vancouver. Hockey and skating events will take place at the Pacific Coliseum and GM Palace. For more information, including ticketing information, go to www.winter2010.com.

LEAVENWORTH

Located 100 miles east of Everett via Highway 2 (which is itself 60 miles south of Bellingham via Interstate 5), Leavenworth is a charming, Bavarian-themed burg on the sunny (as in 300 days of sun each year), dry, and often hot side of the Cascades. It's a true indoor-outdoor wonderland. Along with boasting more than 150 unique shops and galleries, 45 restaurants, and more than 100 lodging facilities—many German influenced and all with storefronts/exteriors boasting a Bavarian feel (including the town's McDonald's and Starbuck's)—Leavenworth is beloved for its riches of outdoor opportunities.

The Wenatchee River flows through town and in summers is littered with kayakers, rafters, tubers, and lollygaggers by the thousands. The Icicle Creek Canyon, which starts literally at the edge of town, has some of the best hiking and backpacking in the West (highlighted by the Alpine Lakes Wilderness), as well as primo rock climbing and camping opportunities. Mountain and road biking are popular too, and Leavenworth's climate ensures plenty of dry sunny days on the area's four golf courses. (At the town's open-air theater on a hillside overlooking the town and the nearby mountain ranges, one can even attend live performances of, what else, *The Sound of Music*.)

In winter, Leavenworth is ideal for cross-country skiing in Icicle Canyon and downhilling at the way-small, in-town Norman Rockwellesque ski hill that boasts its own ski jump. In general, the town itself goes winter crazy, as all buildings are adorned with millions of tiny twinkling white lights. Christkindlemarkt is just one of many festivals and events that take place during the winter months.

But Leavenworth hasn't always been a town best known for its Oktoberfests, Nutcracker Museum (the only all-nutcracker museum in the United States), International Accordian Celebration, and all-around Bavarian schtick. A former boomtown living high off the timber and railroad industries, Leavenworth was hit hard by the Great Depression. Logging companies, looking for more profitable areas, moved out and the sawmill closed. The formerly Leavenworth-based Great Northern Railroad moved its headquarters to Wenatchee, and the town was in dire straits for decades.

But you know what they say: When the going gets tough, the tough get lederhosen. In the mid-1960s, as a way to draw tourists and therefore tourist dollars, community leaders decided to take advantage of the town's Alps-like setting and reinvent itself as a mini-Bavaria. It worked. Today Leavenworth draws more than two million

The North Cascades Highway, State Route 20, closes each November because of snowfall. It opens again sometime in April or whenever the snow level allows. In winter, for people in Bellingham, this means heading south to Everett, east to Wenatchee, north to Twisp and finally to Winthrop, turning what is a summertime three-hour drive into a wintertime six-hour excursion.

visitors each year and is a tourist Mecca.

For information on Leavenworth, contact the Leavenworth Chamber of Commerce at (509) 548–5807 or www.leavenworth.org.

WINTHROP/METHOW VALLEY

For the closest thing you'll get to a visit to the Old West, head to Winthrop and the surrounding Methow Valley. In the early 1970s when the North Cascades Highway was about to be completed and would open up Winthrop, the Methow Valley, and the rest of this part of eastern Washington to west-siders, Winthrop town leaders sought a way to distinguish their small town near the confluence of the Methow and Chewuch Rivers. They hit on the idea of an Old West theme and instantly had a winner.

Instead of sidewalks, Winthrop boasts vintage boardwalks with hitching posts, and all shops, restaurants, and tourist lodgings are decked out in wooden 1880s false facades like something from an episode of *Gunsmoke*. Winthrop's setting—sagebrush and sunflower mountain ridges, dry pine forests, and sparkling lakes and rivers—furthers the Old West effect. As do local annual events such as May's Winthrop '49ers Days festival and August's Oldtime Fiddlers Contest, as well as various rodeos, cowboy jamborees, and square dances held throughout the year. (July's Winthrop

---

Owen Wister, who wrote The Virginian, *America's first Old West novel, honeymooned here and wrote his book shortly afterward. Much of the settings and events in the book are based on experiences Wister had or heard about here in Winthrop.*

Rhythm and Blues Festival, though not Western-themed, is one of the town's biggest events.) Today, though about 400 people call Winthrop their year-round home, more than 600,000 visitors drop in each year.

But as outdoor enthusiasts know, there's lots more to Winthrop than just cowboys and false-front buildings. With its abundant sunshine and wintertime cold temps and powder dry snow, the Methow (pronounced "Met-how") Valley is renowned as a cross-country skier's and snowshoer's wonderland. Managed and maintained by the Methow Valley Sport Trails Association (MVSTA), more than 130 miles of groomed trails crisscross the area, making it a mecca for Nordic types throughout the Northwest.

That's winter. The rest of the year, the MVSTA maintains almost 100 miles of those trails for mountain bikers, equestrians, hikers, and runners. It's become a hotbed for mountain bikers, and events such as the annual Winthrop Boneshaker MTB Bash and the Methow Valley Mountain Bike Festival draw the knobby-tired set from throughout the region.

The MVSTA has its origins in the late 1970s when a few lodging businesses in three valley areas—Mazama, Rendezvous, and Sun Mountain—needed to come up with a way to stay open past Labor Day. They hit on the idea of attracting cross-country skiers by grooming a few kilometers of ski trails. When that was a success, they took the next step of establishing trails that connected all three areas, the farthest of which—Mazama and Sun Mountain—are almost 20 miles apart.

That drew more skiers, all of whom needed a place to stay, which drew new lodges, cabins, motels, and eateries. Those businesses wanted more trails built, which of course drew more skiers. In the 1980s, the MVSTA began sponsoring biking and running events, which attracted year-round business and businesses.

For information on places to stay in Winthrop and the surrounding Methow Valley, call the Winthrop Chamber of Commerce at (509) 996–2125 or (888) 463–8469, or visit www.winthropwashington.com. Or just stay at the Sun Mountain Lodge (www.sunmountainlodge.com), basically top-of-the-food-chain digs with spectacular rooms, stunning vistas, and super access to the trails. For more information on the Methow Valley Sport Trails Association and its events, call (509) 996–3287 or visit www.mvsta.com.

SAN JUAN ISLANDS

Though there are some 173 named San Juan Islands, just four of them are served year-round by the Washington State ferry system (888–808–7977, www.wsdot.wa.gov/ferries). These are drive-on, bike-on, or walk-on ferries, which leave from the Washington State Ferry terminal in Anacortes. (To get there, head south on I-5 to exit 230, and head west on Highway 20 for about 16 miles to Anacortes, following the ferry terminal signs. Once in town, turn left onto 12th Street, and the ferry terminal is about 4 miles ahead.)

Lopez, Shaw, Orcas, and San Juan Islands are each forested gems, and each has its own unique charm. Situated in the Olympic rain shadow, the islands receive about two-thirds as much rain as more inland places such as Bellingham and Seattle. Lopez Island is the friendly one, where it seems that no one passes by without waving. Shaw Island is tiny and rarely visited, with just a single general store as its only commercial enterprise, thus it's the place to get to if you want to get away. Orcas is the largest island, with the most

varied terrain, including the Mount Constitution viewpoint, the highest point in the
islands. San Juan has the hustle and bustle
(kinda) of the islands' biggest town Friday Harbor—as well as the best chance of
seeing orca whales from land. Lopez,
Orcas, and San Juan Islands all have many
places to stay, from campgrounds to bed-
and-breakfasts to posh resorts, fine restaurants, and unique shops and galleries.

The first stop on the ferry and only
about 35 minutes from Anacortes, Lopez is
often called Slow-pez for its slow pace.
Largely agricultural, with rural country
roads popular with bicyclists, Lopez has
several tidewater parks and, despite its
small size with only 2,200 year-round residents, a big community spirit. The annual
Tour de Lopez bike ride in April and Fourth
of July celebration bring out lots of colorful costumes, irreverence, and local charac
ter. Lopez Village, the island's one and only
town, is about 3 miles from the ferry landing. Here, one can fine places to eat (Love
Dog Café, 360–468–2150), spend the night
(Lopez Islander Resort, 800–736–3434,
www.lopezislander.com), and rent a bicycle
(Lopez Bicycle Works, 360–468–2847,
www.lopezbicycleworks.com). For camping, seaside Spencer Spit State Park
(360–902–8844, www.parks.wa.gov) is a
can't-go-wrong. Contact the Lopez Island
Chamber at (360) 468–4664 or www
.lopezisland.com for more information.

Shaw Island is usually the second ferry
stop and certainly the quickest. Only 220
people live here year-round and, with only
the 11-site Shaw Island County Park
(360–378–1842) campground to attract
visitors, Shaw doesn't have much tourism
volume. Still, the peace, the quiet, and the
tranquility make this a worthwhile stop.

In direct contrast to Shaw are Orcas
and San Juan Islands, which draw the lion's
share of San Juan Islands' tourists. Orcas is
the biggest in size and shaped like a giant
horseshoe. Its crowning glory is 5,252-acre
Moran State Park (360–376–2326, www
.parks.wa.gov), with its myriad lakes, trails,
campgrounds, and Mount Constitution, the
highest point in the San Juan Islands, at

2,409 feet high. In a region with no short-
age of amazing vistas, the 360-degree
panorama from the viewing tower might
just be the best. Mount Baker to Rainier to
Vancouver to Bellingham to the Olympic
Mountain to pretty much anything that
comes to mind when you think of the
Northwest—you can see it from here. At
least it sure seems that way.

In the top of the horseshoe is Eastsound, Orcas Island's largest town and a
place to find lots to eat, places to sleep,
and shops to browse. Eastsound is about 8
miles from the ferry landing, and on the
way into town, explore the island's rolling
hills and country roads that pass llama
farms, yoga retreats, and funky galleries.
Just outside Moran State Park, Rosario
Resort and Spa (360 376–2222, 866–
801–ROCK, www.rosario.rockresorts.com)
offers upscale accommodations on a hillside overlooking the water. For more information on Orcas Island, contact the Orcas
Island Chamber of Commerce at (360)
376–8888 or www.orcasislandchamber
.com.

The busiest, and the last of the four
ferry-served islands, is San Juan Island.
Though a little smaller than Orcas in land-
mass, San Juan has the island's only incorporated city, Friday Harbor, and more
year-round residents (about 7,000) than
the other three islands combined. But the
island's temporary residents are probably
its most well-known. Each year about 90

orca whales make the waters of Haro Strait on the west side of the island their home, where they spy-hop, breach, and lob-tail in all their glory and draw tourists by the hundreds of thousands. Lime Kiln Point State Park (www.parks.wa.gov) is a wonderful, rocky day-use park that's one of the best on-land places in the world from which to spot whales. Or if you'd rather get out in the water with them, numerous kayak outfitters (Elakah Expeditions, 800–434–7270, www.elakah.com) and whale-watch boats (Maya's Whale Watch Charters, 360–378–7996, www.mayas whalewatch.biz) are more than willing to offer up-close and personal orca views.

The ferry lands in Friday Harbor itself, which is nice for walk-ons, who can then rent bicycles (Island Bicycles, 360–378–4941, www.islandbicycles.com) or mopeds (Susie's Mopeds, 360–378–5244, 800–532–0087, www.susiesmopeds.com) to explore the island. The town itself is home to many nice eateries, terrific shops and galleries, and the popular Whale Museum (62 First Street North, 360–378–4710, www.whale-museum.org). Roche Harbor (www.roche harbor.com), at the island's northwest corner, boasts the Hotel de Haro, built in 1886 and maintained in a grand turn-of-the-century style. For more information on San Juan Island, contact the San Juan Island Chamber of Commerce at (360) 378–5240 or www.sanjuanisland.org.

RELOCATION 🏠

Any discussion about relocating to Bellingham has to begin with two things: the booming real estate market and a labor force that's undergoing somewhat of a transformation.

Like many towns on the West Coast since just about the most recent turn of the century, Bellingham's housing market has exploded. Between 2000 and late 2005, home prices jumped 70 percent to an average price of about $325,000. The biggest climb was between 2004 and 2005 when home prices rose 23 percent. As of press time, they were continuing to escalate.

The area's vaunted quality of life, with mountains, water, and forests everywhere, and the fact that it's a West Coast university town that's appeared on numerous Top 10 lists as one of the best places to live, recreate, play golf, retire (you pick) are just a couple reasons why so many are choosing to make Bellingham their new home. Ironically, Bellingham's relative affordability was one of the things drawing people here also. But even with the recent housing boom, Bellingham prices are still below other West Coast cities such as Seattle, San Francisco, and Santa Cruz.

That relative affordability has drawn many retirees from California as well as Golden Staters who made their money during the tech boom of the late 1990s and are now buying homes where they can get the most for their money. In 2005, one real estate agent told me that 9 out of every 10 people they take to look at houses is from California.

A lot of those people moving here are folks who lived here during their college days at Western Washington University and vowed that if they ever got established to the point that they could live here permanently, they'd do so in a heartbeat. So there are folks with money. Telecommuters and people who are able to work

via the Internet and aren't tied to an office are also moving here.

That alludes to the one thing that's lamented about a lot in Bellingham: the lack of high-paying jobs. Unemployment is low in Bellingham, but there are a lot of people who are underemployed. One thing you hear people say is that Bellingham has more espresso baristas who have Master's degrees than just about anywhere. Many folks who move here have to take into consideration how much Bellingham's vaunted quality of life is worth to them—is being able to ski, hike, paddle, sail, camp, etc. in one of the most beautiful spots in the country, as well as being able to enjoy all the cultural advantages of living in a university town less than 90 minutes from two great cosmopolitan areas, worth making perhaps not quite as much money as one can make elsewhere? There is not a lot of major industry here, and what industry there is has mostly undergone cutbacks in recent years.

Formerly focused on fishing, logging, heavy industry, and farming, the labor force is much more diversified now. Retail, tourism, health care, the service industry, and education form the economic backbone these days. The median household income for people living in Bellingham and Whatcom County is about $42,000; the state average is about $51,000.

Bellingham might not be for everyone. It's a progressive university town, a bit left-leaning and a bit bookish. Every Friday afternoon at the downtown intersection of Commercial and Magnolia Streets, there's a peaceful demonstration focused usually on whatever the latest governmental agenda is in the news, whether it be the war in Iraq or a local move to fluoridate the town's water supply. (In 2005, voters turned down the fluoride initiative.) Taxpayers vote millions of dollars to buy up prime parcels of land along the waterfront and elsewhere, which they then turn into parks and trails so that everyone can enjoy them. Bumper stickers seen around town decry development.

That said, construction in Bellingham is booming, with much of it focused on infilling—building up instead of sprawling out—in downtown Bellingham and Fairhaven. As of late 2005, the tallest building was the 14-story Bellingham Towers built in the late 1920s. But plans were in the works for several 18- and 20-story buildings—condos with commercial enterprises on lower floors—in both downtown Bellingham, Fairhaven, and even just north of the city. Which brings us to where newcomers to Bellingham are moving and what they can expect to pay.

That $325,000 average price for a three-bedroom, two-bath house increases significantly if there's a water view, whether it's the waters of Bellingham Bay or Lake Whatcom. So neighborhoods such as Edgemoor ($575,000), on the hills above the bay just south of Fairhaven; South Hill ($600,000), on the hillside above Fairhaven and extending toward Western Washington University; Alabama Hill ($475,000), near Lake Whatcom with views overlooking much of the city; Geneva ($475,000), on the south side of Lake Whatcom, and Silver Beach ($425,000), on the lake's north side, tend to be the most pricy. (The priciest, however, are in the Chuckanut area, south of Fairhaven. Nestled in the woods on the flanks of Chuckanut Mountain overlooking Chuckanut Bay are homes that routinely go for $2 million-plus.)

Median- and lower-priced neighborhoods include older in-city ones such as the Lettered Streets ($275,000), just north of downtown and the oldest neighborhood in the city; Columbia ($325,000), just beyond the Lettered Streets; the York neighborhood ($300,000), just east of downtown and on the bay side of Interstate 5; Happy Valley ($275,000) on the South Side between Fairhaven and the freeway; and Fairhaven ($350,000). That Fairhaven price, however, doesn't include the new high-rise condos, many which have spectacular water views. (These have been going for a half-million dollars and more.)

Roosevelt ($250,000) and Sunnyland ($250,000), on the east and west sides of the freeway, respectively, and at the north end of town, are among Bellingham's lowest-priced neighborhoods.

For more house for about the same price—or same house at a lower price—many buyers head for areas on the outskirts of Bellingham's city limits. Sudden Valley, about 8 miles east of downtown Bellingham on the south side of Lake Whatcom, is one such place. Three-, four-, and sometimes even five-bedroom homes here with a much bigger lot than you'd find in Bellingham can be had for $300,000. Even better deals can be found in Glenhaven, about 5 miles beyond Sudden Valley, where three-bedroom homes go for about $225,000.

New subdivisions just north and northeast of Bellingham promise similar deals—more house, more land, for the same or slightly less price than you'll find in town. That's true of outlying towns in Whatcom County such as Ferndale and Lynden. In general, the farther one gets from the city, and thus city services and conveniences, the less expensive the homes.

As for those looking for rental properties, expect to pay about $500 to $700 per month for a one-bedroom apartment, and $900 to $1,200 for a three-bedroom house. This is a college town, so summer is the best time to look for a place.

REAL ESTATE AGENCIES

Coldwell Banker
3610 Meridian Street
(360) 734-3420
www.coldwellbankermiller.com
The local office of the national real estate company offers everything you need to relocate—from mortgage to appraisal to finding reputable contractors for new building projects to even supplying a list

of potential babysitters for families new to the area.

John L. Scott
2930 Newmarket Street, Suite 111
(360) 671-9640
www.johnlscott.com
In business since 1931, John L. Scott has 129 offices in Washington, Oregon, and Idaho. A full-service agency, Scott offers Compass Relocation Service, which assists long-distance buyers with moving, storage, and securing interim rental housing if needed.

Johnson Real Estate Team
1215 Old Fairhaven Parkway, Suite E
(360) 527-8766, (888) 713-3056
www.johnsonteamrealestate.com
A full-service agency, the Johnson Team, as they're known, even have their own moving truck to help out with your move. This is a family operation, with three Johnsons on the team.

Misty Mountains Realty, Inc.
8193 Kendall Road, Maple Falls
(360) 599-2093
www.mistymtsrealty.com
Misty Mountain focuses on residential and vacation properties in eastern Whatcom County, especially the Maples Falls-Glacier area at the edge of the Mount Baker–Snoqualmie National Forest. It offers homes and lots in both Snowline and Glacier Springs, the two gated communities in the area.

Mt. Baker Homes and Land, Inc.
9937 Mount Baker Highway, Glacier
(360) 599-1900
www.mtbakerhomesandland.com
Working the Maple Falls–Glacier area for more than 30 years, this company also deals in vacant land at the edge of the National Forest for future residences or vacation homes. As with Misty Mountains, Mount Baker Homes deals in homes and properties that are as close as one can get to the Mount Baker Ski Area.

Re/Max Whatcom County
913 Lakeway Drive
(360) 647-1313, (800) 723-1313
www.nwhomes.net
This full-service agency opened in 1991 and has five offices throughout Whatcom County—Bellingham, Sudden Valley, Ferndale, Lynden, and Point Roberts. One of the area's fastest-growing agencies, Re/Max Whatcom County offers mortgage, home warranty, and relocation services along with working directly with builders on new homes. The agency also deals in commercial properties.

Windermere Real Estate Whatcom
515 W. Bakerview Road
(360) 734-7500
www.windermerewhatcom.com
With four Whatcom County offices in the Bellingham area—Bellingham, Lynden, Blaine, and a kiosk at Bellis Fair Mall—Windermere is a full-service agency with a commercial division as well.

Wm. T. Follis, LLC, Realtors
108 Prospect Street
(360) 734-5850
www.follisrealtors.com
A true family-run business, Follis was founded in 1921 by William T. Follis Sr. and it has had at least one Follis or another on staff ever since. (Currently, there are two Follises on staff.) So, along with offering the full range of real estate services, including property management, Follis has one of the longest histories in local real estate.

LICENSES

Driver's licenses: Newcomers must apply for a driver's license within 30 days of becoming a Washington resident. The legal age to obtain a Washington State driver's license is 16. A first-time license costs $45, and it's good for five years. Renewals cost $25 and are good for five years.

You are also required to register your vehicle within 30 days of becoming a resident. This costs $30. Contact the licensing division of the Whatcom County Auditors Office at (360) 676-6740 for more information.

Tabs are required for your auto's rear license plate. They display the month and year of your car registration renewal. For more information contact the Department of Licensing at 3800 Byron Avenue, Suite 136, (360) 676-2097.

Auto Inspections: Car inspections are not required in Washington.

Registering to vote: All voting in Whatcom County is now done by mail-in ballot. You may register to vote at anytime by calling the Whatcom County Auditor at (360) 676-6742. In order to vote in an upcoming election, your mail-in registration form must be postmarked 30 days before the election or you must register in person at least 15 days prior to the election.

ECONOMIC/DEMOGRAPHIC INFORMATION

Bellingham/Whatcom
Chamber of Commerce and Industry
1201 Cornwall Avenue, Suite 100
(360) 734-1330
www.bellingham.com

Bellingham/Whatcom
County Convention and Visitors Bureau
904 Potter Street
(360) 671-3990
www.bellingham.org

Bellingham Whatcom
Economic Development Council
105 East Holly Street
(360) 676-4255, (800) 810-4255
www.bwedc.org

Birch Bay Chamber of Commerce
4880 Beachcomber Drive, Suite C
Birch Bay
(360) 371-5004
www.birchbaychamber.com

Blaine Chamber of Commerce
728 Peace Portal Drive, Blaine
(360) 332-4544, (800) 624-3555
www.blainechamber.com

Everson Nooksack
Chamber of Commerce
P.O. Box 234
Everson, 98247
(360) 966-3407
www.eversonnooksackchamber.org

Ferndale Chamber of Commerce
5640 Riverside Drive, Ferndale
(360) 384-3042
www.ferndale-chamber.com

Lynden Chamber of Commerce
518 Front Street, Lynden
(360) 354-5995
www.lynden.org

Mt. Baker Foothills
Chamber of Commerce
P.O. Box 866, Maple Falls 98266
(360) 599-1518
www.mtbakerchamber.org

Point Roberts Chamber of Commerce
P.O. Box 128, Point Roberts 98281
(360) 945-2313
www.pointrobertschamber.com

Sumas Chamber of Commerce
(360) 988-2028
www.sumaschamber.com

SUPPORT GROUPS

Adoptive Parent Support Group
(360) 647-2643

Alcoholics Anonymous
(360) 734-1688

Cancer Support—All Adult Cancer Group
(360) 738-6701

Caregivers Support Group
(360) 715-6410

Down Syndrome Outreach
(360) 384-9518

Family and Friends of Cancer Patients
(360) 738-6701

Fibromyalgia Education and Support
Group
(360) 715-6420

Heart Disease (CARDIAC) Support
Group
(360) 738-6719

HIV/AIDS Support Group
(360) 671-0703

Manic Depression & Depressive Support
Group of Whatcom County
(360) 733-1627

National Multiple Sclerosis Society
(800) 344-4867

Parkinson's Disease Support Group
(360) 724-3382

Sexual Assault Support Group
(360) 715-563

Survivors of Suicide
(360) 738-9539

Women's Cancer Support Group
(360) 734-3314

RESOURCES FOR RESEARCH

Center for Pacific Northwest Studies
Goltz-Murray Archives Building,
Western Washington University
Bellingham
(360) 650-7747
www.acadweb.wwu.edu/cpnws

Northwest Indian College
2522 Kwina Road
(360) 676-2772, (866) 676-2772
www.nwic.edu

Whatcom Museum of History and Art
121 Prospect Street
(360) 676-6981
www.whatcommuseum.org

RETIREMENT 🌴

A mong the many Top 10 and 10 Best lists on which Bellingham and Whatcom County have appeared over the past decade are several that have to do with retirement. *AARP* Magazine named Bellingham the nation's second-best "dream town" in which to settle down. *Money Magazine/* CNN rated Bellingham one of the eight best places to retire. Kiplinger rates B'ham one of the top college towns to retire in. Bellingham is fourth in *AARP's* "clean and green" category and within the top 50 when it comes to "most alive places" in which to retire.

Why the accolades? Well, along with similar reasons for why people of all ages are flocking here—the scenic beauty, recreation opportunities, Western Washington University, quality of life, etc.—Bellingham is known for its top-notch hospital and retirement-living communities. This is important not just for potential retirees but also for those who aren't nearing retirement age but have parents who are.

Bellingham and Whatcom County's retirement communities, which run the gamut from independent retirement living to assisted-living to full-care facilities, are located throughout the city and county, thus adding to Bellingham's diverse culture. They're not shunted off to their own little "district" but rather can be found in family neighborhoods, in downtown Bellingham's commercial core, in outlying towns, as well as in suburban subdivisions. As of 2005, 13 percent of Bellingham's population was 65 and older. In Whatcom County as a whole, the percentage is slightly less (11.6 percent); 26,000 people in Whatcom County (or 16 percent) are age 60 or over.

Bellingham's relatively mild weather—rarely too hot, rarely too cold, little snow—its proximity to cultural centers such as Seattle and Vancouver, B.C., and a lack of big-city traffic jams are a further draw to retirees looking for a new home.

HOUSING

Independent Living

Bellingham/Whatcom Housing Authorities
208 Unity Street
(360) 676-6887
www.bellinghamhousing.org
This local government agency helps seniors and low-income families procure affordable studios to two-bedroom apartments in Bellingham as well as various towns throughout Whatcom County.

The Leopold
1224 Cornwall Avenue
(360) 733-3500
www.retmgmtco.com
Located in a historic Bellingham building, the Leopold offers the vibrancy of the downtown Bellingham experience as well as excellent water and mountain views in the upper floors. (Excellent soundproofing ensures that it's not *too* vibrant, however.) One- and two-bedroom apartments have their own kitchens. Along with assisted living options, the Leopold also has a secret garden, a patio area, and a ballroom, favored by big bands and tango clubs. The building is named for Leopold Schmidt, a former owner of the building when it was part of the grand Byron Hotel in the early 1900s.

Merrill Gardens at Cordata
4415 Columbine Drive
(360) 715-8822
www.merrillgardens.com
Along with studio to two-bedroom apartments, this retirement community north of Bellingham near Whatcom Community

College also offers the option of two-bed-room cottages with single-car garages. There are loads of amenities, including Anytime Dining—eat when you want, restaurant-style. The facility also has an assisted-living option. This community is owned by Seattle-based Merrill Gardens, which operates a number of retirement facilities throughout the West and South-east. In 2004, Merrill Gardens won the Business of the Year Award from the Ore-gon and Western Washington Better Busi-ness Bureau.

Parkway Chateau
2818 Old Fairhaven Parkway
(360) 671-6060
www.parkwaychateau.com
Conveniently located between the historic Fairhaven district and a small shopping center, the Parkway Chateau offers 109 studio and one- and two-bedroom units. The facility offers organized trips and activities, and the Parkway Chateau is located near a couple of Bellingham's popular walking/hiking trails—the Interur-ban Trail and the Connelly Creek Nature Area. The company is part of the Holiday Retirement Corporation.

The Willows
3115 Squalicum Parkway
(360) 671-7077, (877) 370-5407
www.willows-bellingham.com
Two blocks from St. Joseph Hospital, The Willows has 137 units—studios to two bed-room/two bath—in a splendid wooded setting offering a true Northwest experi-ence. A fitness trail winds through the woods, and The Willows provides all the amenities you'd expect from a quality retirement community, including flexible dining, a guest suite for visitors, a full activity schedule, and doorstop transit service.

Assisted Living

Bellingham Highgate Senior Living
155 East Kellogg Road
(360) 671-1459
www.highgateseniorliving.com
This 48-unit facility is located close to shopping near Bellis Fair Mall. It offers var-ied levels of care, from assisted living to more comprehensive care for those requiring full assistance due to memory loss. Along with a full-time registered nurse, Highgate also offers an in-house doctor.

Fairhaven Estates
2600 Old Fairhaven Parkway
(360) 647-1254
www.emeritus.com
With a great location near Fairhaven at the edge of a forest with paved walking paths, Fairhaven Estates offers 50 studio and studio suites. Along with sightseeing tours, the facility offers myriad shopping trips and various outings, and it has hos-pice services.

Lynden Manor Assisted Living
905 Aaron Drive, Lynden
(360) 354-5985
www.lyndenmanor.com
Located in Lynden, about 15 miles north of Bellingham, Lynden Manor's studios, and one- and two-bedroom apartments are set in a small-town environment. Round-the-clock supervision, activity rooms, and easy access to walking trails and local ball fields are available. The facility also has a 29-unit Specialty Care Center for those suffering from Alzheimer's and other dementia-related illnesses.

Summit Place Assisted Living
2905 Connelly Avenue
(360) 734-4181
www.summitplaceassistedliving.com
Located just east of Fairhaven, this small facility offers 34 studio apartments as well as its unique personal touch. Adjacent to

the Mount Baker Care Center, it provides support for acute medical issues as well as short-term rehabilitation. This facility is popular with couples requiring varying levels of care.

SENIOR RESOURCES

Apria Healthcare
709 West Orchard Drive, #6 and #7
(360) 738-8300
www.apria.com
Offers comprehensive home health care including home-infusion therapy, in which patients can receive treatment and intravenous medication at home.

Catholic Community Services
133 Railroad Avenue, Suite 100
(360) 676-2164, (888) 300-2493
www.ccsww.org
CCS provides affordable in-home care and services such as housework and grocery shopping as well as personal care such as dressing, bathing, and the like. Care options range from a few hours a day to 'round-the-clock care.

Northwest Regional Council/Area Agency on Aging
600 Lakeway Drive
(360) 738-2500
www.nwrcwa.org
This invaluable agency provides the elderly and their families with free information on the wide range of local public and private resources. Areas covered include in-home care, medical insurance, caregiver support, housing, long-term care options, and more.

Social Security Administration Office
Federal Building
104 West Magnolia Street, Suite 109
(800) 772-1213

St. Francis Extended Healthcare
3121 Squalicum Parkway
(360) 734-6760
www.stfrancisbellingham.com

This 118-bed skilled nursing and rehabilitation facility is located right on the St. Joseph Hospital campus. It offers both private and semiprivate rooms and numerous services, including physical, occupational, and speech therapy; recreation therapy; dietary services; and postoperative recovery. A unique feature is that the on-site preschool links children and seniors through the facility's St. Francis Intergenerational Program.

St. Joseph Hospital Adult Day Health
St. Joseph Hospital South Campus
809 East Chestnut Street
(360) 715-6410
www.peacehealth.org
Along with providing social activities such as music and crafts, meals, and personal care, St. Joe's offers rehabilitation and special programs for those with dementia.

SENIOR CENTERS

In partnership with the Whatcom County Council on Aging, Whatcom County Parks and Recreation offers eight senior centers throughout Whatcom County. They host a wide variety of classes and social programs, from foreign languages to arts and crafts to music and dancing to Bible study to exercise classes and lots more. In addition, simple health care such as glaucoma screening, hearing tests, and flu shots are available, as are low-cost nutritious meals. Call the individual center to find what services are provided.

Whatcom County Council on Aging
315 Halleck Street
(360) 398-1995, (360) 733-4030
www.wccoa.org

Whatcom County Parks & Recreation Department
Senior Services Administrative Office
315 Halleck Street
(360) 733-4030
www.co.whatcom.wa.us/parks/seniors

Here are the individual senior centers.

Bellingham Senior Activity Center
315 Halleck Street
(360) 676-1450

Blaine Senior Center
763 G Street, Blaine
(360) 332-8040

Everson Senior Center
111 West Main Street, Everson
(360) 966-3144

Ferndale Senior Activity Center
1998 Cherry Street, Ferndale
(360) 384-5113, (360) 384-6244

Lynden Community Senior Center
401 Grover Street, Lynden
(360) 354-4501

Point Roberts Community Center
1487 Gulf Road, Point Roberts
(360) 945-5424

Sumas Community Center
461 Second Street, Sumas
(360) 988-2714

Welcome Valley Senior Center
Mosquito Lake Road, Deming
(360) 592-5403

LIFETIME LEARNING

Between Bellingham's local university, community college, and technical college, opportunities for lifelong learning abound. Whether your interests are culinary or artistic, computer-based or linguistic, whether you want to learn more about Native American history, or, now that you've got the time, how to finally get that novel published, extended learning programs at these area institutes offer something that should meet your needs and interests.

Bellingham Technical College
3028 Lindbergh Avenue
(360) 752-7000
www.btc.ctc.edu

**Western Washington University
Academy for Lifelong Learning**
405 32nd Street, Suite 209
(360) 650-3308

**Whatcom Community College
Community Education Classes**
237 West Kellogg Road
(360) 647-3277
www.whatcomcommunityed.com

COMMUNITY ACTIVITIES

Both Bellingham's and Whatcom County's parks and recreation departments offer outings and classes that, while they may not be geared specifically for seniors, are certainly senior appropriate. Some examples include introductions to kayaking, cross-country skiing, and snowshoeing, low-impact yoga, travelogue series, and day trips to Leavenworth and Sucia Island. Check the quarterly printed Leisure Guide in the *Bellingham Herald*.

Bellingham Parks and Recreation
3424 Meridian Street
(360) 676-6985
www.cob.org/parks

Whatcom County Parks and Recreation
3373 Mount Baker Highway
(360) 733-2900
www.co.whatcom.wa.us/parks

VOLUNTEER OPPORTUNITIES

Whatcom Volunteer Center
411 York Street
(360) 734-3055, (800) VOLUNTEER
www.whatcomvolunteer.org
This agency is a one-stop clearinghouse that channels the energies and talents of

more than 350 nonprofits, schools, government, and health care organizations to places where they're needed most. Through the Volunteer Chore Program, the center provides housework, yardwork, and minor repairs and does errands for hundred of elderly and disabled people who might otherwise not be able to live independently. Seniors looking to help others are always welcome.

TRANSPORTATION

Whatcom Transit Authority (WTA)
(360) 676–RIDE
www.ridewta.com
Along with offering bus service throughout Bellingham and to some towns and destinations in western Whatcom County, WTA also offer Specialized Transportation for seniors and those with disabilities. Specialized Transportation is curb-to-curb service available to the disabled and those age 65 and older. With its 40-plus wheelchair-lift-equipped vehicles, WTA makes more than 10,000 Specialized Transportation trips per month. The Specialized Transportation fare is 50 cents. On all regular WTA buses, the fare for seniors (age 65 and older) is 25 cents, half the regular fare.

PUBLICATIONS

Pacific Northwest Retirement
(360) 733–589
www.pacificnwretirementmagazine.com
This free monthly for the 50-plus set is distributed at hundreds of outlets throughout the Northern Puget Sound area. Along with stories focusing on retirement, health and fitness, money management, travel, and the like, the magazine offers jokes, short stories, and word puzzles.

EDUCATION AND CHILD CARE 🚫

Bellingham is a college town with more than 25,000 students enrolled at four local institutes of higher learning. They are Western Washington University (WWU) (about 13,000 students), Whatcom Community College (7,000 students), Bellingham Technical College (4,000 students) and Northwest Indian College (1,000 students). Because it's a four-year university that also offers myriad post-graduate programs, not to mention its beautiful 215-acre campus atop Sehome Hill, and the fact that it's Bellingham's largest employer, WWU is the most well-known. *U.S. News & World Report* perennially ranks Western as one of the top public universities that grant master's degrees in the West. (As of 2006, it had ranked second for nine years in a row.)

Bellingham itself is served by one public school district—Bellingham Public Schools—while outlying Whatcom County, including its small towns, is served by six others. Those are the Blaine, Ferndale, Lynden, Meridian, Mount Baker, and Nooksack Valley school districts. Bellingham's district is the largest, with about 11,000 students enrolled in its 13 elementary schools, 4 middle schools, 3 high schools, and an alternative high school. Throughout Whatcom County, about 25,000 students attend public or private K-12 schools.

Like Bellingham's population, enrollment at just about all the schools, including the college and pre-college level, has increased. And just as construction has boomed, school construction has done the same. In the past 15 years, Western has undertaken $220 million worth of construction and renovation projects—a new science, math, and technology complex; a new student rec center; renovation of the library and student union—with another $52 million to be completed by 2007. At the north end of town, Whatcom Community College, which didn't have a single building until 1985, now has a 65-acre campus that seems to be growing all the time. Meanwhile, Bellingham Technical College is set to open its newest and largest building on campus—a $12 million welding center. And as for K-12 education, Bellingham and Whatcom County have added three new high schools, one middle school, and six elementary schools.

For those too young for public school, Bellingham has a number of fine child-care facilities as well.

HIGHER EDUCATION

Bellingham Technical College
3028 Lindbergh Avenue
(360) 752-7000
www.btc.ctc.edu
Along with career counseling and advising, this facility at the west side of Bellingham offers professional programs in fields such as business, computer technology, culinary arts, fisheries and aquaculture, engineering, health sciences, and human services, and more.

Northwest Indian College
2522 Kwina Road
(360) 676-2772
www.nwic.edu
This accredited two-year school located just west of Bellingham on the Lummi Reservation offers programs in the arts and sciences to members of American Indian, Canadian First Nations, and Alaska Native tribes. Academic advising and career counseling are offered as well.

Western Washington University (WWU)
516 High Street
(360) 650-3000
www.wwu.edu

In 1899 the first courses were offered at what would eventually become Western Washington University. Housed in a three-story brick building up on Sehome Hill—today's Old Main building—it was a teacher's college named the New Whatcom State Normal School. Twenty-four students enrolled that first year, mostly women, who intended to become teachers in one of the area's burgeoning logging, mining, fishing, or farming communities. Back then only a year of training was required to become a teacher, and because parts of the state didn't have high schools, the Normal School offered secondary classes, too.

In the 1920s the school began offering more general-education classes, and during the following decade, it became a four-year college and changed its name to Western Washington College of Education. Total enrollment was still low, a little less than 500 total students, and that number that was cut in half during World War II. After the war, enrollment rebounded and, along with construction as the campus expanded, boomed. By 1960 enrollment topped 3,000. Ten years later it was more than three times that.

These days, the school, which changed its name to Western Washington University in 1977, is the place of higher learning for 13,000-plus students and is perennially ranked one of the top public universities in the West. It's Bellingham's biggest employer, too, with more than 2,200 people drawing paychecks from the school.

As the center of Bellingham's intellectual life, WWU is a comprehensive, modern university consisting of seven colleges and encompassing everything from arts to education, humanities to social sciences, environmental studies to business technology. About 700 students attend Western's Graduate School.

Athletically, Western Washington University is a NCAA Division II school with Viking (that's the mascot) teams competing in 16 varsity sports. In 2005, Western's Women's Rowing team won the school's first and only national championship.

Whatcom Community College (WCC)
237 West Kellogg Road
(360) 676-2170
www.whatcom.ctc.edu

Located just north of Bellingham city limits, just past Bellis Fair Mall, WCC is a beautiful newer campus that offers 90 associate degrees for transfer as well as a number of professional/technical programs. Among those are programs in computer information, graphic design, business administration, massage, medical assistance, registered nursing, physical therapy, and lots more.

PUBLIC SCHOOLS

Bellingham Public Schools
1306 Dupont Street
(360) 676-6400
www.bham.wednet.edu

In the 1850s and 1860s, the first settlers were making inroads into what would eventually become thriving logging, coal mining, and fishing industries. It wasn't long before those settlers realized that their children were in need of some book learning. In 1861 the Sehome School House became Whatcom County's first public school. It was located near the Sehome Coal Mine, which was a major employer of the day, at what today would be the corner of Maple Street and Cornwall Avenue. As the population grew, and more settlements on Bellingham Bay sprung up, more and more schools emerged as well, though they only went as high as grade school. In 1890, Central High School opened, becoming the first high school in the region, at a site that serves now as Bellingham Public Schools' administration building. By the time of Bellingham's consolidation as a single city, there were 14 schools spread throughout the bayside area.

Today some 11,000 students attend the 21 schools in Bellingham's district. It's a highly regarded district that's garnered statewide recognition as a model high-achieving school system. As a result, in 2005 the district received its second Bill and Melinda Gates Foundation Grant for $2.1 million. At 7 of the district's 13 elementary schools, at least 90 percent of the students read at or above the Washington State standard. More than 80 percent of high-school students graduate on time, compared to the state average of 70 percent, and the high schools' dropout rate is about half Washington State's average. SAT scores exceed the state and national average, also.

Each elementary school offers kindergarten on a half-day basis. (Though there has been talk in recent years of switching to full-time.) To enter kindergarten, children must be five years old by August 31. To register your child, contact the Bellingham Public Schools (registration is ongoing throughout the year); your child's birth certificate and immunization records are required.

PRIVATE SCHOOLS

Assumption Catholic School
2116 Cornwall Avenue
(360) 733-6133
www.school.assumption.org
Opened in 1913, Assumption is Bellingham's oldest private school. Located in downtown Bellingham, it offers a quality preschool through eighth-grade education with daily instruction in the Catholic faith. The school opened under the guidance of the Tacoma Dominican Sisters, who led most of the teaching duties until the early 1970s; sisters from various orders and lay principals have comprised most of the education staff since then.

Bayside Montessori
1027 Samish Way
(360) 650-9465
www.baysidemontessori.com

The first school in Whatcom, which would eventually become Bellingham, was opened in the 1850s by Edward Eldridge, one of the town's founding fathers. It was a night school for coal miners but it was quickly shut down when mine management realized that the school was having a diminishing effect on the money the miners had been spending at the company-owned saloon.

One of several Montessori schools in Bellingham, Bayside is the largest and the only one in either Whatcom or Skagit County that offers a Montessori curriculum for children in preschool to sixth grade. Established in 1993, the school is located on Bellingham's east flank, on Samish Way near Lake Padden.

Lynden Christian Schools
417 Nooksack Avenue, Lynden
(360) 318-9525
www.lyncs.org
Located in downtown Lynden, about 15 miles north of Bellingham, Lynden Christian Schools offer quality education with a definite Christian emphasis for kids in preschool through high school. With roughly 1,100 students attending Lynden Christian's elementary, middle, and high schools, it's the largest private school system in Whatcom County. And with a history that dates from 1910, it's also the oldest.

Whatcom Day Academy
5217 Northwest Road
(360) 312-1103
www.whatcomdayacademy.org
This school, located about 5 miles northwest of Bellingham, opened its doors in 1988 and is renowned for its high-quality education. The nonsectarian school offers small class sizes on its 2.5-acre campus at the edge of wetlands.

Whatcom Hills Waldorf School
941 Austin Street
(360) 733-3164
www.whws.org
This Association of Waldorf Schools of North America–approved school, one of 800 worldwide, opened in 1986. The small K-8 school is located on a two-acre site about 3 miles east of downtown Bellingham, overlooking Lake Whatcom and the surrounding foothills. It's the site of the former Geneva School, which opened in 1890 and was one of the Bellingham area's first schools.

CHILD-CARE CENTERS

What follows is a sampling of the many businesses and agencies that offer child care. Parents should check the school out ahead of time to ensure that they're comfortable with the prospective center's environment, staff, and policies. Also see above for private schools that offer preschool child care.

A Little Darling School
912 W. Illinois Street
(360) 676-KIDS
Located near Cornwall Park, Little Darling is for three- to five-year olds. Among its many calling cards, including a seven-to-one child to caregiver ratio, the school serves home-cooked organic meals.

A Loving Space
1200 Ellis Street
(360) 676-1355
This highly regarded downtown establishment also has a full-time kindergarten option, something some working parents find helpful.

Barkley YMCA Child Development Center
2415 Rimland Drive
(360) 714-0450
www.whatcomymca.org
Bellingham's two YMCA child centers offer care for everyone from infants as young as four weeks old to toddlers to preschoolers. They also offer before- and after-school care for grade schoolers.

Downtown YMCA
Child Development Center
1256 North State Street
(360) 733-8630
www.whatcomymca.org

Little Epistles Preschool
St. Paul's Episcopal School
2117 Walnut Street
(360) 738-3321
www.spesnet.com
Located near Elizabeth Park in the homey Columbia neighborhood, Little Epistles encourages families from all faiths to enroll. (In fact, three-quarters of enrolled kids are from non-Episcopalian families.) St. Paul's also offers K-8 and high-school education at a campus at the northwest end of town.

Whatcom County College Parent Cooperative Preschools
Whatcom Community College
(360) 676-2170, ext. 3231
There are six WCC-affiliated co-op preschools in Whatcom County, three of which are in Bellingham. Geared for three- to five-year-olds, these schools offer parents a hands-on role in their child's preschool education. Parents are encouraged to help out in the classroom and with school management, and to attend monthly meetings and WCC parent education classes.

HEALTH CARE (H)

With one of the top hospitals in the Northwest, noted for its cardiovascular center and emergency room services, among other things, Bellingham and Whatcom County are in good hands when it comes to health care. Throughout the city and county, there are more than 200 physicians and surgeons, almost 100 dentists, 80 chiropractors, and 14 naturopathic physicians.

As it is just about everywhere across the country, health care is one of the area's true growth industries. As of 2000, just more than 16,000 individuals in the area were employed by various health care businesses, social services, or membership organizations.

HOSPITALS

St. Joseph Hospital
2901 Squalicum Parkway
(360) 734-5400
www.peacehealth.org/Whatcom
Bellingham and Whatcom County are served by St. Joseph Hospital, a member of Peace Health, which has hospitals in Washington, Oregon, and southeast Alaska. Peace Health was started in 1890 by a couple nuns from the Sisters of St. Joseph of Peace, who headed west from Newark, New Jersey, to Fairhaven to start a hospital to care for the area's loggers, mill workers, and fishermen as well as their families.

Along with being the city's second-largest employer (almost 1,800 people work for the hospital), the 253-bed, two-campus hospital is famous for its Cardiovascular Center, which offers the latest in interventional cardiology, heart surgery, and cardiac rehabilitation. Likewise, the St. Joseph Hospital Community Cancer Center uses state-of-the-art equipment and

techniques to ensure the best possible care for patients. The hospital provides the full range of specialized senior health care, orthopedic surgery and rehabilitation, and mental health; boasts the most up-to-date childbirth center; provides 24-hour emergency room services; and more.

St. Joseph's South Campus (809 East Chestnut Street, 360–715–6410), closer to downtown Bellingham, is a seven-acre campus that focuses on services relating to behavioral health, physical rehabilitation, wellness programs and education, therapeutic touch, massage, and acupuncture.

The hospital's main campus is in the midst of major expansion, but it's safe to say that as more and more people move to Bellingham, thus increasing the need for health care, it's always in the midst of major expansion. (Since 1990, St. Joe's has pretty much doubled in size, and it's expected to double again over the next 20 years.) As of press time, St. Joe's was about to embark on a $13 million project to expand the childbirth and cardiovascular centers as well as the intensive care unit. Completion is expected in fall 2006.

EMERGENCY SERVICES

St. Joe's has a 24-hour fully equipped and staffed emergency room and has been designated by Washington State as a Level-II Trauma Program, the highest designation of any emergency room north of

---

St. Joe's Hospital just keeps growing by leaps and bounds. In 1964 it was a 61,000-square-foot facility. Forty years later it was almost 10 times that size, at 590,000 square feet. By 2025 it's projected to be 1.1 million square feet.

Seattle. In extreme emergencies, patients are airlifted to Seattle's Harborview Medical Center.

PUBLIC HEALTH CARE

Whatcom County Health Department
509 Girard Street
(360) 676-6724
www.co.whatcom.wa.us/health
Public health information, referrals, and assistance are provided by the Whatcom County Health Department. Working with participating physicians, dentists, and various agencies, the health department helps to set up relationships between patients and various health care providers in areas such as pediatrics, oral health, maternity, nutrition, alcohol and drug abuse, and many other areas.

LOW-COST HEALTH CARE

Interfaith Community Health Center
220 Unity Street
(360) 676-6177
www.interfaithchc.org
Interfaith is a not-for-profit clinic providing affordable medical and dental services for low-income individuals. Fees are charged on a sliding scale.

Sea Mar Community Health
Bellingham Medical Clinic
4455 Cordata Parkway
(360) 671-3225
www.seamar.org
Sea Mar offers a wide range of health, behavioral, dental, and visual services to diverse populations, specializing in service to Latinos. Fees are based on income and size of household.

PHYSICIAN'S GROUPS

Madrona Medical Group
4545 Cordata Parkway
(360) 738-2200
www.madronamedical.com

After St. Joseph Hospital, Madrona Medical is the region's largest multispecialty physicians group, with more than 65 doctors specializing in numerous areas. Started in 1995 as a somewhat loose network of health care providers with offices throughout the city and Whatcom County, the professionals came together in 1999 with the opening of a 70,000-square-foot facility on the north side of Bellingham. Along with primary care, Madrona professionals provide care in a wide range of areas, including pediatrics, dermatology, allergy and immunology, cardiology, orthopedics, oncology, pulmonology, and general surgery.

Family Care Network
www.familyhealth.org
With 40-plus physicians, Family Care is the area's other large network of doctors. However, unlike Madrona, this group has 11 offices throughout Whatcom County, including 6 in Bellingham. These range from 1-doctor offices to a clinic with 10 doctors and 2 nurse practitioners. Here are some of the larger offices.

Family Health Associates
3500 Orchard Place
(360) 671-3900

Ferndale Family Medical Center
5616 3rd Avenue, Ferndale
(360) 384-1511

Lynden Family Medicine
1610 Grover Street, Suite D-1, Lynden
(360) 354-1333

North Sound Family Medicine
2075 Barkley Boulevard, Suite 105
(360) 671-3345

Squalicum Family Medicine
3015 Squalicum Parkway
(360) 733-7974

MINOR-EMERGENCY CLINICS

Bellingham also has several private walk-in clinics that treat more minor health issues and concerns. They're open from 8:00 A.M. to 8:00 P.M. Monday through Friday and from 9:00 A.M. to 5:00 P.M. on weekends.

Care Medical Group/ExpressCare
4280 Meridian Street, Suite 120
(360) 734-4300
www.caremedicalgroup.com

Walk-In Health Clinic Incorporated
4029 Northwest Avenue
(360) 734-2330

2940 Squalicum Parkway
(360) 734-2330

REFERRAL AGENCIES

Whatcom County Medical Society
3130 Squalicum Parkway, Suite 300
(360) 676-7630
www.whatcom-medical.org
Founded in 1889, this group helps match potential patients with doctors and other medical professionals located nearby. It also provides information on local social services, has Web sites where you can gather detailed medical information, and helps mediate in grievances with physicians.

SPECIALIZED HEALTH CARE

AIDS/HIV Care

Sean Humphrey House
1630 H Street
(360) 733-9357, (360) 733-0176
The Sean Humphrey House is one of only three Adult Family Homes in the state to provide room, board, counseling, and medication services to low-income individuals living with AIDS/HIV. It was started

in 1996 as the realization of the last dream of R. Sean Humphrey, a 30-year-old Bellingham man who died of AIDS in 1992. The Sean Humphrey House can accommodate six individuals.

Mental Health

St. Joseph Hospital Behavioral Health Services
809 East Chestnut Street
(360) 715-6400 for outpatient
(360) 715-6526
(360) 715-6413 for inpatient
www.peacehealth.org/Whatcom/behavioralhealth
St. Joe's offers a wide range of both outpatient and inpatient treatment for those with mental health and/or chemical dependency issues. Their staff includes psychiatrists, mental health specialists, social workers, physicians, recreational and occupational therapists, and more.

Massage Therapy

Ancient Healing Works
1209 11th Street, Suite 3, Fairhaven
(360) 312-3186
www.ancienthealingworks.com
This Fairhaven concern offers both massage therapy and energy work to help clients release stress, stimulate blood circulation, and reach their best potential for achieving Serenity Now.

Naturopathy

Bellingham Natural Family Medicine
119 North Commercial Street, Suite 910
Bellingham Towers building
(360) 738-7654
www.bnfm.com
This naturopathic clinic uses such modes and methods as herbal medicine, home-

opathy, nutrition, exercise, and hydrotherapy to help patients achieve wellness.

Physical Therapy

Performance Physical Therapy
Barkley Medical Building
2075 Barkley Boulevard, Ste. 200
(360) 733-4008
www.performancephysicaltherapy.com
Performance offers quality outpatient physical therapy in everything from rehabilitation for spinal conditions to issues with extremities to orthotic to benign paroxysmal positional vertigo to women's health issues, particularly post-partum. Renowned for their work with athletes, Performance also has an office at Bellingham Athletic Club (1616 Cornwall Avenue, Suite B, 360-714-0870).

MEDIA

B ellingham and Whatcom County are not exactly media hotbeds. They have two television stations, one of which broadcasts only about 90 minutes of local content per day. The other is city-owned and mostly broadcasts city council meetings and the like. There are a number of radio stations, most of which are owned and operated by a single entity, Cascade Radio Group. Fortunately, however, Bellingham and Whatcom County residents are able to pick up a wide number of television and radio stations from Seattle, Vancouver, and Victoria, B.C.

When it comes to print media, Bellingham is fairly thriving. Along with a daily, we have an alternative weekly, a couple business monthlies, and a hip monthly music 'zine, among others. And most of the small cities in the outlying county have their own weekly newspapers.

NEWSPAPERS AND MAGAZINES

Bellingham Business Journal
The Bellingham Business Journal
1321 King Street #4
www.businessjournal.org

Northwest Business Monthly Magazine
1732 Iowa Street
(360) 671–3933
www.nwbusinessmonthly.com
These two Bellingham monthlies are where to find out about Whatcom County business trends and hirings and firings, as well as who's building and who's gone bankrupt. The Business Journal features a useful Web site that provides useful up-to-the-moment scuttlebutt. Northwest Business Monthly also provides coverage of Skagit, Island, and San Juan Counties.

Bellingham Herald
1155 North State Street
(360) 676–2600
www.bellinghamherald.com
Bellingham and Whatcom County are served by one daily newspaper, the Bellingham Herald, which is owned by the McClatchy Company. Started in 1890 as the thrice-weekly Fairhaven Herald, it, like the bayside towns it covered, enjoyed a number of ups and downs—suspending operations for a bit, merging with other papers, etc. It became the Bellingham Herald in 1903 and moved to its current location at the corner of North State and East Chestnut streets in 1926. The building is now one of Bellingham's landmarks.

Owned by the Gannett Corporation from the 1970s through 2005, Gannett recently traded the Bellingham Herald to Knight-Ridder, which in turn sold it to McClatchy.

The Herald covers local news, sports, business, weather, and education, as well as national stories (usually via the wire services), and it offers special coverage on outdoor recreation on Fridays. Thursday's Take 5 pull-out arts and entertainment guide is an invaluable resource for finding out what's going on during the upcoming weekend. Seasonally (usually in early September, December, March, and June), the Herald publishes a pull-out Leisure Guide that's stuffed with recreation and educational events, programs, camps, and such.

Throughout the year, the Bellingham Herald *and* Cascadia Weekly *devote special coverage and guides to long-running Bellingham events, such as the* Ski to Sea *race and festival each Memorial Day weekend and the Northwest Washington Fair in early August.*

Cascadia Weekly
1329 North State Street
(360) 676-1966
www.bellinghamweekly.com
As a member of the Association of Alternative Newsweeklies, the *Bellingham Weekly* offered a somewhat alternative slant on local news coverage. Started in 1997 as *The Every Other Weekly* (which, as the name suggests, came out every two weeks), it became a weekly in 2003 and has since become an invaluable source of local news and opinion, as well as handling local arts, entertainment, and outdoor coverage. After a brief hibernation in winter of 2005–2006, it reemerged as the *Cascadia Weekly*. The *Weekly* is free; it comes out on Thursday, and it's available at most shopping outlets and high-traffic areas such as the YMCA and the Bellingham Cruise Terminal.

Mount Baker Experience
225 Marine Drive, Blaine
(360) 332-1777
www.mountbakerexperience.com
Focusing on things to do and places to go in the foothills and mountains of eastern Whatcom County, this free quarterly often features some terrific mountain photography. It also carries lots of Mount Baker Ski Area–related info.

Whatcom Independent
1201 Cornwall Avenue, Suite 107
360 676-9411
www.whatcomindy.com
This weekly started publication in 2003 and offers yet another take on local news and politics. This is an alternative to the alternative *Cascadia Weekly*, which is an alternative to the corporate-owned *Bellingham Herald*. The *Independent* is free of charge.

Whatcom Magazine
The Bellingham Herald
1155 North State Street
(360) 676-2600
www.whatcommagazine.com
A publication of the *Bellingham Herald*, this quarterly active-lifestyle magazine is geared toward the age 45 and older set and runs features on local personalities, day trips, the arts, the outdoors, restaurants, and more. It's available for free at local Haggen grocery stores and various other retail outlets.

What's Up! Magazine
P.O. Box 2173
(360) 714-9310
www.whatsup-magazine.com
This is a monthly guide to Bellingham's night life with an emphasis on the local music scene. Band interviews, show reviews, calendar of events, and more make this invaluable for B'ham's young hipster set.

RADIO STATIONS

Cascade Radio Group
2219 Yew Street Road
(360) 734-9790
www.kism.com
Five of the most popular local radio stations are owned by the Cascade Radio Group, which itself is owned by Saga Communications, a Michigan company in the business of acquiring radio stations. All have their studios at the same Yew Street Road address and can be contacted at the above phone number. Here's the CRG station followed by its format.

KISM FM 92.9—Classic Rock.

KAFE FM 104.3—Soft Rock. (Nickname: Soft Rock Kafé.)

KGMI AM 790—News, Rush Limbaugh, Bill O'Reilly, et al.

KBAI AM 930—Oldies.

KPUG AM 1170—News and lots of sports, local and national.

KLYN FM 106.5
1843 Front Street, Lynden
(360) 354-5596
www.praise1065.com
This Lynden-based station plays contemporary Christian music as well as airing Christian-themed talk shows and similar programs.

KRPI AM 1550
5538 Imhof Road, Ferndale
(360) 384–5117
www.krpiradio.com
This Ferndale-based station broadcasts mostly East Indian music and talk programming in Punjabi.

KUGS FM 89.3
700 Viking Union
Western Washington University
(360) 650–KUGS
www.kugs.org
You never quite know what you're going to hear on Western's radio station. Could be surf rock. Could be Apocalyptic Folk. Could be progressive news and public affairs programming. Could be Putomayo World Music. Could be Honky Tonk Country. Could be just about anything. And that's what makes KUGS so fun to listen to.

TELEVISION STATIONS

BTV10 Channel 10
Information Technology Services
625 Halleck Street
(360) 738–7385
www.cob.org/btv10
BTV10, which stands for Bellingham TV 10, is run by the city of Bellingham. It broadcasts community-oriented programming: city and county council meetings, feature pieces on local personalities, current events, public safety and health issues, etc. Because it is city-funded, there are no commercials.

The Zone, a daily 3:00 P.M. sports radio program on KPUG AM 1170 hosted by locals Doug Lange and Mark Scholten, is definitely worth a listen. They're smart and funny as heck, and they rarely get bogged down by sports minutiae—just by the minutiae of daily life (hilariously so). You'll wonder why some bigger market hasn't yet scooped them up.

KVOS Channel 11
1151 Ellis Street
(360) 671–1212
www.kvos.com
KVOS produces a local program, *News View,* which features local news, sports, and weather as well as personality and lifestyle pieces. The show airs weekdays from 6:30 to 8:00 A.M. The rest of KVOS's programming is syndicated talk shows, reruns, and movies.

WORSHIP

As Bellingham and the towns by the bay developed, their houses of worship did also. In fact many of today's area churches trace their beginnings to those early days when much of the region was impenetrable forests and muddy bays.

Records show that a number of today's churches got their start about 1883, or about 30 years after Roeder and Peabody first rowed upon the shores of Bellingham Bay. That was the year a few hearty individuals began meeting and, after coming up with some handwritten articles of incorporation, they formed the Tabernacle Church. Their first church was at the corner of F and Astor Streets, at what is today's Lighthouse Mission parking lot in Old Town. Eventually the group changed its name to First Congregational, and after various moves to several locations throughout town, they settled in today's church building on Cornwall Avenue.

Also starting in 1883, just up the hill from the Tabernacle Church, was the Church of the Messiah at Whatcom, an Episcopal congregation. The following year they built their first church on Walnut Street in the Columbia neighborhood, the same year they changed their name to St. Paul's. That building still stands, right across the street from the present St. Paul's, a beautiful, heavy stone cathedralesque building built in 1927.

The area's first Presbyterian congregation experienced similar beginnings. They started meeting in 1883 in a drafty log cabin in Fairhaven. Seven years later, not long after the cabin burned down, the congregation was incorporated and today's St. James Presbyterian Church was born.

The Church of the Assumption, the area's largest Catholic church, dates from 1889. Area Lutherans began gathering about 1890. Cornwall Church, which these days averages 2,500 people in attendance at its services at its large facility on Northwest Road, also traces its humble beginnings to the turn of the 20th-century, when early worshipers gathered in people's homes and basements.

Early Jewish settlers, most from Lithuania and Germany, arrived about 1898 and gathered for several years at various locations around town, including the old Odd Fellows Hall. When the Tabernacle Church left for bigger digs, the congregation that would eventually become today's Beth Israel purchased their old church at F and Astor Streets. Beth Israel moved into their current synagogue in 1925.

Any talk of worship in the Bellingham area would not be complete without some mention of Lynden, the small town about 15 miles north of Bellingham. Along with the early Dutch immigrants' affinity for windmills, tulips, and clogs—which now give the city much of its character—the immigrants brought over their Christian Reformed Churches, of which Lynden these days has several. Over time, churches and congregations from other denominations have flocked to Lynden, and today the town boasts that it has more churches per capita than just about any place in the United States. In a town of not much more than 10,000 residents, there are more than 30 churches.

These days, just about every religion is represented in Bellingham and Whatcom County, and worshippers of just about every denomination can find a place to worship.

BAPTIST

Community Baptist Church
810 Samish Way
(360) 734-7392
www.cbcbellingham.com

First Baptist Church
110 Flora Street
(360) 734-4500

First Korean Baptist Church of
Bellingham
3545 Northwest Avenue
(360) 738-4781

BUDDHIST

Bellingham Dharma Hall
1101 North State Street
(360) 398-7008
www.bellinghamdharmahall.org

CATHOLIC

Church of the Assumption
2116 Cornwall Avenue
(360) 733-1380
www.assumption.org

Sacred Heart
1110 14th Street, Fairhaven
(360) 734-2850

CHRISTIAN REFORMED

Bethel Christian Reformed Church
1105 Liberty Street, Lynden
(360) 354-2361
www.bethelcrc.org

Hope in Christ Church
710 East Sunset Drive
(360) 733-6177

Mountain View Christian
Reformed Church
6678 Old Guide Road, Lynden
(360) 398-9292

CHRISTIAN SCIENCE

First Church of Christ Scientist
118 Grand Avenue
(360) 733-6070

CHURCH OF GOD

Cornwall Church
4518 Northwest Drive
(360) 733-2150
www.cornwallchurch.com

CONGREGATIONAL

First Congregational United
Church of Christ
2401 Cornwall Avenue
(360) 734-3720
www.fccbucc.pair.com

EPISCOPAL

St. Paul's Episcopal Church
2117 Walnut Street
(360) 733-2890
www.stpaulschurchbellingham.org

JEHOVAH'S WITNESSES

Kingdom Hall of Jehovah's Witnesses
1525 Electric Avenue
(360) 734-1251

JUDAISM

Beth Israel Synagogue
2200 Broadway
(360) 733-8890
www.bethisrael.com

LATTER-DAY SAINTS

The Church of Jesus Christ
of Latter-Day Saints
2925 James Street
(360) 734-2841

LUTHERAN

Central Lutheran Church
925 North Forest Street
(360) 734-7180
www.centrallutheran.net

Christ The Servant Lutheran Church
2600 Lakeway Drive
(360) 733-1277
www.ctslutheran.org

METHODIST

Garden Street United Methodist Church
1326 North Garden Street
(360) 733-7440
www.gbgm-umc.org/gardenstreetumc

NONDENOMINATIONAL

Christ The King Community Church
4173 Meridian Street
(360) 733-1337
www.ctkbellingham.com

123 North 17th Street, Lynden
(360) 318-9446
www.ncctk.com

3440 Birch Bay-Lynden, Custer
(360) 366-0306
www.northbayctk.com

ORTHODOX

St. Sophia Greek Orthodox Church
510 East Sunset Drive
(360) 734-8745

PRESBYTERIAN

St. James Presbyterian Church
910 14th Street
(360) 733-1325
http://groups.msn.com/stjpres

SEVENTH-DAY ADVENTIST

Seventh Day Adventist Church
910 North Forest Street
(360) 733-7056
www.bellinghamsdachurch.org

UNITARIAN

Bellingham Unitarian Fellowship
1708 I Street
(360) 733-3837
www.buf.org

INDEX